1382

THE DIALOGUE WITH DEATH

The
Dialogue with Death

(Shri Aurobindo's Savitri,
a Mystical Approach)

R OHIT M EHTA

MOTILAL BANARSIDASS PUBLISHERS
PRIVATE LIMITED ● DELHI

First Edition: Ahmedabad, 1972
Reprint: Delhi, 1983, 1994, 1996, 2003

ISBN: 81-208-1222-0 (Cloth)
ISBN: 81-208-1223-9 (Paper)

Also available at:

MOTILAL BANARSIDASS
41 U.A. Bungalow Road, Jawahar Nagar, Delhi 110 007
8 Mahalaxmi Chamber, 22 Bhulabhai Desai Road, Mumbai 400 026
120 Royapettah High Road, Mylapore, Chennai 600 004
236, 9th Main III Block, Jayanagar, Bangalore 560 011
Sanas Plaza, 1302 Baji Rao Road, Pune 411 002
8 Camac Street, Kolkata 700 017
Ashok Rajpath, Patna 800 004
Chowk, Varanasi 221 001

Printed in India
BY JAINENDRA PRAKASH JAIN AT SHRI JAINENDRA PRESS,
A-45 NARAINA, PHASE-I, NEW DELHI 110 028
AND PUBLISHED BY NARENDRA PRAKASH JAIN FOR
MOTILAL BANARSIDASS PUBLISHERS PRIVATE LIMITED,
BUNGALOW ROAD, DELHI 110 007

PREFACE

IN NOVEMBER 1970, my friend, Mr. Rambhai Amin invited me to give a series of eleven talks on Sri Aurobindo's *SAVITRI* under the auspices of Smt. Manibahen Rambhai Amin Trust which he has created in memory of his wife. The talks were held on the spacious lawns of Mr. Rambhai's beautiful house in Ahmedabad, India, and attracted a large and an appreciative audience. Mr. Rambhai Amin is a great devotee of Sri Aurobindo and the Mother, and so was his wife.

Earlier I had given a series of thirty talks on *SAVITRI* under the auspices of Sri Aurobindo Society, Varanasi, India. The present book is the outcome of these talks given by me at these two places. Mr. Rambhai desired that I should write out these talks so that they may be published in a book form. It is hardly necessary to point out that the style followed for lecturing is inappropriate for a book, and so the present book is entirely different both in method as well as content from the lectures delivered on the subject.

Without any exaggeration, one may say that Sri Aurobindo's *SAVITRI* is not only a monumental work, it is indeed a Book of the Century. In this book, we see Sri Aurobindo's many-splendoured personlity. Here he is seen as a yogi and a philosopher, a mystic and an occultist, a poet and a lover— all at once. Once in many centuries a personality of this high calibre makes its appearance on the world stage, and still more rarely does one come across a master-piece of such rich quality as *SAVITRI*.

[iii]

In this book I have tried to present the superb mysticism of Sri Aurobindo as he has expounded it in his own inimitable style, in exquisite poetry covering twentyfour thousand lines. I have attempted to do this with only one desire, and that is, to induce more and more people to turn to the original work of Sri Aurobindo, for, no interpretation, however elevated it may be, can take the place of the original poem. *SAVITRI* is a book of perennial inspiration, for, it contains the quintessence of Sri Aurobindo's great spiritual adventure which had only one aim: To bridge the gulf between Heaven and Earth so that:

The Spirit shall look out through Matter's gaze
And Matter shall reveal the Spirit's face.

Rohit Mehta

Varanasi : India.
December 25, 1971

CONTENTS

CHAPTER I

THE UNLIT TEMPLE

SRI AUROBINDO belongs to that illustrious galaxy of sages and saints who have been, in all ages, the great Fire Pillars of Humanity. He has indeed given a new turn to the thinking of the world, and has symbolised, in his own thought and action, a new dimension of living. While he has written a large number of books on a great variety of subjects, there are two of them which stand out pre-eminently, for both clarity and originality. These are the *Life Divine* and *Savitri*. These two books give a clear exposition of his philosophy of life. While in the first, we see Sri Aurobindo as a great occult scientist, in the second, we meet him as a mystic of Mystics, using the medium of exquisite poetry to convey to humanity his deep and profound experiences of spiritual life. Thus *Life Divine* and *Savitri* are complementary to each other. Sri Aurobindo was both a *Manishi* and a *Kavi*, an intellectual genius and a sensitive poet at the same time. The epic of *Savitri* reveals to us Sri Aurobindo as a *Kavi*, even as *Life Divine* presents him as a *Manishi*, soaring into great heights of intellectual and occult understanding of man and the universe. While occult science deals with the super-physical structure of the evolutionary drama of Man and the Universe, in Mysticism one comes across the very content of spiritual life, unfettered by the limitations of one's normal consciousness. In a mystic approach one is indeed concerned with an Expansion of Consciousness, and not just with an extension of it. In Sri Aurobindo's *Savitri*, we have the story, told in exquisite poetry, of man's journey into new dimensions of consciousness. It speaks of the Ascent of Man

1

and the Descent of the Divine. While the Ascent of Man has its limitations, the Descent of the Divine has no limits whatsoever. It has no frontiers, whether of range or content, forming a boundary. Man must ascend as far as his powers and capacities can lead him, and, from there, call out to the Divine to descend. It is this which constitutes the Yoga of Ascent and the Yoga of Descent so beautifully described by Sri Aurobindo in his *Savitri*.

In the sub-title of this book on *Savitri*, we have an indication of the nature of the theme presented by the author in his monumental epic. The sub-title says that the epic is "a legend and a symbol". There are many who are familiar with the legend of Savitri. It is a story narrated by the sage Markendeya to King Yudhisthira when the latter was in a despondent mood. The legendary story appears in the *Vana-parva* of the great Hindu epic of Mahabharata. Here the entire story is narrated in barely seven hundred lines. But Sri Aurobindo has expanded this narration to cover nearly twenty-four thousand lines. He has not deviated from the basic narration of the legend, but in expanding the legendary story—, Sri Aurobindo has transformed the legend into a symbol.

One may ask: A Symbol of what? It is said that a mystic is one who sings of the sunrise in the darkness of the night. In all ages, the mystics have been the Heralds of a New Dawn, the proclaimers of a New Age. When all humanity slumbers in the dark night, it is these mystics who watch the coming of the Dawn, and burst into songs of Hope and Cheer even before the first rays of the Rising Sun appear on the horizon. Sri Aurobindo, like a great mystic, has transformed the legend of Savitri into a symbol of the New Dawn. The entire epic is indeed a poem of the New Dawn. The Dawn which the epic depicts is the Dawn of a New Consciousness, for, man must rise above the mind if he is to find solutions to the many baffling problems of life. The consciousness of man, cribbed, cabined and confined within the narrow space of the mind, cannot solve the perplexing problems with which he is faced today. The hope for humanity lies in the dawn of a new consciousness. In the long and arduous journey of Ashvapati, the father of Savitri, we come across the gropings of the mind in search of a new consciousness. In the birth of Savitri, we see the fulfilment of the promise, indicating the arrival of the New Dawn, the descent of a new consciousness. The new consciousness cannot be forged by the efforts of the mind. It descends like the Grace of the Divine.

When does the grace of New Consciousness come? How does it come? Are the efforts of man utterly futile? How far can man go by his own endeavour, and when must he stop? These are the questions with which the epic of *Savitri* is concerned. It speaks of man's journey through the Night and of the promise concerning the arrival of the New Dawn. The subject of Dawn is indeed the under-current of the whole epic poem of Sri Aurobindo. He begins it with a reference to the Dawn, and ends with even a more explicit mention of "a greater Dawn". However, the two Dawns connote two different moods of Nature and also of human consciousness.

Sri Aurobindo ends his great epic with the following lines:

Night, splendid with the moon dreaming in heaven
In silver peace, possessed her luminous reign,
She brooded through her stillness on a thought,
Deep, guarded by her mystic folds of light,
And in her bosom nursed a greater dawn.

What was the greater dawn that the night nursed in her bosom? For an answer to this question one must traverse back to the very beginning of the great epic. Sri Aurobindo begins his story with a reference to another dawn which was to become the turning point both for

Savitri as well as Satyavan, her husband, who was destined to die on that fateful morning. Sri Aurobindo, the
superb poet that he was, begins the story of his great
epic in a manner in which only a poet of his calibre
could have done. The epic poem of Savitri begins with
the following lines:

It was the hour before the Gods awake.
Across the path of the divine Event
The huge foreboding mind of Night, alone
In her unlit temple of Eternity,
Lay stretched immobile upon Silence' marge
. . . .
. . . .
A fathomless zero occupied the world.

In these lines the author has presented a background,
a fitting background, for the fateful event that is to take
place. It is this event which forms the very core of the
entire epic. It is the death of Satyavan which constitutes
the main theme round which the whole story is woven.

The poet says: "It was the hour before the Gods
awake", meaning all was utterly silent. The Dawn is yet
to arrive. The author describes the Dawn as the divine
Event. He tells us that across the path of the Dawn lies
stretched, the Night, completely immobile, along the
margin of deep silence. The poet gives a very significant description of the Night before the arrival of the
Dawn. He says: "A fathomless zero occupied the world".
There is a nothingness that lies stretched, but it is a
nothingness which contains a fathomless depth. It is a
Zero that has occupied the world, but it is a Zero whose
depth cannot be measured. There is a deep silence, but
it is an ominous silence, for, as the poet says: "This
was the day when Satyavan must die".

As a legend, one can understand this description of
the ominous night prior to the death of Satyavan. But
what is its meaning as a symbol? Who is Savitri, and

once again who is Satyavan? What does his death signify? What indeed is the meaning of the "fathomless Zero"? Is it fathomless because it contains an infinity of numbers? Is it the seed of all manifestation? If so, what is the nature of manifestation that lies concealed in its bosom?

For answers to these questions, we must turn to the story of Savitri as narrated by Sri Aurobindo, the poet and the mystic. But before we turn to find answers to the above questions, it needs to be enquired as to what indeed is the relevance of Savitri to the modern man? Savitri as a symbol, depicted by Sri Aurobindo, has indeed great relevance to the modern age. Ours is an age of the Mind and its unprecedented adventures. But strangely enough this civilization of man is a witness to the triumphs and the tragedies of the mind at the same time. Man has launched himself into the outer space of universe, but he remains an utter stranger to the inner space of consciousness. An adventure into outer space without a mastery over inner space would result in the utilization of scientific powers for the fulfilment of self-centred motives. To have scientific power without a spiritual insight is a dangerous proposition. If science is not linked with spirituality, then the future of humanity is dark and dismal. But such linking cannot be done by the mind, for, mind knows not what spiritual insight is. It is only when the mind is inspired by a vision descending from realms beyond the mind, that a spiritual insight can be vouchsafed to man. There has to be a union of Heaven and Earth, so that in the earth-consciousness comes the living touch of Heaven. This indeed is the imperative need of today. Mind has created immense problems. It is obvious that mind cannot solve them by its own effort and understanding. Into the mind of man must come the inspiring presence of the Super-Mind. The civilization of the mind is masculine in its nature, not in the biological, but in the psy-

chological sense. It is because of this that one sees in
all its expressions and activities elements of aggressive-
ness, of argumentativeness, of arrogance, of acquisitive-
ness, of animal propensities. Into this Masculine civilization must come the touch of the Feminine, once
again not the biological, but the psychological feminity.
In terms of consciousness, man must be both masculine
and feminine simultaneously. The *Ardha-narishwar* is the
symbol of a perfectly integrated human being. Today in
humanity we see only the masculine consciousness at
work, whether in man or in woman. This has caused
wars and dissensions, conflicts and divisions. It is due
to this that we see mind in the throes of a great tragedy even in the hour of its most phenomenal triumph.
If man is to save himself then the masculine consciousness
must receive the inspiration and guidance of the feminine consciousness. It is in the close association of the
masculine and the feminine aspects of consciousness, that
there can arise the linking of science and spirituality.

In the great epic of Savitri, Sri Aurobindo speaks
of the close association of Savitri and Satyavan. They together can build heaven on earth—not either of them
singly. Satyavan alone is powerless. It is only when
Savitri joins him that he is endowed with a sense of Immortality. Man must realize his immortality, but for that
the masculine consciousness must be united with its
feminine counterpart..

The mind of man, barren in its efforts, cries out today for a gift from Heaven. And the gift from Heaven is
indeed the birth of Savitri. If modern civilization is to
save itself from doom and disaster, then it must understand the great mystery of the birth of Savitri. It is in
unravelling this great mystery that man will witness the
linking of science and spirituality, the close association
of the Masculine and the Feminine consciousness, the
marriage of Earth and Heaven.

CHAPTER II

A NAMELESS MOVEMENT

The legend of Savitri has become a symbol of great spiritual significance under the poetic magic of Sri Aurobindo. In dealing with this subject of symbol, one has to understand very clearly its distinctiveness from an image. A symbol and an image are not identical. An image is filled with the projections of the mind. And so when one looks at it, the image returns what has been projected into it. But a symbol contains nothing of the mind. It is like an open window, completely empty and therefore capable of conveying the vision of transcendental reality. Man seeks to transform symbols into images, and, then remains for ever confined to the world of mind's projections. But when he empties image after image of his manifested world then he begins to live in a world of symbols. The image-world is dead, but the world of symbols is ever alive and new. A really cultured individual is he who continually transforms the world of images into a world of symbols. But this demands a complete cessation of the interpreting and projecting activities of the mind. The mind that is involved in its own explanations cannot know what the significance of a symbol is. The symbol is a channel through which the refreshing waters of heaven reach the earth, irrigating the parched fields of logic and intellect. It is symbol which opens the way to the Descent of the Divine. Savitri as a legend is an image built by the imagination of man; but Savitri as a symbol is the communicating link between Heaven and Earth. In Sri Aurobindo's *Savitri*, we find symbol after symbol conveying deep and profound truths of spiritual life. But *Savitri* as a symbol cannot be understood by mere intel-

lect. The way of the mind is too slow and tardy. It
can understand the message of an Image, but not the
sublime intimations of a Symbol.

The philosophy of Sri Aurobindo centres round the
principle of Evolution, not merely of form and structure
but of consciousness. Conscious evolution forms one of
the cardinal principles of his approach to life. In *Savitri*
too we see an exposition of the principle of evolution.
His whole thesis of Higher Mind, Illumined Mind, Intuitive Mind, Over-Mind and Super-Mind is an original
contribution to the subject of Psychology. In the journey
of Ashvapati, in search of an answer to the imperative
need of the human race, we see these evolutionary
stages in terms of consciousness. In *Savitri* the author has
again and again referred to the symbolism of the Night
and the Dawn. Now Night and Dawn represent a rhythm
of evolutionary drama. They are the Infinite Rest and
the Infinite Motion in the vast panorama of evolutionary
growth. The march of evolution has periods of action
and inaction. During the Night all is still and quiet;
there is no movement at all. And then gradually there
begins a stir—an imperceptible stir — in the silence of
the Night. Every such stir indicates an evolutionary jump
or a Mutation. The utter stillness of the Night is a pre-
condition for the arrival of a Mutation. The Dawn of
each evolutionary stage is a Mutation or a fundamental
change. The Birth of Savitri and the death of Satyavan
represent such revolutionary periods of Human evolution.
Satyavan must die if he is to realize his Immortality. Man,
coming to the realization of his Immortality, is surely one
of the finest Dawns in the march of evolution. But the
saying is "the night is darkest before the Dawn". There
is no doubt that the Night prior to this Great Dawn is
even more dark. In the mystical literature of the world
there is to be found a mention of what is known as the
Dark Night of the Soul. This is not the Night prior to
realization; in fact, it is a Night of separation after

the first meeting with the Beloved. It is a night of intense suffering—it is the Darkest Night in the life of a mystic. The Night before the Dawn which was to see the death of Satyavan was indeed a Dark Night for Savitri; for, it was to be a day of separation after the short-lived bliss of having spent a year in the company of Satyavan. It was to be a day when the Lover and the Beloved would be separated after their first meeting. But the Dark Night of the Soul is a precursor to a life of Bliss Eternal. Such a bliss is in the womb of the future. When the Dawn breaks, after the dark night, Savitri must become a witness to the death of her dear Satyavan. There is a deep poignancy in this experience of the Night. And Sri Aurobindo has portrayed this Night and the slow arrival of the Dawn like a superb painter. He says:

> Athwart the vain enormous trance of Space,
> Its formless stupor without mind or life,
> A shadow spinning through a soulless Void,
> Thrown back once more into unthinking dreams,
> Earth wheeled abandoned in the hollow gulfs
> Forgetful of her spirit and her fate.
> The impassive skies were neutral, empty, still.
> Then something in the inscrutable darkness stirred;
> A nameless movement, an unthought idea
> Insistent, dissatisfied, without an aim,
> Something that wished but knew not how to be.

Here we see not only an exquisite description of Night gradually giving way to Dawn, but we also notice an imperceptible suggestiveness of human mood as well. Will the dawn of yesterday be born out of this dark night? Since Night and Dawn are evolutionary symbols in the *Savitri* of Sri Aurobindo, one may be tempted to ask: Will another day, similar to the many yesterdays be born out of this dark and dismal night? The story of evolution says that the past, in the psychological sense is a die-hard, and therefore pulls the moment of the present eternally towards it. Sri Aurobindo gives expression to this tendency of the past conditioning the new dawn with the colours of yesterday in the following· significant lines:

> Like one who searches for a bygone self
> And only meets the corpse of desire.
> It was as though even in this Nought's profound,
> Even in this ultimate dissolution's core
> There lurked an unremembering entity,
> Survivor of a slain buried past
> Condemned to resume the effort and the pang,
> Reviving in another frustrate world.

The story of evolution is a tale of continuity. But a mere continuity does not explain the mystery of evolutionary growth. Scientists talk of jumps in nature, and it is in these jumps that a new direction to the stream of evolution is given. Sri Aurobindo speaks in the very beginning of his epic about the great event of mutation, for, the day that will follow the new dawn will see the death of Satyavan, and Satyavan's death was not meant to be an ordinary event. The day is destined to bring, not only the death of Satyavan, but, with it, a sense of Immortality to the mortal man. A turn in the evolutionary stream seems imminent. But the past seeks to overshadow the moment of the present and thereby tries to lead the new dawr along the footsteps of the old, for the revival of another frustrate world.

Sri Aurobindo describes the arrival of the Dawn in phrases that are very delicate and extremely suggestive. He writes:

> The darkness failed and slipped like a falling cloak
> From the reclining body of a god.
> Then through the pallid rift that seemed at first
> Hardly enough for a trickle from the suns,
> Outpoured the revelation and the flame.
> The brief perpetual sign recurred above.

A glamour from the unreached transcendencies
Iridescent with the glory of the Unseen,
A message from the unknown immortal Light
Ablaze upon creation's quivering edge,
Dawn built her aura of magnificent hues
And buried its seed of grandeur in the hours.

The Dawn buries its seed of grandeur in an hour—the seed that shall grow into a magnificent tree in the course of the day. This dawn with its aura of majestic hues awoke the people from their nightly rest. With the coming of the dawn started numerous activities of human beings. The poet says:

There was the common light of earthly day.
Affranchised from the respite of fatigue;
Once more the rumour of the speed of Life
Pursued the cycles of her blinded quest.
All sprang to their unvarying daily acts.

People started hurrying to their various tasks. But, as the poet says, behind this activity there was hardly to be seen anything more than the blinded quest. People knew not where they were going and why. It was just the pursuing of a cycle of occupations with which they were long habituated. For them there was no dawn; it was only the arrival of another day, like the many yesterdays that they had experienced. They had not even seen the aura of magnificent hues with which the dawn had heralded its arrival. The poet says in the above lines that "all sprang to their unvarying daily acts". The acts were the same, absolutely unvarying. The new day was like any other day. But for Savitri it was a different day. She was conscious of even the faintest step of the coming Dawn. Sri Aurobindo says that while Savitri too was awake, "akin to the Eternity whence she came, no part she took in this small happiness, a mighty stranger in the human field". Why was this so? Savitri had kept awake throughout the night. She had watched every step of the coming dawn, for,

> Time's message of brief light was not her.
> In her there was the anguish of the gods
> Imprisoned in our transient human mould,
> The deathless conquered by the death of things.

Within her heart was the deep anguish, for, she will soon have to "confront death on her road". She was awake like everybody else and was engaged in the usual routine of the day, and yet, as the poet says:

> A dark foreknowledge separated her
> From all of whom she was the star and stay.

Savitri had known all along about this fateful day. Even when she lived with apparent joy and happiness with all in the household, in her mind there was all the time the shadow of the destined day cast over the sunshine of her life, lived in the company of Satyavan. How could she tell about this day to her husband? And how could she share this grief with sorrow-stricken parents of Satyavan? The secret of the fateful day was kept by Savitri all to herself for one long year, giving to none even a faint hint of what was to happen. As Sri Aurobindo says :

> Unknown her act, unknown the doom she faced,
> Unhelped she must foresee and dread and dare.

There is the darkness of the night on the one hand, and, on the other, there is the bursting of the morning light. Savitri seems to be standing between Darkness and Light, for, was she not both human and divine? Savitri's anguish was all the more because she was poised between Humanity and Divinity, between the Darkness of the Night and the Light of the Dawn. If she had been just human she would have broken down and sought the help of others in the hour of the great misery. If she had just been Divine she would not have cared for the woes of the mortals. But being both, at the same time, greatly intensified her anguish. Her inner state is most graphically described by the poet in the following lines:

> Even in the moment of her soul's despair,
> In its grim rendezvous with death and fear,
> No cry broke from her lips, no call for aid;
> She told the secret of her woe to none:
> Calm was her face and courage kept her mute.

For Savitri, this was not just the dawning of another day; It was a day that demanded all her courage, for, she must face death singlehanded. She was torn between her Divinity and her Humanity. Sri Aurobindo has drawn a remarkable character of Savitri in his epic. As an incarnation of Divinity, Savitri was far away, but as the finest gem of Humanity she was near to the pains and the aches of human beings. Her mission was to impart the quality of the divine to the struggling and suffering humanity. Being both divine and human made her task extremely difficult. The burden of anguish which she was carrying was not just her own. In the words of the poet she had taken up the "load of an unwitting race". The difficulty of her great mission becomes evident when we peruse the following lines of the poet:

> The mortal's lot became the Immortal's share.
> Thus trapped in the grip of earthly destinies,
> Awaiting her ordeal's hour abode,
> Outcast from her inborn felicity,
> Accepting life's obscure terrestrial robe,
> Hiding herself even from those she loved.

On this day while Savitri was with her people, her mind was far far away. For her it was a day with grim significance, the day which had been lying heavily on her mind all through the year. The poet beautifully says about her that "aloof, she carried in herself the world". She indeed was aloof from the world. And on this fateful

morning it was more so. But while aloof she carried the
burden of the whole world, for, "even her humanity was
half divine". It is difficult to portray a character that
is divine and yet at the same time human. It was easy
for Savitri to retire into her divinity and be deaf to the
cries of the world. In Savitri's character, Sri Aurobindo
has expressed deepest truths of his philosophy. He believed
neither in the denial of the materialist, nor in the rejection
of the ascetic. The materialist denies the world of the
Spirit, and the ascetic rejects the world of Matter. His
philosophy is a poise between Spirit and Matter. And
this is exactly the character of Savitri. How could she
forget her divine heritage, and once again how could she
reject the world and its suffering? And so in the hour
of this deep crisis, posed by the fateful morning, we find
in Savitri divinity alternating with humanity. Sri Aurobindo
describes this alternating mood of divinity and humanity
in the following lines.

> In a deep cleft of silence twixt two realms
> She lay remote from grief, unsawn by care,
> Nothing recalling of the sorrow here.
> Then a slow faint remembrance shadowlike moved,
> And sighing, she laid her hand upon her bosom
> And recognised the close and lingering ache.

But how could she afford to be swayed by human
frailties? The sun had arisen and was moving towards the
noon. Soon, very soon, she would be called upon to
confront Death who was to take away Satyavan into those
realms where all mortals have to go. Savitri realized that
the God of Death had remained unappeased even though
she had offered "daily oblations of her unwept tears."
She must stand up and cross swords with Death itself,
for, there was none who could help her in the hour of
deep crisis which was approaching fast. Savitri regains her
composure and is ready to meet the challenge of Death.
Sri Aurobindo describes her new mood thus:

Awake she endured the moments' serried march
And looked on this green smiling dangerous world,
And heard the ignorant cry of living things.
Amid the trivial sounds, the unchanging scene,
Her soul arose confronting Time and Fate.
Immobile in herself, she gathered force.

She could meet the challenge of Death only if she was composed and quiet, not in an agitated frame of mind. She must gather up all her strength, for, she had to meet Death alone, with none by her side. She was nearing the great moment of crucifixion, and the strange irony was that she had herself to carry her cross on which she would be crucified.

One may ask: Why must Savitri go through all this agony? Can she not seek her escape in the quiet regions of Heaven from where she had come? Or can she not become completely one with humanity, forgetting her divine origins? Was she not attempting to do the impossible by bridging the enormous gulf that separated Earth from Heaven? Was she not seeking Immortality for the mortal man? Can this ever happen? Why can she not reconcile herself to her fate as most human beings do? From the base of humanity, can she ask for the rights that belong to divinity? She was indeed attempting to do the impossible, and yet she had come down to earth exactly to achieve this. It is the bridge between Earth and Heaven which characterises the new dawn of consciousness. The mortal must put on Immortality—to achieve this, Savitri had come down from her heavenly abode to live within the restricted campus of humanity. Is it possible for the mortal to put on Immortality? Sri Aurobindo gives an answer to this question in the symbolical narration of *Savitri*, and so we must move with the poet as he unveils the great mystery of the Birth of Savitri and the Death of Satyavan, in canto after canto, of his immortal epic.

CHAPTER III

A PARABLE OF DAWN

The subject of Immortality occupies a place of great importance in the Hindu View of Life. But in the context of the all pervading realm of Death, the concept of Immortality seems a little out of place. The Bhagavad Gita says, that, that which is born must die. If that be the case then where does Immortality come in? Unless there is a conquest over Death, to talk of immortality seems meaningless. And can Death be conquered? In the *Kathopanishad*, Nachiketa describes Yama as the *Antaka*, meaning one who brings everything to an end. And this description seems to be very apt, for, we see death all around as a universal phenomenon. There is no escape from Death. One must, indeed, settle one's accounts with Death before one talks of Immortality. Nachiketa did this in his own way. He went to the palace of death while alive in order to extract from the King of Death the very secret of death itself. But for Nachiketa, death was not an imperative problem. He went himself seeking death. If he had refrained from provoking his father, he need not have come to an encounter with death. With Savitri, the problem of death was completely in a different context. It appears that death came seeking her. Unable to carry Satyavan away, Death and Savitri came face to face. The problem for Savtiri was not to find the secret of Death; her problem was how to vanquish death. And death can be vanquished in his own realm only. To go with death into his kingdom and come back to earth after vanquishing him—this was the great adventure to which Savitri was called. It was no mean adventure. Savitri knew, even before her marriage, that death would come at the appointed hour to take Satyavan

16

from her. For one full year, Savitri was inwardly preparing herself for this encounter with death. To know that death will come on the appointed day, and to find oneself actually facing the morning of that day, are two different things. In the course of one year, Savitri had not even once entreated death to put off his appointment. She had not pleaded with Gods to ward off the evil day. She had not sought escape from this encounter with death. All that she had done was to prepare herself for the fateful event, and that too all alone, without giving even a hint to any one. The year had passed on and now the dawn had come heralding the arrival of the fateful hour. As Sri Aurobindo says: "Immobile in herself, she gathered force".

But with Mighty Death almost around the corner, Savitri's mind naturally goes back in retrospect, for, her mind is crowded with the memories of the twelve months spent in joy and happiness with Satyavan. How soon the year has gone! It was as if only yesterday that she was united in marriage with Satyavan, and how quickly these months have gone! On the one hand she makes herself ready to meet the Lord of Death; on the other, the events and happenings of the past twelve months pass in her mind in a flowing movement. Let us not forget that while she was Divine, she was at the same time intensely human. Her divinity had not eclipsed her humanity. Like any sensitive human being, her mind was seeing the pictures and the images of events that had quickly moved on during the last twelve months. The poet describes the state of the mind of Savitri thus:

Awhile, withdrawn in secret fields of thought,
Her mind moved in a many-imaged past.

The images flew past the screen of memory. And the images bore events and happenings which were lived in love and rapture. As the poet says: "Twelve passionate months led in a day of fate". Between the intensely happy

past and the prospect of the immediate future, Savitri
must have felt inwardly torn and tormented. How could
she stop the stream of memory, and how could she stop
the arrival of the fateful hour? Sri Aurobindo says:

> Along the fleeting event's far-backward trail
> Regressed the stream of the insistent hours,
> And on the bank of the mysterious flood
> People with well-loved forms now seen no more
> And the subtle images of things that were,
> Her witness spirit stood reviewing Time.

It is Death that presides over the realm of Time, for,
it is in the flow of time that one hears the silent footsteps
intimating the arrival of the King of Destruction. He
knocks, in turn, at the door of every human being, and
when he knocks, one must open the doors and go whither
he takes us. His imperceptible presence can be felt in
time-succession. But Savitri's witness spirit was engaged
in reviewing the time-sequence, the moments that had
flown one by one. One is hardly aware of the flying
moments; one becomes aware of the passage of time when
a major change occurs. But what comes at the end of
time was being gradually built up moment by moment.
One realizes the significance of the moment only when,
perched on the precipice of time, one looks back to see
how each moment was leading up to the final event. On
this fateful morning Savitri is in such a retrospective
mood, giving free vent to memory so that moment after
moment may be projected on its wide screen. The poet
says:

> All that she once had hoped and dreamed and been,
> Flew past her eagle-winged through memory's skies.

But what does she see in this wide screen of memory?
In the flash of a moment she sees as it were the whole
panorama of life, from the days of her childhood to the
fateful morning when Death would snatch Satyavan

away from her. It was a past, rich in content, such as any one would like to relive. The poet gives us in the following lines the whole range of her life cast on the screen of memory. He says:

As in a many-hued flaming inner dawn,
Her life's broad highways and its sweet bypaths
Lay mapped to her sun-clear recording view,
From the bright country of her childhood's days
And the blue mountains of her soaring youth
And the paradise groves and peacock wings of Love
To joy clutched under the silent shadow of doom
In a last turn where heaven raced with hell.

In the above lines Sri Aurobindo has drawn a perfect picture of Savitri's life from childhood onwards until she comes to the point where heaven raced with hell. Who will win in this race? On that fateful dawn it looked as if Hell had scored over Heaven.

Savitri in a reminiscent mood shows human qualities at their best. It looks as if the Divine aspect has receded so that Savitri as a perfect representative of womanhood may shine out with all the rich emotional content that one associates with womanliness. As Sri Aurobindo says: "All in her pointed to a nobler kind". She was indeed a jewel of womanhood, and that too at its noblest. And yet what a bleak prospect lay in front of her! Why should she, the fairest of the fair, and the noblest of the noble, be faced with such a situation as would break even the strongest heart? The poet replies:

An absolute supernatural darkness falls
On man sometimes when he draws near to God.
That hour had fallen now on Savitri.

This is indeed the history of humanity where we find sages and saints facing situations that they do not seem to deserve. But as Sri Aurobindo says, when a person draws near to God he is required to walk through an inferno in the psychological meaning of the term. Suffering and sorrow seem to be their lot. Perhaps this is so in order that the best out of the saints and sages may be evoked. Savitri, otherwise a soft and a tender woman, rises to her stupendous heights of strength and valour when faced with a situation that would have broken the hearts of many a man. She faces a crisis that demands the focussing of all her inner strength, for as the poet says:

> Her being must confront its formless Cause,
> Against the universe weigh its single self,
> On the bare peak where Self is alone with Nought
> And life has no sense and love no place to stand,
> She must plead her case upon extinction's verge,
> In the world's death-cave uphold life's helpless claim
> And vindicate her right to be and love.

She has to stand on the bare peak, alone with Nothingness as her companion, and she has to plead her case from the verge of extinction. Truly speaking, it is not her case alone that she has to plead; she has to plead the case of entire humanity. But before she can speak on behalf of the whole humanity, she must as the poet says:

> An old account of suffering exhaust,
> Strike out from Time the soul's long compound debt
> And the heavy servitudes of the Karmic Gods,
> The slow revenge of unforgiving Law
> And the deep need of universal pain
> And hard sacrifice and tragic consequence
> Out of a Timeless barrier she must break,
> Penetrate with her thinking depths the Void's
>   monstrous hush,
> Look into the lonely eyes of immortal Death.

This was the stupendous task to which she was called —"to look into the lonely eyes of Death". Death is indeed lonely, for, who would keep company with him? Into the eyes of this lonely Death, Savitri must look. She must penetrate the monstrous hush of Void, for, death is indeed the messenger of the Void. But how will she have the courage to do this? She can find that courage if she is willing to settle her own account and thus free herself from the servitude of the Karmic Gods. She must pay back her debt with compound interest, so that she has no personal burden of her own to carry. Even the last vestige of the Karmic bond must be snapped so that she has not to submit to the slow revenge involved in the opera- tion of the Karmic Law. She herself must be utterly Karma-less if she is to free humanity from its burden of the past. This is surely the mission to which all truly great have been called, and it is because of their hard sacri- fice and tragic consequence that mankind has been saved from total destruction. Once again humanity needs the healing touch of Savitri, and she can heal only if she is ready to go through the fire. The fateful dawn puts this terrific demand on Savitri, for, as the poet says:

> The great and dolorous moment now was close.
> A mailed battalion marching to its doom,
> The last long days went by with a heavy tramp,
> Long but too soon to pass, too near the end.

The last days were too long and yet too soon to pass. The poet gives an expression to a very subtle feeling agi- tating the heart of one who knows what is to come. One feels: Why does not that moment come quickly, and yet at the same time one feels how the last moments are passing away so rapidly! There is a subtle inner conflict through which Savitri must be going as she woke up on that fateful morning. Savitri had, during the whole year, prepared a battalion, properly armoured, but she has to see this entire battalion marching towards its doom. Though tender, Savitri has to be like tempered steel so that she remains unbroken in the face of the greatest tragedy. If she breaks down then what will happen to humanity?

There will be none left to plead the case of mankind. She must vanquish death so that man may discover his immortality. But to vanquish death was not a mean assignment. Savitri has been given an assignment with Death. Even the bravest heart would shudder to keep this assignment, for,

No helper had she save the strength within;
There was no witness of terrestrial eyes;
The Gods above and Nature sole below
Were the spectators of that mighty strife.

Even Gods and Nature too were only spectators of the great strife to which Savitri had been invited. Savitri had grown up in the beauties of nature where she had risen to the stature of her Spirit. The poet says that in these sylvan surroundings of nature was enacted "her drama's radiant prologue". It was in these beauties of nature that "Love came to her hiding the shadow, Death". The poet says, that inspite of this, Love will find in Savitri his perfect shrine, for, never "a rarer creature bore his shaft". Savitri was made of a stuff of which gods are made, and yet, even though godly, she was most intimate with man. Sri Aurobindo describes the character of Savitri in words which are superb. He says:

Near to earth's wideness, intimate with heaven,
Exalted and swift her young, large-visioned spirit
Voyaging through worlds of splendour and of calm
Overflew the ways of Thought to unborn things.
Ardent was her self-poised unstumbling will;
Her mind, a sea of white sincerity,
Passionate in flow, had not one turbid wave.

In her heart there was a passionate flow, and yet there was in it not even one turbid wave. The flow was crystal clear with not even one muddy ripple. She overflew the ways of Thought and moved on to unborn things. She could not be measured in terms of the mind, for, she transcended the ways of the mind. She seemed to be in communion with the Unborn and the Unmanifest.

Sri Aurobindo calls her "a priestesss of immaculate ecstasies". She was not merely pure, she was Purity itself. How can there be a turbid wave in that crystal clear stream of life?

Savitri was near to earth's wideness and yet at the same time she was intimate with heaven. She was, according to the poet,

A heart of silence in the hands of joy
Inhabited with rich creative beats
A body like a parable of dawn
That seemed a niche for veiled divinity
Or golden temple door to things beyond.
Immortal rhythms swayed in her time-born steps;
Her look, her smile awoke celestial sense
Even in earth-stuff, and their intense delight
Poured a supernal beauty on men's lives.

As one reads the description of Savitri in the superb words of the author, one feels that even the pen of Sri Aurobindo must have experienced the limitations and the inadequacies of language while drawing a picture of such a being as Savitri. He says about Savitri that "Love in her was wider than the universe, the whole world could take refuge in her single heart". The Poet says that "earth's breath had failed to stain that brilliant glass", for, even while moving with man "her walk kept still the measure of the gods". Could there be anything more cruel than that a being like Savitri should be faced with such dark and dismal situation? Why could not the gods spare her from such a fate? But as Sri Aurobindo says:

But joy cannot endure until the end:
There is a darkness in terrestrial things
That will not suffer long too glad a note.
On her too closed the inescapable Hand:

It is said that the sweetest flower soonest withers. On earth, too glad a note does not last long. There seems to be a strange factor at work which pulls down all who seek to climb higher than others. To bring him down to the level of others seems to be the usual tendency among men. Nature too works in ways that are inscrutable. In the midst of the sunshine of life there comes a deep shadow from somewhere. In the midst of pleasure there is invariably cast the long shadow of pain. Savitri is no exception to the working of this strange law. Savitri was brought to a point where she must choose. Will she go along the path that humanity chooses? Or will she carve out a new path? She is faced with a great Issue of her life. On the choice she makes depends whether her mission will be fulfilled or whether she too will go down under the merciless hoof of time. The poet· has entitled this canto of his Book as The Issue, and in the following lines he formulates the issue with which Savitri is faced. He says:

To wrestle with the Shadow she had come
And must confront the riddle of man's birth
And life's brief struggle in dumb Matter's night.
Whether to bear with Ignorance and Death
Or hew the ways of Immortality,
To win or lose the godlike game for man,
Was her soul's issue thrown with Destiny's dice.

It is a big issue that stared Savitri in the face. This is indeed the issue which each man must face sooner or later. Man has not to achieve immortality; he has only to recognise it and allow it to act within him. Savitri was faced with this problem: How to bring to man the awareness of his immortality? The issue has become clouded because of the fear of death. To be aware of immortality does not mean to run away from death, rather it is to face death and have a free dialogue with it. When man is free from the fear of Death, then, in that very freedom, he becomes

aware of his Immortality. Man must have a straight talk
with Death if he is to be free from the spell of fear that
has been cast over him. Savitri had entered this game with
death so that she could bring to humanity a sense of
Immortality. She was determined to break the spell of
death. "Whether to bear with Ignorance and Death, or to
hew the ways of Immortality"—that indeed was the issue
before Savitri. Even within the frame of tender womanhood, Savitri had the indomitable will. It was not difficult for her to make the choice. Her choice is expressed
by Sri Aurobindo in the following lines:

> Accustomed to the eternal and the true,
> Her being conscious of its divine founts
> Asked not from mortal frailty pain's relief,
> Patched not with failure bargain or compromise.
> A work she had to do, a word to speak;
> Writing the unfinished story of her soul
> In thoughts and actions graved in Nature's book,
> She accepted not to close the luminous page,
> Cancel her commerce with eternity,
> Or set a signature of weak assent
> To the brute balance of the world's exchange.

She was not willing to cancel her commerce with
eternity by putting a signature of weak assent to the demands of fate. She had made her choice so that the issue
with death could be settled once and for all. Immortality
is man's lawful heritage. He must claim it from the
pretender that is death. But man has been too weak to fight
his own battles, for, the only weapon that he has is the
mind with its tardy processes of logic. Savitri comes with
a new weapon with which to fight the hordes of Death,
and it is the mission of Savitri to endow man with this
new weapon—weapon not of the mind, but of that which
transcends the limitation of the mind. Will Savitri be able
to wield that weapon? Can a mere man possess powers
that can match the strength of death? Man feels too

powerless, and Savitri has come down to give to man a
sense of confidence so that he can match his own strength
against the giant will of death. Man has no faith; how
can he, a mere pigmy, cross swords with a giant that the
Lord of Death is? It is true that man with the powers of
the mind cannot wrestle with the strength of Death. But
how to call to that strength which lies beyond the frontiers
of the Mind? Can the Higher strength be available to
man? If so, how? Sri Aurobindo points to this great
miracle of Supreme Power working through man. He
says:

> A magic leverage   suddenly is caught
> That moves the veiled Ineffable's timeless will:
> A prayer, a master act, a king idea
> Can link man's strength to a transcendent Force.
> Then miracle is made the common rule,
> One mighty deed can change the course of things;
> A lonely thought become omnipotent.

Man must know the secret of linking his puny strength
to the Great Force Above. Sri Aurobindo says that this
can happen through ordinary things of life—a prayer, a
gesture, an idea, even a lonely thought may become a
window through which the Transcendental Vision may
be vouchsafed to man. What matters is the opening
made in one's normal consciousness. Our mind moves in
a closed circle, and so goes round and round the same
mental region. It may re-decorate its own furniture lying
within that closed circle, but it can never come upon
something entirely new by its own movement. Man needs
to find an opening within his consciousness so that something transcendental may reach him from realms above.
It is this descent from above which performs the miracle
whereby man achieves what he otherwise, depending
upon his own strength, would never have been able to
achieve. The opening in the consciousness cannot be made
by the mind. It happens mysteriously, but he who

knows the secret can indeed send a Call to the Divine. This is what saints and mystics of all ages have done. The so-called miracles in their lives were due to the fact that they were able to call to the Supreme to achieve something which they, by their own power, could not do. But who can send such a call to the Divine? He who asks nothing for himself; he who is ready to pay back his own debts to Karma with compound interest; he who is crystal clear in all that he does or thinks. It is only when the turbid waters of the mind have settled down that the Vision of the Supreme is vouchsafed to him. Such a person indeed was Savitri.

Sri Aurobindo says that "even a lonely thought can become omnipotent". This is possible only when there is a Descent from above. The Great Miracle to which the poet refers in the above lines is possible only when the Divine descends into the life of man. If we see miracles in the lives of saints and sages it is because of this descent. In such a descent, it is not the man who acts, it is the Divine that acts through him. And the descent of the Divine may happen in the most undemonstrable manner. There is no fanfare attached to the descent of the Divine. It comes silently in the night. The night in this sense means that the receiver is not even conscious of it. If the receiver were conscious of the descent of the Divine, then he would be filled with subtle pride and arrogance. He would begin to regard himself as superior to others. And therefore the Divine comes with silent steps, so as not to awaken the receiver of the grace. The poet refers to this in the following lines:

. . . wisdom comes, and vision grows within;
Then Nature's instrument crowns himself her King;
He feels his witnessing self and conscious power;
His soul steps back and sees the Light supreme.

The light supreme is seen when the soul steps back, and yet there is a feeling that one has been endowed with

some mysterious power of which there was no awareness
earlier. When this mysterious power comes then all can
be accomplished — even the vanquishing of the great foe,
Death itself. Then, as the author says, a victory is won
for God in man. Savitri in her great hour of crisis stands
completely transformed. She possesses a strength which
she never knew before. As soon as she made the choice,
when the issue was clearly seen by her, then there came
the Divine Power pouring down. It was this Descent
which performed the miracle. But what was the miracle?
The poet says:

> A living choice reversed fate's cold dead turn,
> Affirmed the Spirit's tread on Circumstance,
> Pressed back the senseless dire revolving Wheel
> And stopped the mute march of Necessity.
> A flaming warrior from the eternal peaks
> Empowered to force the door denied and closed
> Smote from Death's visage its dumb absolute
> And burst the bounds of consciousness and Time.

The poet says that Savitri had made a living choice,
not a mere conceptual choice of the mind. We choose but
with the mind. Such a choice has no living power in it.
But when Savitri made the choice then the fate's cold and
dead turn was reversed, and Savitri was able to affirm
the tread of the spirit on outer circumstance. Not only
that, she was able to stop the mute march of Necessity.
In our lives there is just a mute march of Necessity. It is
compulsion that directs our course—the compulsion of fate
and circumstance. But Savitri was able to reverse this
process. How did this happen? It happened because she
made a living choice. It needs to be noted that a living
choice is made only when one faces the situation of life
without any effort to escape or to explain. There stands
nothing between the situation and ourselves—no image, no
idea, no theory. The Divine Grace pours down its benedic-
tion only on those who make a living choice. The choice

made by the mind has an element of commerce in it; it is polluted by motives. In the living choice there is just the challenge of life with no effort to cover it up with mind's explanations. Savitri made this living choice on that fateful morning, and with it she was transformed from a tender woman to a flaming warrior from the eternal peaks. She had the power to force open the door of Great Mystery kept closed by Death. It was a door to which Death had denied entry to man. With forcing open of this door, Savitri, as the poet says, burst the bounds of consciousness and Time. It is interesting to note that Sri Aurobindo places here consciousness and time together. Ours is a time-bound consciousness, and so long as it is confined within the limits of time, so long there must remain the fear of death. For, Death is the un-challenged ruler over the regions of Time. So long as consciousness is bound by time it cannot challenge the might of Death. But Savitri burst open the bounds of consciousness and thereby broke down the limitations of Time. She rose above Time where Death has no sway, and from there challenged the supremacy of Death. Here we see Sri Aurobindo speaking about the Great Miracle of Descent.

What was possible for Savitri can be made possible in the life of each human individual. One may ask : How? The Miracle of Descent comes only when there has been the purification of Ascent. The Divine Grace does not come to one who is idle and indolent — a spiritual parasite. There is a descent only when there has been an ascent. And the ascent is an act of purification, or, to put it differently, it is an act of making oneself light. Even in the physical sense one cannot be air-borne unless one travels light. On the spiritual flight too one has to dis-card the enormous luggage gathered by the mind. With all that burden one cannot become air-worthy. The burden of the mind must be dropped so that one can ascend to the utmost capacity of oneself. There comes a point in the ascending journey when man cannot proceed any further. It is at that point that the miracle of descent takes place. Man must ascend upto that point, but he must not attempt to go beyond it. This is the point where the Ascent and the Descent meet. When this meeting takes place then can one return to earth, the starting point of the ascent, but the return is filled with joy indescribable. One returns from that point, possessing transcendental power and strength. It is a strength which enables him to challenge the mighty ·empire of Death itself. He who returns is endowed with that power—but he is just a trustee of that Power, not its owner.

The entire epic of Savitri written with the exquisite pen of Sri Aurobindo contains the secret of Ascent and Descent. It is an epic which initiates one into the secrets and mysteries of both the Yoga of Ascent as well as the Yoga of Descent. The Yoga of Savitri is the Yoga of Descent, and the Yoga of Ashvapati is the Yoga of Ascent. There is no wonder, the poet assigns to the Yoga of Ashvapati a major portion of his great epic. It is in mastering the Yoga of Ashvapati that one can be vouch-safed the great miracle of the Birth of Savitri. The secret of spiritual experience lies in Descent, but one can come to it only as one undertakes the journey of Ascent, even as Ashvapati , the father of Savitri did. And so we must travel with King Ashvapati on his long and arduous journey before we can know how to burst open the door, denied and closed by Death.

CHAPTER IV

THE AVENUES OF THE BEYOND

SRI AUROBINDO says that it was the living choice made by Savitri which reversed the cold and dead turn of fate. What indeed is a living choice? It is essential to know this for it has the power to reverse the turn of fate. It has to be remembered that there is nothing more living than the facts of life. All concepts, beliefs, ideas, ideals, imaginations are dead — it is only the fact which is living. There may be any number of ideas and beliefs with reference to facts, but they are all mental constructs, and, therefore, have no living quality about them. And so the living choice of Savitri indicates her choice relating to facts. But is there any scope of choice with regard to facts? A fact is something unalterable; it is there for one to accept it, or not, as the case may be. There can be choice with regard to opinions about facts. But facts by themselves admit of no choice. Then what is the meaning of Savitri's living choice? It really means Savitri became aware of the fact, or, to put it differently, she saw clearly the fact without any superimpositions or explanations of the mind. To see the fact as a fact is indeed a living choice. In fact, it is an awareness without any element of rejection or selection. A living choice is indeed a choiceless awareness. Savitri came to this awareness with regard to the fact of Satyavan's imminent death. She became intensely aware of it, brushing aside all wishful thinking. It is this which endowed Savitri with tremendous strength so as to be able to force open the doors closed by death. It is the seeing of the fact which releases from one unsurpassed energy. It is in the awareness of the fact that one experiences the miracle of Descent from on high. If in the awareness

31

of the fact one experiences the Descent of the Divine, then surely in arriving at the state of awareness one comes to the fulfilment of the Yoga of Ascent. Does the Yoga of Ascent merely mean becoming aware of the fact of life? Is that all, or does Ascent mean something more? Regarding spiritual matters man generally has no faith in a simple approach. He thinks that spiritual life must mean going through complex practices involving austerities of a difficult nature. A simple approach is never considered seriously by a spiritual aspirant. And yet things that are sublime can be reached only through approaches that are utterly simple. We stated in the last chapter that ascent demands rendering oneself light. And so it is a process of shedding burden after burden. In other words, an ascent requires a continual process of negation. It is by constant negation that one can rise higher and higher, A spiritual flight needs a consciousness that is ceaselessly engaged in negations. While Descent is intensely positive, Ascent is a constant act of negation. It is in the negative soil created by the Ascent, that the positive plant of Descent can take root. It is by constant negations that one comes to an awareness of the facts of life. One may ask : What is it that is being negated? Ordinarily the facts of life are covered over with the projections and super-impositions of the mind. Behind the Golden Veil, woven by the mind, is concealed the face of Reality, so says the Isavasya Upanishad. To negate the Golden Veil is to become aware of the Fact of Life. The Fact and the Reality are not two different things. Reality reveals itself in the fact. When one is aware of the fact then there is the possibility of listening to the still small voice of Reality. It is in the awareness of the fact that one is enabled to listen to the Voice of the Silence. But in order to see the fact, and, be aware of it, there has to be a continual process of negating the super-impositions of the mind. It is thus that man comes to the pinnacle of ascent where alone he can meet the descending stream of the Divine. The Yoga of Ascent is the Yoga of Negations even as the Yoga of Descent is the Yoga of Affirmation. It is the Divine that affirms, the mind only asserts. Assertion and Affirmation are poles apart; one is of the mind, the other arrives only when the mind stands completely divested of all its contents and accumulations. Negation is indeed the secret of Ascent.

In the epic of Savitri, Sri Aurobindo deals exhaustively with the Yoga of Ashvapati which indeed is the Yoga of Ascent. And Ashvapati's Yoga is a series of negations. It is only when all is negated that the Voice of the Divine is heard promising the descent of one of its most brilliant rays for dispelling the darkness of the earth. And so the Birth of Savitri cannot be understood unless one understands the Yoga of Ashvapati in which the latter ascends higher and higher by a never-ending process of negations.

But one may ask : Who is Ashvapati ? And why did he undertake the stupendous jouney of ascent? What was it that induced him to face many a hazard on this upward journey? The legend of Savitri says that Ashvapati was a King of Madra Desha. He appears to have been a very wise and a benevolent ruler. He was ever active in relieving the suffering of the people, and therefore was loved and respected by all in his vast kingdom. He was, however, unhappy about one thing. He was childless, and for eighteen long years had performed austerities and offered oblations to propitiate the gods so that he may be blessed with a child. Sri Aurobindo has slightly altered the legendary story. Instead of showing Ashvapati performing austerities and offering oblations in various sacrifices, he has introduced the journey of the King in quest of a divine blessing so that he may have a child for which he was longing. And so Ashvapati's long journey is for obtaining the blessing of a child. But what is the symbolical meaning of the journey of King Ashvapati ? Ashvapati indeed takes a very hazardous journey in the course of which he goes to realms subtle and invisible — but all, in search of the Divine Blessing for a child.

Ashvapati is not just an individual; he is a king and therefore the leader of men. In fact, he is the representative of humanity, and that too the best and the noblest. He represents the Humanity of the Mind, for, he is the leader of a civilization built and nurtured on the triumph and the accomplishments of the mind. The civilization of the Mind has, as it were, chosen its representative — and this is King Aswapathy. But Ashvapati·, the representative of the human race, is childless. It is hardly necessary to point out that mind is ever barren. Mind can be clever, but it can never be creative. In the Shvetashvatara Upanishad, the Guru tells his pupil that the esoteric teaching which he had imparted to him must not be given to one who is *Aputra* or childless. This means that the esoteric wisdom must not be cast in the barren soil of the mind. It is like casting pearls before the undeserving. Ashvapati , the representative of the Mind-civilization, is *aputra* or barren. Our civilization of today built on the triumphs of the mind is utterly barren. One sees in it an expression of the cleverness of the mind. But it lacks completely the element of creativity. Ashvapati goes in search of the Creative Urge of life, for without this his kingdom must remain utterly barren. It is this creative urge that induces him to take a long and arduous journey. He must discover the fount of creative energy, for without it his kingdom will have comfort but no happiness. Mind's cleverness has invented numerous means of comfort in this age. But where is happiness? Happiness surely comes from creative living. But mind is an utter stranger to creativeness. Ashvapati must find that factor by which he can discover the secret of creative living. It is for this that he goes on a journey into realms invisible and obscure. On his journey he carries the imperative need of humanity. He is the voice of the human race and so must speak out in the court of the Divine about the urgent need of man.

It is in this background that one can appreciate fully the opening line of the Third Canto of the First Book of the epic of Savitri. Here the poett says :

A world's desire compelled her mortal birth.

The birth of Savitri was indeed an answer of the Divine to the imperative need of man conveyed by its best representative, King Ashvapati . If the need of humanity is conveyed from the highest point of ascent then the Divine is compelled to descend. And so Ashvapati climbs higher and higher until he reaches the highest point of Ascent, and from there, cries out to the Divine. Man can compel the Divine, but for this he must reach the highest point of his ascent. The cry sent from the lower reaches of the mind is not heard. Man must climb the hill of mind's negations and from there convey his demand. This is what Ashvapati does. But in order to understand this, we must journey with him into strange and weird lands, negating even the fairest spots on that journey so as to reach that point where nothing further has to be negated. Sooner or later each man must undertake this journey and discover for himself the source of Creative Living. But from where must the journey begin? How did Ashvapati start this stupendous journey? What was his starting point?

In the third Canto of the First Book, Sri Aurobindo gives us a bird's-eye view of the jouney of Ashvapati . The King begins the great journey with an intense feeling of inner dis-satisfaction. There is an awakening of the Higher Mind in Ashvapati , and it is from here that the arduous journey begins. The spiritual journey must begin from the point of inner dissatisfaction. Speaking about this awakening, the poet says about Ashvapati that —

Humanity frames his movements less and less.

Having seen the utter meaninglessness of life that lacks creativity, Ashvapati is in a state of tremendous discontent, wanting to break through the barrier that keeps humanity away from the joys of creative living. It was not just a superficial and an intellectual dissatisfaction with things. Ashvapati was seized with a deep discontent which impelled him to go to the very root of the problem and find the fountain of Eternal Joy. The poet describes this state of Ashvapati in the following lines:

His soul lived as eternity's delegate
His mind was like a fire assailing heaven,
His will a hunter in the trails of light.
An ocean impulse lifted every breath;
Each moment was a beat of puissant wings.
The little plot of our mortality
Touched by this tenant from the heights became
A playground of the living Infinite.
This bodily appearance is not all;
The form deceives, the person is a mask;
Hid deep in man celestial powers can dwell.
His fragile ship conveys through the sea of years
An incognito of the Imperishable.

The man of spiritual discontent is indeed on fire—there is a divine afflatus in him. One can say about him in terms of the Christian hymn that he is "restless until he finds his rest in Thee". Ashvapati was indeed in this condition. The poet says "his mind was like a fire assailing heaven". Ashvapati was in a state of tremendous urgency, for, the problem of humanity must be solved and that too without delay,–otherwise man will degenerate into a machine with all creative urges smothered within him. As long as the mind seeks explanations and justifications, so long man never comes to a state of urgency. Ashvapati was past that stage, for, no explanation could satisfy him; he wanted to assail the very citadel of heaven. Ashvapati suddenly became a mere tenant on the little plot of mortality. He was a king, but to him his earthly kingdom seemed meaningless without the touch of heaven. He realizes that the body is not all, "the form deceives and the person is a mask". No longer was he prepared to accept the masked existence. He felt that there must be something greater and vaster than the life to which he had been linked so far. About Ashvapati, the poet says:

> He feels his substance of undying self
> And loses his kinship to mortality.
> A beam of the Eternal smites his heart,
> His thought stretches into infinitude,
> All in him turns to spirit vastnesses.

When a real discontent arises in the life of man then no risk is regarded by him as too great. He steps out of the normal routine of life, and feels within him the strength to challenge all hordes. Such was the condition of Ashvapati. He had risen to the state of the Higher Mind. In Sri Aurobindo's Philosophy, Higher Mind has a special significance. It is not just a modification of the lower mind and its propensities. The Higher Mind is a state where the individual has discarded all the pettiness and the smallness of worldly existence. No longer does the world of ordinary interest attract him. One comes to this state when one sees the utter meaningless-ness of what one was doing so far. Whether there is another way of life or not, one does not want to remain in the suffocating atmosphere of the world with its petty interests. Ashvapati had done with the ways of the world, and was now in search of something that would contain his soul in tremendous revolt. Sri Aurobindo gives expression to the new mood of Ashvapati thus:

> Out of apprenticeship to Ignorance
> Wisdom upraised him to her master craft
> And made him an arch-mason of the soul,
> A builder of the Immortal's secret house,
> An aspirant to supernal Timelessness;
> Freedom and empire called to him from on high;
> Above mind's twilight and life's star-led night
> There gleamed the dawn of a spiritual day.

He had done with his apprenticeship, his craftsmanship, and had become the arch-mason of the soul engaged in building a New Temple for Humanity. The poet says that Ashvapati was an aspirant to supernal Timelessness. He had seen for long the endless succession of Time, but the flow of Time by itself made no sense. He wanted to know the meaning of Time-succession. But for this he must touch the realm of Timelessness, for it is the Timeless that contains the meaning of time. And so as Sri Aurobindo says, Ashvapati must move on to the twilight of the Mind, he must journey from the darkness of the Mind to the Dawn of the Spirit. Ashvapati had indeed undertaken a stupendous task, and such was the nature of his discontent that no half-measures could give him rest. The state of the Highr Mind impelled him to climb higher and higher, until he reached the point beyond which he could not go by his own effort. He must arrive "on the frontiers of Eternity". He had heard the call of the Beyond. How could he remain chained to the futile movement of time?

The poet says that Ashvapati in his journey must come to a point where he shall own "the house of undivided Time". It is a steep climb towards which he must move until he comes to the Silence of Space itself. Sri Aurobindo gives in this bird's-eye view of the journey, a peep into the states of consciousness to which Ashvapati must rise. The poet says:

> Silent and listening in the silent heart
> For the coming of the new and the unknown.
> He gazed across the empty stillnesses
> And heard the footsteps of the undreamed Idea
> In the far avenues of the Beyond.

Ashvapati voyaged from plane to plane so that his consciousness widened into cosmic dimensions. From the world of the Form into the realm of the Formless, he

moves, and the world of the Formless has no frontiers.
There as the poet says:

. . . one can be wider than the world;
. . . one is one's own infinity

To what stupendous heights of consciousness does Ashvapati
rise can be guaged by the following lines of exquisite beauty.
The poet says:

His centre was no more in earthly mind,
A power of seeing silence filled his limbs :
Caught by a voiceless white epiphany
Into a vision that surpasses forms,
Into a living that surpasses life,
He neared the still consciousness sustaining all,
The voice that only by speech can move the mind
Became a silent knowledge in the soul;
The strength that only in action feels its truth
Was lodged now in a mute omnipotent peace.

There was a mute omnipotent peace in which his entire
strength was lodged, but it was a stillness that sustained
all. The journey of Ashvapati was long and arduous, but
the end was sublime. He had moved on in a world
that was completely different not merely in outer form but
in content. He had risen to a dimension of living unimagined by the mind. About his new abode of consciousness, Sri Aurobindo says:

The fate that punishes virtues with defeat,
The tragedy that destroys long happiness,
The weeping of Love, the quarrel of the Gods,
Ceased in a truth which lives in its own light.
His soul stood free, a witness and a king.
Absorbed no more in the moment-ridden flux
Where mind incessantly drifts as on a raft
Hurried from phenomenon to phenomenon,
He abode at rest in indivisible Time,
As if a story long written but acted now,

In his present he held his future and his past,
Felt in the seconds the uncounted years
And saw the hours like dots upon a page.

To feel moments in uncounted years and to see hours
like dots upon a page is indeed to transcend the field
of time as it is understood by us the mortals. He found
his abode in Indivisible Time — or in the Eternal Now.

Before describing the actual journey of Ashvapati into
invisible planes, Sri Aurobindo gives us in this First Book,
in the last three Cantos, a preview of whither the Royal
traveller is going. He tells us about the elevated state of
consciousness which will be the end of his journey. We are
invited to have a peep into the end of the long journey
from where the King will return to earth bringing happy
tidings. Ashvapati is going into regions where no frontiers of time exist. In fact he comes to the experience of
Indivisible Time so that the past, the present and the
future lie before him like an open book. He was going
to realms where according to the poet : "Mind screened
no more the shoreless infinite". The land towards which
Ashvapati was moving was indeed a country where the
sway of the mind was no more. It was a region which
transcended the mind. The poet says that in that state
of high altitude, Ashvapati came to transcendental
experiences. These are expressed in the following lines:

Across a void retreating sky he glimpsed
Through a last glimmer and drift of vanishing stars
The superconscient realms of motionless peace
Where judgement ceases and the word is mute
And the Unconceived lies pathless and alone.
There came not form or any mounting voice;
There only was Silence and the Absolute.

Sri Aurobindo says that "out of that stillness, mind new-
born arose". The renewal of the mind is possible only
in absolute stillness. It is in silence that man's regenera-

tion takes place. But this silence is not merely where the "word is mute", It is a silence where no movement of thought occurs. In this regeneration of the mind happens a fundamental transformation of man. In the words of the poet:

A transfiguration in the mystic depth,
A happier cosmic working could begin
And fashion the world-shape in him anew,
God found in Nature, Nature fulfilled in God.

Ashvapati experiences a true release of the soul. And after this release he feels within himself power and energy unheard of. He was freed from ignorance to which he had been chained so long. He realized that life was not a movement of chance; in fact he saw in the world "a living movement of the body of God". One must first be free from ignorance before one comes to understand the Secret Knowledge. Such was the transformation of Ashvapati that the poet says:

The days were travellers on a destined road,
The Nights companions of his musing spirit.
A heavenly impetus quickened all his breast;
The trudge of time changed to a splendid march;
The Divine Dwarf towered to unconquered worlds,
Earth grew too narrow for his victories.

The last three cantos of the First Book are a prelude to the actual journey of Ashvapati. And these cantos have been named most appropriately. First there is a release from Ignorance, then is the awakening into Secret Knowledge, and lastly with that Knowledge comes the Freedom of the Spirit. The soul is more akin to one's psychic personality. One must be free first from the ignorance of this personality. Then alone comes the understanding of the Secret Knowledge. Here the Secret Knowledge is indeed the occult knowledge which Ashvapati finds in the course of his journey. But the occult knowledge is not enough.

One must be free even from the subtle framework of this occult knowledge. It is only then that there comes the Freedom of the Spirit which is indeed a profound mystical experience. Breaking the shell of ignorance, Ashvapati acquires Occult knowledge, but when even this is put aside then comes to the Royal traveller an experience of deep mysticism. How does Ashvapati move on to these stages? These are narrated in the cantos which deal with the actual journey, plane by plane. Ashvapati returns to earth not merely with Secret or Occult knowledge. He returns with a deep mystical experience. The poet says that "the human in him paced with the divine". In Ashvapati ,

> A Power worked, but none knew whence it came.
> The universal strengths were linked with his;
> Filling earth's smallness with their boundless breadths,
> He drew the energies that transmute an age.
> His walk through Time outstripped the human stride.

Ashvapati drew the energy that enabled him to transmute an age. He could usher in a new Age, for, there was some mysterious power that was working through him. From the Timeless region he came to the field of Time, but here his walk outstripped the human stride.

Ashvapati moves from Ignorance to Secret Knowledge, and from thence into the Freedom of the Spirit. From the negative to the positive, and from thence to the Transcendental—this is the road which Ashvapati traverses. From the ignorance of the body and the mind he rises to the gathering of the Secret Knowledge. What is the nature of this Knowledge? For this we must turn to the Fourth Canto of the First Book.

CHAPTER V

THE VOWELS OF INFINITY

The journey of spiritual ascent begins from one's release from Ignorance. Unless man steps out of ignorance, he cannot proceed further, for, it is ignorance that pulls him down. But how does one step out of ignorance? Is it by acquiring knowledge? Is it by gathering information? The man who says he knows is indeed the most ignorant person. For, how can any one say that he knows? One can know about building a bridge or constructing a house, one can know about a mathematical equation or about some geographical details. But how can he say that he knows about something which is constantly in a state of flux. In order to say that one knows, the thing has to be stationary. One can say that one knows about things that are static. But life is never static; it is in a state of flux, and, therefore, new from moment to moment. The flux of life is not a theory; it is not just a mental concept. One can see for oneself the flow of life and be aware of the constant state of flux. That which is living is not the same any two moments. And so one can never approach life from the base of knowledge. Knowledge is rooted in the past, but that which is living exists only in the moment of the present. And so to step out of one's ignorance ·is to be aware that one really does not know what life is. The mind that says that it does not know has by that very statement come to an extraordinary state of enquiry. And the journey of spiritual ascent can be undertaken only by one in whom the Flame of Enquiry has been lighted. Without this enquiry, no movement on the spiritual path is possible. But enquiry is not to be mistaken for curiosity. In curiosity mind wants to gather more knowledge, whereas in enquiry mind's process of gathering knowledge is brought to a halt. When one looks at what the mind has gathered then does one put it aside without any struggle whatsoever. When the hollowness of mind's knowledge is seen then the process of gathering knowledge is brought to a stop. In that interval where the process of gathering knowledge by the mind is halted, real enquiry begins. He who says that he knows is an individual with a closed mind. The mind that has come to conclusions has extinguished the flame of enquiry. And so the first requisite on the Path of Ascent is a tremendous sense of enquiry. This comes only when the knowledge gathered by the mind is totally negated. This is the first factor of negation on the upward journey.

Ashvapati negates the knowledge that had been his guide till now. And in this negation he finds his freedom from ignorance. Man's release from ignorance comes when he discards the knowledge which the mind has gathered. There is no greater ignorance than the holding on to the knowledge gathered by the mind. Here we do not refer to mathematical knowledge or knowledge regarding measurable things. It is when we enter the field which defies all measurement that knowledge becomes a hindrance. It is this knowledge that has to be negated so that freed from ignorance one may experience the lighting of the Flame of Enquiry. When Enquiry or *Jijnasa* is active then man steps out of ignorance and is ready to learn. A readiness to learn is the pre-requisite for undertaking a spiritual journey. Ashvapati had begun to feel that the body and the mind were not all. With that realization he had negated the entire base of his knowledge from where he was accustomed to act so far. To negate the very base of knowledge is to be free from ignorance. It may seem paradoxical but that indeed is the truth.

Man begins by negating the sensorial knowledge. That truly is the base from where most people act and react. When the sensorial knowledge is negated then there opens out to man a new category of knowledge. This is the Secret or the Occult knowledge. Ashvapati on his journey becomes acquainted with that knowledge on plane after plane. It is Secret and Occult because it is outside the purview of the senses. Sri Aurobindo has entitled the Fourth Canto of the First Book as "Secret Knowledge". And so into this field he takes us for a bird's eye-view of Ashvapati's journey along the planes and sub-planes of subtler regions. Sri Aurobindo says:

This world is a beginning and a base
Where Life and Mind erect their structured dreams;
An unborn Power must build reality.
A deathbound littleness is not all we are:
Immortal our forgotten vastnesses
Await discovery in our summit selves:
Unmeasured breadths and depths of being are ours.
Neighbours of Heaven are Nature's altitudes.
To these high-peaked dominions sealed to our search
Too far from surface Nature's postal routes,
Too lofty for our mortal lives to breathe,
Deep in us a forgotten kinship points
And a faint voice of ecstasy and prayer
Calls to those lucent lost immensities.

Each man has his *Vishva-rupa*, his Universal Form. This lies extended in realms invisible. We ourselves have lost a sense of our own immensities. As the poet says we have "unmeasured breadths and depths of being".

Man can go in search of his own immensities only when he realizes that he is not merely a death-bound littleness. This demands an inward turn, an inquiry into depth. Man knows the breadth of life through the vast sensorial knowledge he gathers. But he has to discover his depth. And depth is hidden below the surface. It is this which

demands a probe into the Occult nature of things. Somehow man in his reflective moments feels that what appears on the surface of things is not all. There are
hidden and subliminal layers. When he steps out of the
ignorance of mind's knowledge then he begins to inquire
about deeper aspects of life. Behind this deeper inquiry
there is an urge to find something that does not get corrupted by time. Man is eternally in search of—

> A mind unvisited by illusion's gleams,
> A will expressive of soul's deity,
> A strength not forced to stumble by its speed,
> A joy that drags not sorrow as its shade.

In the realm of sensorial experiences man knows only
that joy over which the shadow of pain is invariably cast.
But there must be that Pure Joy which is for ever free
from the touch of pain and sorrow. But this is not to be
found on the surface of life with which he has been accustomed so far. He must dive deeper, for, perchance, he
may discover a source of pure joy in the hidden recesses
of his being. But as the poet says "all is screened, subliminal" and one needs other eyes with which to look at
the deeper things of life. This urge for deeper things arises
only when one misses something in his surface existence.
He who does not miss, does not hear the call of the deep.
But Ashvapati had seen the hollowness of surface existence. He missed something which urged him to move
on into realms hidden and invisible. What was it that he
missed in his surface existence? The poet has expressed
it beautifully thus:

> We must fill the immense lacuna we have made,
> Re-wed the closed finite's lonely consonant
> With the open vowels of Infinity,
> A hyphen must connect Matter and Mind,
> The narrow isthmus of the ascending soul.

Here the word Mind signifies the Spirit, for, as the
poet says there must be a hyphen connecting Spirit and

Matter. But it can be only a narrow isthmus, a narrow strip of land connecting the two vast areas of Spirit and Matter. The hyphen has to be very subtle, almost intangible. But will Ashvapati find this isthmus on the occult lands, will he find there the Vowels of Infinity to wed the finite's lonely consonant? The answer can be given only by Ashvapati after he has travelled into those regions. Today man wants to speak a language which contains only the consonants. How can such a language be spoken? And how can it become intelligible? The consonant is the masculine nature of consciousness. Unless the vowels of feminine consciousness are wed to the consonants, the language of life can never become intelligible. How miserable is our language of consonants without the soft and the feminine touch of the vowels can be understood by what Sri Aurobindo says in the following lines:

As if an unintelligible phrase
Suggested a million renderings to the Mind,
It lends purport to the random world.
A conjecture leaning upon doubtful proofs,
A message misunderstood, a thought confused
Missing its aim is all that it can speak
Or a fragment of the universal word.

It leaves two giant letters void of sense. Will a journey into the occult worlds bring Ashvapati to the discovery of the Vowels of Life? Or will he find there only an extension of consonants? The occult world is inhabited by gods. Do they know the secret of uniting the finite consonants with the Vowels of Infinity? The infinite is not ever-lasting. While the latter connotes an extension of time, the first indicates the extinction of time. The occult world is only an extension of the world in which we live. Ashvapati's movement into the occult world is a movement from the *Kshara* to the *Akshara*—from the Perishable to the Imperishable. But these are only the opposites. There must be something that transcends the

opposites. Bhagavad Gita calls it the *Purushottama* or the
Purusa. Ashvapati must get the secret knowledge that
is in the keeping of the Gods.

But the world of man and the world of the gods are
the two opposites of creation. The Seen and the Unseen
worlds are like the two poles. Stepping out of the meaninglessness of the Seen world, one naturally feels like exploring the Unseen, for, perchance, one may find there an
answer to one's unceasing query. One must explore the
two opposites for without this exploration one cannot
know what the Transcendental *Pursusa* is. While Man is
restless, Gods are unmoved. The unmoved gods many a
time seem too cold and aloof. They seem by their cold-
ness to deny the world. Can the answer to life's query
be found by denying the world? Neither in indulgence
nor in denial must lie the answer. Ashvapati negated the
indulgence of the world, he must come to the negation of
world-denial too. But for this he must know the ways
of the gods. And that is what he attempts to do as he
moves into worlds hidden and invisible. But Sri Aurobindo indicates as to what he may find. He says in the
following lines,

> Careless they seem of the grief that stings the world's
> heart,
> Careless of the pain that rends its body and life;
> Above joy and sorrow is that grandeur's walk;
> They have no portion in the good that dies,
> Mute, pure, they share not in the evil done;
> Else might their strength be marred and could not
> save
>
> Undriven by a brief life's will to act,
> Unharassed by the spur of pity and fear,
> He makes no haste to untie the cosmic knot
> Or the world's torn jarring heart to reconcile.

From the identification of man to the aloofness of
the gods—this seems to be the journey from the Seen to

the Unseen realms. Having known man's identification, Ashvapati y must know the aloofness of the gods too. As the poet says in the above lines the gods make no haste to untie the cosmic knot nor to reconcile the world's torn jarring hearts. They seek to remain aloof lest their strength be marred. The gods would rather have the Law take its own course than that they interfere in its working. If man is a slave to Fate, Gods seem to be slaves to Law. There must be something greater than the Law but this cannot be found in the realm of the Gods. Sri Aurobindo says :

> . . . a spiritual secret aid is there;
> While a tardy Evolution's coils wind on,
> And Nature hews her way through adamant,
> A divine intervention thrones above.

This throne above is indeed of the Purusa who transcends, the *Kshara* and also the *Akshara*, he is beyond man and also beyond the gods. He is to be found not through occult knowledge but through mystic communion. About the Purusa, Sri Aurobindo says:

> One who has shaped this world is ever its lord:
> Our errors are his steps upon the way;
> He works through the fierce vicissitudes of our lives,
> He works through the hard breath of battle and toil,
> He works through our sins and sorrows and our tears.
> He is the Maker and the world he made,
> He is the Vision and he is the seer;
> He is himself the actor and the act;
> He is himself the knower and the known,
> He is himself the dreamer and the dream.

The mystery of life is not with the gods but with Him who is both Immanent and Transcendent. It is in the *Lila* or the Play of the *Purusa* and the *Prikriti* that one can unravel the mystery of life as also of death.

The secret of life as well as of death is to be found neither in the indulgence of man nor in the aloofness of

the gods. The introduction of the word ·"gods" by Sri
Aurobindo has its own significance. "Gods" are not
necessarily certain entities living on invisible planes of the
universe; they are indicative of certain states of consciousness. Man is lost in the indulgence of participation,
and gods are committed to a state of aloofness. In the
first we see the factor of unrighteousness, while in the
second we see the element of self-righteousness. Man is
eternally concerned with the problems of unrighteousness,
of fighting the evil. But the factor that operates in the
lives of the gods is that of self-righteousness out of which
arise elements of aloofness and self-centred neutrality. And
so gods represent the state of consciousness, the distinguish-
ing feature of which is self-righteousness. The creator of
the universe is neither lost in the indulgence of his own
creation, nor is he aloof from his creation, standing away
as a neutral being, watching the movement of creation.
He is not just a participant nor is he just a witness of his
creation. He is a participant and a witness at the same
time. This is the dynamic concept of the Creator that
Sri Aurobindo places before us in his *Savitri*. The relationship between the Creator and his Creation is a living
relationship. The Creator is not one who is resting on
his oars after having brought creation into existence. He
is not just watching his creation from a distance. He is
all the time present in his creation, and yet he is away
from it. He is both near and far; he is both immanent
and transcendent; he is *nirguna* and *saguna* at the same time.
Sri Aurobindo has portrayed this dynamic relationship of
the Creator with his Creation in his references to the play
of the *Purusa* and *Prakriti*. He says:

> He knows her only, he has forgotten himself;
> To her he abandons all to make her great.
> He hopes in her to find himself anew,
> Incarnate, wedding his infinity's peace
> To her creative passion's ecstasy.

Sri Aurobindo has described the play of *Purusa* and *Prakriti* as the play of the Lover and the Beloved. His conception of Godhead is in terms of the Creator pervading the Creation. The Creator willingly accepts the limitations of creation. This is known in Hindu philosophy as the Eternal Sacrifice of God. The Bhagavad Gita says that "the Eternal, the All-permeating, is ever present in sacrifice". However, the word sacrifice does not convey the concept of Godhead which Sri Aurobindo has placed in his philosophy. In a relationship of love one does not talk of sacrifice, and for Sri Aurobindo the relationship of the Creator with his creation is that of love. What will not the Lover do for his Beloved ? As Sri Aurobindo says, "the Purusa has forgotten himself", for, he abandons himself to make her great. This dynamic relationship of *Purusa* and *Prakriti* is nowhere to be seen in Eastern or Western philosophy. Sri Aurobindo did not accept the concept of Maya or Illusion. But even the traditional *Lila-vada*, the doctrine of Play, does not completely explain what Sri Aurobindo wishes to convey. The creation is not just the play of the Creator. In play there is a certain amount of dualism. But Sri Aurobindo says : "They are Two who are One". In Play one does not find those deeper overtones of relationship which one associates with Love. And so neither the Mayavada of Sri Shankaracharya, nor the Lila-vada of Sri Vallabhacharya can convey what Sri Aurobindo indicates in the relationship of Two who are One. Love and Love alone can explain this relationship between *Purusa* and *Prakriti*, between the Creator and his Ceation. It is the relationship of Krishna and Radha where Krishna forgets himself in his love for Radha. The following lines of the poet make this relationship clear. He says :

A rapt solicitor for her love and grace,
His bliss in her to him is his whole world.
Or, a courtier in her countless retinue,
Content to be with her and feel her near

He makes the most of the little that she gives
And all she does drapes with his own delight.
A glance can make his whole day wonderful,
A word from her lips with happiness wings the hours
This whole wide world is only he and she.

In this canto which we are considering, the poet
gives us a pre-view of , Ashvapati's journey. From the
world of men, he goes to the world of the gods, but this
is a movement from involvement to aloofness. This is
what the Occult journey implies. But Ashvapati must
proceed further from the aloofness of the gods to the
ecstasy of Love, for, thus alone can he understand the
meaning of all existence. In the eyes of the Beloved is
enshrined the image of the Lover; in Creation, and there
alone, one meets the Creator. The Secret Knowledge
conveyed by Occultism is not enough, Ashvapati must
move on to the ecstasy of the mystic union. It is in
the moment of mystical ecstasy that one can feel the
loving touch of the Divine. The Poet says :

In Nature's instrument loiters secret God.
The Immanent lives in man as in his house.
Eternal, he assents to Fate and Time,
Immortal dallies with mortality.

/ Ashvapati was an intrepid traveller in search of the
secret of Creative Living. The problem of /Ashvapati,
and, therefore, of the entire humanity, has been expressed
beautifully by the poet in just one line. He says: "Our
life is a paradox with God for key". Without finding this
key, our paradoxes cannot be resolved. And /Ashvapati
is in search of this key. Having found the world of men
as utterly barren, he probes the plane of the gods, for,
perchance the key to the paradoxes may be found there.
But even here it is not found, and so he moves further to
enquire from God Himself the meaning of his Creation.
The poet says:

He has made this tenement of flesh his own,
His image in the human measure cast
That to his divine measure we might rise;
Then in a figure of divinity
The Maker shall recast us and impose
A plan of godhead on the mortal's mould
Lifting our finite minds to his infinity,
Touching the moment with eternity.
This transfiguration is earth's due to heaven:
A mutual debt binds man to the Supreme:
His nature we must put on as he put ours.

Here the poet tells us about Humanity transforming itself into Divinity. But how will this be? Earth has a debt to discharge to heaven, for, did not the Divine take the human form so that humanity may reach perfection? How is the earth going to discharge this debt? Man must ascend to the highest peaks of his perfection, for, thus alone can he find the key that shall resolve the many paradoxes of his life. For this man must discover the Creator in his vast Creation. Sri Aurobindo says that Purusa forgot himself in Prakriti, but in the game of hide and seek, Prakriti must re-discover Purusa, for, that is the debt which Prakriti must discharge to Purusa. The poet tells us :

He is the Player who became the play,
He is the Thinker who became the thought;
He is the many who was the silent One.

To re-discover the Player who became the play is the sublime mission that animates Ashvapati in his long journey. He must explore the greater world, and bring down to the suffering and confused humanity a message of New Hope. And Ashvapati does return to earth with a message from the Heaven. Mother Earth had entrusted him with a mission. Did he know what that mission was. and whither was he going for the fulfilment of that mission?

It is true that Ashvapati felt within himself a divine
discontent. Humanity seemed to him utterly barren and
he cried out to earth for humanity's redemption. And
it is in answer to that cry that Mother Earth sent him to
a hazardous journey so that he may find the Elixir of Life.
But perhaps Ashvapati himself did not know what the
nature of the journey would be and what would be his
destination. Sri Aurobindo says:

Across   the noise and multitudinous cry,
Across the rapt unknowable silences,
Through a strange mid-world under supernal skies,
Beyond earth's longitudes and latitudes,
His goal is fixed outside all present maps.
But none learns whither through the unknown he
                                                    sails
Or what secret mission the great Mother gave.
In the hidden strength of her omnipotent Will,
Driven by her breath across life's tossing deep,
Through the thunder's roar and through the windless
                                                    hush,
Through fog and mist where nothing more is seen,
He carries her sealed orders in his breast.
Late will he know, opening the mystic script,
Whether to a blank port in the Unseen
He goes or, armed with her fiat, to discover
A new mind and body in the city of God
And enshrine the Immortal in his glory's house
And make the finite one with Infinite.

Ashvapati   undertakes the stupendous journey with
the sealed orders of the Mother Earth. He does not know
what his mission is, and whither is he going. But impelled
by the inner discontent he goes through the "thunder's
roar and the windless hush, through fog and mist where
nothing more is seen". But there is the hidden strength
of the indomitable will of the Mother Earth, and it is this
which is impelling him to move on across life's tossing deep.

Undaunted by the strange and unknown forces, Ashvapati carries on his journey. The poet says:

> And never can the mighty traveller rest
> And never can the mystic voyage cease,
> Till the nescient dusk is lifted from man's soul
> And the morns of God have overtaken his night.

Ashvapati cannot rest until the Dawn has overtaken the night—for these are his orders. He goes as earth's representative to bring from heaven a new light which shall dispel the darkness of man. The Mother Earth has sent her noblest son to wrest from heaven the secret of Immortality. Ashvapati must bring with him the Key with which to unlock the paradoxes of man's life. But for this he must understand the Supreme Paradox of the Divine, for, what greater paradox there can be than the Divine incarnating as Man, the Immortal taking upon itself the sheath of mortality? Why did the Absolute plunge into the limitations of the relative? Why did the Eternal come into the slow and the tardy processes of Time? What was the purpose of it all? The poet says:

> To evoke a person in the impersonal Void
> That the eyes of the Timeless might look out from
> Time.
> For this he left his white infinity
> And laid on the Spirit the burden of the flesh,
> That Godhead's seed might flower in mindless Space.

The seed of Godhead can flower only in mindless Space. But for this Ashvapati must come to the condition of absolute space, the space not broken up by mind. It is only then that he can understand the Divine Purpose; only then can he resolve the Great Paradox of the Immortal putting on mortality. This is not something which the mind can understand. Along with many other things, Ashvapati must negate mind itself, for, the mind cannot go into the rarefied atmosphere of the spirit. It is only by communing with the Divine that the purpose of the Divine can be understood. But mind stands as the greatest hurdle in the way of Communion. How does Ashvapati⁄ negate the mind? Before the mind is negated, he must know how the mind comes into being. The mind of man is the product of Evolution, and so one must know the story of Evolution before one can commune with the Mindless Space where alone the mystery of the eternal play of Purusa and Prakriti can be understood. Through Ashvapativ's journey, Sri Aurobindo has narrated the fascinating story of Evolution, not merely of forms but of life and consciousness. And so we must travel with him, plane by plane, to know the significance of Evolution. Evolution is a movement in Time. We must know what this movement is, for, it is in this movement of Time that one can feel the intangible presence of the Timeless. Then shall we know why the Spirit took upon itself the burden of flesh, why Divinity took its incarnation in humanity, why Freedom chose to function in the campus of limitation.

CHAPTER VI

A CONE OF FIRE

IN the last three cantos of the First Book of *Savitri*, Sri Aurobindo has, as it were, given both the prelude and the epitome of Ashvapati's journey. We see in this, both the beginning as well as the end, of the travels of the King who undertakes the journey on behalf of the entire humanity so as to convey to the Divine the urgent need of Man. In these three cantos, the poet refers to the Release of the Soul, the gathering of the Secret Knowledge and the Freedom of the Spirit. There is a Book of the Golden Precepts, held in great esteem by the Buddhists. From this book, Madam H.P. Blavatsky has chosen some fragments and published a book with her annotations, entitled *The Voice of the Silence*. In this, there is a reference to the Three Halls through which the spiritual neophyte must pass. These Halls are the Hall of Ignorance, the Hall of Knowledge, and the Hall of Wisdom. It is only when he steps out of the third hall that he comes to the Valley of Bliss. The Book is surcharged with Occult traditions, and yet it indicates the Way of Mystic Union. Now the three Halls of this Buddhist book have some relevance to what Sri Aurobindo suggests in the last three cantos of the First Book. The release of the soul is akin to leaving behind the Hall of Ignorance. Here the soul means the personality of man which obviously is his acquired nature built through the passage of time as a result of resistances and indulgences. The spiritual traveller must step out of the prison of his own personality, and this is tantamount to the release of the soul. Then comes the acquiring of the secret or the occult knowledge. The spiritual pilgrim, no doubt, tarries a while in this region, but he cannot

57

settle down there, for, there is much that is missed in
this land. The leaving behind of this region is comparable to the stepping out of the Hall of Knowledge. Then
according to the Buddhist book one comes to the Hall of
Wisdom. This is the state of the Intuitive Mind in terms
of Sri Aurobindo's philosophy. The other two stages
refer to the Higher Mind and the Illumined Mind, respectively, in the context of Sri Aurobindo's classification. It
is the Hall of Wisdom which represents the realm of the
Spirit. In fact, one might say it lies on the outskirts of
the Land of the Spirit. The spiritual pilgrim must step
out of the Hall of Wisdom too, for, then alone he can
move from the Intuitive Mind to the State of the Over-
mind. It is only when the traveller moves out of the
Hall of Wisdom that he knows the real freedom of the
Spirit. And the experience of this freedom brings the
neophyte to the Vale of Bliss. It is a Vale of Bliss because
it is in the state of Over-mind that the intimations of the
Super-mind are received. It is the Freedom of the Spirit
with which the last canto of the First Book is concerned.
It is here that the cord of the mind is snapped. Here the
mind is negated in a complete and an absolute manner.
But then what is that state where the mind is not? The
poet tells us:

> When life had stopped its beats,
> Death broke not in.

It is an interval of Nothingness, of Creative Void,
and it is in this Void that the Voice of the Silence is heard.
It is in this Void that the intimations of the Super-Mind
come. This Creative Void is described by Sri Aurobindo
as "when breath and thought were still". What one finds
in this Void is something beyond even the wildest imagination of the mind. The poet says:

> Here even the highest rapture Time can give
> Is a mimicry of ungrasped beautitudes,
> A mutilated statue of ecstasy,

A wounded happiness that cannot live,
A brief felicity of mind or sense.

Even the highest joy that the mind can conceive of
is like a mutilated statue of ecstasy compared to what
one experiences in this Vale of Bliss, the interval of Creative void. The complete negation which is the very quintessence of Ashvapati's journey is hinted at by the poet
in the following lines:

His soul retired from all that he had done.
Hushed was the futile din of human toil
Forsaken wheeled the circle of the days;
In distance sank the crowded tramp of life.
The Silence was his sole companion left.

When all is negated what remains is Silence, absolute Silence. This is the highest peak of spiritual experience. It is negative and therefore intensely positive. The
vision that came when Silence was the only companion
of Ashvapati has been superbly described by Sri Aurobindo. He says:

A call was on him from intangible heights;
Indifferent to the little outpost Mind,
He dwelt in the wideness of the Eternal's reign.
His being now exceeded thinkable space,
His boundless thought was neighbour to cosmic sight:
A force came down into his mortal limbs,
A current from eternal seas of Bliss.

The poet says that Ashvapati had become "a living
centre of the Illimitable". It is most significant that the
poet, in the above lines, describes Mind as a little outpost. And it is only when the mind becomes thus a little
outpost that a current from the eternal seas of Bliss can
be felt. This is the state of the Over-mind where the
pilgrim comes to the Vale of Bliss. This is the state of
true spiritual or mystical experience. It is here that the
Freedom of the Spirit is known. Sri Aurobindo has entitled

the last canto of the First Book as the "Yoga of Spirit's Freedom and Greatness'. It is here that the Spirit awakens to its intrinsic greatness. So far he had moved with borrowed greatness, but now, in knowing the Spirit's Freedom, he comes to the awareness of his own true greatness, his own Uniqueness. And absolute freedom is known only when the vision of one's own Uniqueness comes. To such a one there is an irresistible urge to transform the very earth into Heaven. The poet says that Ashvapati felt like:

> An arrow leaping through eternity
> Suddenly shot from the tense bow of Time,
> A ray returning to its parent sun.
> Death lay beneath him like a gate of sleep.
> One-pointed to the immaculate Delight,
> Questing for God as for a splendid prey,
> He mounted burning like a cone of fire.

"Burning like a cone of fire" that is what one feels when one comes to the experience of spiritual ecsatsy. This is the highest bliss of the mystic, for, "His Spirit mingles with Eternity's heart and bears the silence of the Infinite". By a process of continual and unrelenting negation, Ashvapati comes to the summit of the ascending path. Sri Aurobindo, speaking about Ashvapati coming to this state, says:

> His being towered into pathless heights,
> Naked of its vesture of humanity.
> A strong Descent leaped down, A Might, a Flame,
> A Beauty half-visible with deathless eyes,
> A violent Ecstasy, a Sweetness dire,
> Enveloped him with its stupendous limbs.
> His nature shuddered in the Unknown's grasp.
> In a moment shorter than Death, longer than Time,
> By a power more ruthless than Love, happier than
>   heaven.

Sri Aurobindo's *Savitri* is not just a book. Here Sri Aurobindo narrates his own spiritual experience. It is because of this that the language is so living, and so powerful. In this supreme mystical state, Ashvapati felt that his "soul and cosmos faced as equal powers". Such was the stupendous strength that he felt within himself. Now nothing was impossible to him, for, his consciousness had so widened that it had no limits or boundaries whatsoever. He saw a new order and a new design in the vast universe—not the plan his mind had superimposed, but the intrinsic plan of the Creator Himself. Very often man complains that in the creation of God there is much sorrow and injustice where the man of evil intentions flourishes, and the man of good actions suffers. But man has no right to say this so long as he does not even look at the creation of God. We live most of the time in our own creations, in the world projected and super-imposed by the mind. It is only when the super-imposition of the mind ceases that one can view the Creation of God. Man sees his own creation and blames the creator. When Ashvapati stood in the total silence of the mind, then he saw for the first time the Great Design of the Creator. He saw not only the pattern but the purpose of entire creation. Man is destined to be a collaborator with God, but such collaboration is possible only when he destroys his own world of mental projections and super-impositions. In the total negation of the mind, Ashvapati saw the Great Vision, and this view of the Great Design inspired him to change the face of the earth, and to rebuild it nearer to the Heart of the Creator. Ashvapati returns to earth inspired and strengthened by the Vision that was vouchsafed to him. This is how the the poet describes the inspired state of Ashvapati :

An answer brought to the torn earth's hungry need
Rending the night that had concealed the Unknown,
Giving to her her lost forgotten soul.

A grand solution closed the long impasse
In which the heights of mortal effort end.

Sri Aurobindo tells us that the mortal effort at best can go upto that point where only an impasse is created. All efforts of the mind lead upto a deadlock. The civilization of ours built on the stupendous efforts of the mind faces today deadlock after deadlock. Who will end this impasse created by the mind? The poet tells us that Ashvapati brings with him the answer to the hungry need of the torn earth. He heralds the coming of the New dawn where the night is rent asunder, revealing the secret of the Unknown which it had long concealed in her bosom. In Ashvapati's return, earth finds once again its lost soul. Has not the modern civilization lost its soul? It needs the miracle of Descent whereby it can re-discover its soul. And without the re-discovery of the soul, man must rapidly slide down the inclined plane of degeneration and disintegration. The poet says that Ashvapati's ascent indicated a movement:

From Matter's abysses to the Spirit's peaks.
Above were the Immortal's changeless seats,
White chambers of dalliance with Eternity
And the stupendous gates of the Alone.

Ashvapati had reached right upto the gates of the Alone, and he saw on the journey "homelands of beauty shut to human eyes". He had gone upto the point where the realm of the mind ended. He found a place of quiet and silence where he could abide awhile. This was the Creative Interval, the great Spiritual Void where he was destined to hear the Voice Divine. The stupendous height to which he had come has been described in exquisite lines by the poet. He says:

A voyager upon uncharted routes
Fronting the viewless danger of the Unknown,
Adventuring across enormous realms,
He broke into another Space and Time.

The great spiritual adventure which Ashvapati had undertaken brought him to a new dimension of living. He broke into another Space and Time. The poet significantly uses the word "broke". He does not say he "came" to another Space and Time. The experience of another Space and Time can never be gradual. It is always sudden, and that is why the poet says Ashvapati broke into a new dimension. True spiritual awakening is always sudden. The mind of man knows only the slow and gradual process of logic and reason. But logic can never enable him to enter the realms of new dimension. It is in the jump of consciousness, in the great inner leap, that one comes upon suddenly the Indescribable Beauty of Reality itself. One has to come upon it; one cannot go to it.

Having given us an insight into Ashvapati's journey from Matter to Spirit, the poet takes us into the realms visited by him so that we can have a closer look at the experiences through which the royal pilgrim had gone. The poet has entitled the Second Book as one dealing with the Traveller of the Worlds. We shall have a close look at the travels of this intrepid traveller in the subsequent pages of this book.

CHAPTER VII

THE BRILLIANT COURTYARD

IT is said that ideas rule the world. If so, there has been no idea more powerful than the Principle of Evolution enunciated by Charles Darwin towards the latter part of the 19th Century. This principle of Evolution has had a revolutionary impact on the thinking of the people for the last nearly one hundred years. This is so because Evolution gave to the scientists and the intellectuals of the world a connecting thread which brought together in one whole, immense diversities in the field of nature and man. Until the enunciation of this doctrine of evolution everything seemed so utterly scattered that it was difficult to see any design or plan in the workings of nature. It is through Evolution that we now are able to get a connected story of all that has happened and is happening in the field of nature as also of man. What at one time seemed just random happenings is no longer so. A clear design is visible and it looks, as if, nature is moving in terms of teleology. The principle of Evolution has influenced the thinking of people in all walks of life in the course of the last one hundred years.

It is true that Evolution, as it was enunciated by Charles Darwin, has undergone many modifications. In this the contributions of Lamark and Mendel are specially noteworthy. Nevertheless the original framework of Evolution remains, and it is this which has given a "wholeness" to the seeming meaninglessness behind the phenomenon of nature. Today science is able to tell us a connected story from the unicellular creature like amoeba to the complex entity like man. But there is one lacuna

64

in scientific propositions of Evolution. Science is able to describe to us the process as to *how* evolution has proceeded from the simple to the complex, from the homogenous to the heterogenous forms of life. While it tells us about the process, it is unable to indicate to us the purpose of evolution. While it speaks of the *"how"* of evolution, it cannot tell us about the *"why"* of evolution. This is so because science studies only the evolution of form and structure. The changes in form and structure by themselves make no sense. Unless one studies evolution of consciousness along with the evolution of form, the whole concept of Evolution must remain a mere meaningless movement of nature. It is significant to note that to the science of biology mutation is still a mystery, for, mutation cannot be put in the framework of structural changes. It is mutation that breaks down the phenomenon of structural continuity. Why does nature produce giant dinosaurs at one time, lording the earth, and at another time wipe them out to be replaced by creatures small and structurally insignificant? There is no answer to this in terms of biological continuity. Why should nature suddenly break this continuity, and, from this break, start a new evolutionary stream? Evidently nature is moving towards the fulfilment of a purpose. But by analysing the process, one cannot arrive at the purpose. For this, one must examine the problem of evolution from an entirely different dimension. In other words, without understanding the evolution of consciousness, the structural changes will seem meaningless. It is consciousness that gives meaning to structural changes. Without Evolution of Consciousness, the Evolution of Form seems devoid of purpose. But science knows nothing about the evolution of consciousness. Sri Aurobindo has dealt with the subject of consciousness comprehensively in his *Savitri*. The entire journey of Ashvapati is nothing but a description of the Evolution of Consciousness. In fact, Ashvapati 's journey is a journey in consciousness. In terms

D.–5

of consciousness Sri Aurobindo has indicated three main landmarks of Evolution. These are Matter, Life and Mind. Evolution moves on from Matter to Life and thence to the development of the Mind. According to Sri Aurobindo, evolution so far has passed these three landmarks. But there must be a movement further, for, mind cannot be the last word in evolutionary progress. Ashvapati in his journey goes from Matter to Life and then to Mind in its various aspects. He stops at a point beyond which Mind cannot go, and it is there that he comes to a communion with something which transcends the Mind. He gets the intimations of the Super-Mind. And ·Super-mind is the next landmark towards which the evolutionary stream must move. But before one can move on to that, one must be fully conversant with the evolutionary drama of Matter, Life and Mind. In Ashvapati 's journey, Sri Aurobindo tells us the fascinating story of Evolution in terms of Matter, Life and Mind. It is as we move with the royal traveller that we shall be able to understand the meaning and the significance of the Evolutionary Drama as narrated by the great poet.

In *Savitri*, Sri Aurobindo is not concerned just with narrating the story of evolution, starting from Matter and ending upto Mind. He seems to be pointing to a new turn in the evolutionary stream. He indicates how the evolutionary drama, having come to the state of Mind, appears to have reached a deadlock. Something from above must come to break the deadlock, for, it is always the factor from above that frees the evolutionary movement from a stalemate, whether it is at the biological level or it is at a psychological level. This factor from above is known as Mutation. Man has come to a point in his evolutionary growth when a Mutation must happen as otherwise the stream of life will get blocked in the uncreative processes of the Mind. There must be a breakthrough from the confines of the Mind if the evolutionary stream is to move further. Sri Aurobindo, referring to Ashvapati's journey, says that he came to know all that can be known and all that cannot be known by the human mind. Ashvapati reached the highest summits of the mind, but even there missed something. What was it that he missed even at these heights of the mind? The poet says:

The integer of the Spirit's perfect sum
That equates the unequal All to the equal One,
The single sign interpreting every sign,
The absolute index to the Absolute.

The integer obviously means the whole number or the undivided quantity. It is with this whole number that one can equate the unequal All with the equal One. It is this whole number that was missed by Ashvapati even at the height of the mind. He missed the single sign which can interpret every sign. The mind knows only the synthesis of parts, and that too when it is at its highest. But a synthesis of parts is not the Whole, and without this Whole "the unequal All cannot be equated with the One." Mind cannot by its own efforts know the Whole; the Whole comes to it, and when it does, then there takes place a breakthrough in the otherwise closed circle of the mind. Ashvapati must find the Integer of the Spirit's perfect sum if he is to solve the intricate equation of Life. But why cannot Mind give this integer? For this we must understand Spirit's involvement in, and, release from, Matter. Ashvapati was climbing the giant stair of Nature, but as the poet says this movement "swelled upwards but none could see its top". Climbing the giant staircase of Nature, Ashvapati frees himself from the world of gross matter and enters the realm of subtle matter. The poet calls this "The Kingdom of Subtle Matter". We ordinarily know of the three states of matter—the solid, the liquid and the gaseous. But physical science speaks today of the Fourth State of Matter. In Hindu philosophy the states of matter have been indicated by the term *Loka*. It is said that there are fourteen *Lokas*, seven above and seven below. These fourteen lokas only indicate different states of matter. Even when one talks of the Atomic plane, one refers only to the subtlest form of matter. Similarly when one speaks of Patala, one is referring to a form of matter more gross than the physical. Today science talks of Matter and Anti-Matter. Perhaps this may have relevance to the states of matter indicated in the fourteen lokas of Hindu Cosmography. Whatever it is, Ashvapati's journey begins from the gross matter to the subtler states of matter. This is the first lap of his stupendous journey. The poet says:

> He came into a magic crystal air
> And found a life that lived not by the flesh,
> A light that made visible immaterial things.

This kingdom of subtle matter is only a finer counterpart of the physical. But the gross physical cannot completely enshrine the beauty that belongs to the subtler planes. And so compared to the dense physical, Ashvapati finds this realm of subtler matter magnificently beautiful. As the poet says:

> A world of lovelier forms lies near to ours,
> Where, undisguised by earth's deforming sight,
> All shapes are beautiful and all things true.

Physical science looks at evolution always from below. It does not realize that the "below" is only a reflection from the "above", and that it is the above that holds the key to the understanding of the lower realms of evolution. The gross physical matter is just a shadow of the realms of subtler matter. Sri Aurobindo says: "All that here seems has lovelier semblance there". The dense physical is only the working out of the subtle matter. Looked at from the standpoint of form and pattern, the entire universe, from the dense physical to the sublime spiritual, is matter existing in different states or conditions. Even the Atomic plane is matter in its subtlest and the most refined condition when seen in terms of form and structure. But in evolution there is revealed not merely the patterns of structural formations. There is behind all that the Content of Evolution. But it is this content which is missed in scientific examination and investigation. Sri Aurobindo, while not oblivious of structural patterns and their growth, draws our attention unmistakably to the spirit and the content of Evolution. Ashvapati is engaged in the journey of Ascent, and so in this journey, where he has to ascend higher and higher, he must experience in an ever-increasing manner a feeling of being rendered light, for, in the journey of Ascent one must travel light. And so the the poet says:

> After the falling of mortality's cloak
> Lightened is its weight to heighten its ascent.

The mortality's cloak is obviously the gross physical body. In rising to the realms of subtler matter, Ashvapati naturally feels that he has become lightened in his weight. When Ashvapati returns to earth after having accomplished his task he has to resume the "heavier dress" of the mortal world. But now on his upward march, he must move on to greater and greater weightlessness so that he may travel easily into the realms of Space, not so much the space of nature as the Space of Consciousness. The subtle is indeed the source of all that exists in the gross material. Evolution is preceded by the Law of Involution. There is first the involvement of spirit in matter before the evolutionary process starts. It is in this involvement that the subtler becomes the gross and the dense. It is not because the physical has any evil tendencies but it is because of the fact that the gross physical is a very crude medium for the expression of the subtle and the intangible. When

the subtle impulses pass through this medium they get
completely distorted. It is to this distortion that the
poet refers in the following lines wherein he says:

> Its knowledge is our error's starting point;
> Its beauty dons our mud-mask ugliness,
> Its artist good begins our evil's tale.

Can this distorting factor of the 'gross physical medium be corrected? If it cannot be, then the Spiritual
and the Material must remain separate with an unbridgable gap. But the whole theme of Sri Aurobindo's
philosophy centres round the possibility of spiritualizing
matter itself. This implies the eliminating of the distorting factor from the medium of the gross physical. How
is this to be done? For this we will have to travel with
Ashvapati into subtler and subtler realms. The poet
describes the realm of subtle matter, just above the gross
physical, as "the brilliant roof of our descending plane".
The involvement of the Spirit into gross matter has obs-
cured the light from above—but the flame is not extinguished. There must be a release from this involvement,
but it is a slow process. The poet says:

> Here in a difficult half-finished world
> Is a slow toiling of unconscious Powers.

The story of Evolution is a movement from imperfec-
tion to perfection so that:

> Earth's great dull barrier is removed awhile,
> And we grow vessels of creative might.

The earth must become a perfect expression of
heaven. In the words of the poet the destiny of earth
is that:

> This mire must harbour the orchid and the rose,
> From her blind unwilling substance must emerge
> A beauty that belongs to happier spheres.
> An immortal godhead's perishable parts

She must re-constitute from fragments lost,
Re-word from a document complete elsewhere
Her doubtful title to her divine Name.

But will this be possible? Will man be able to
transform the earth in the likeness of the Heaven? He
can, but for this man must fulfil one condition. This
condition is described by the poet thus:

Only when we have climbed above ourselves,
A line of the Transcendent meets our road
And joins us to the timeless and the true.
It brings to us the inevitable word,
The godlike act, the thoughts that never die.

We must come to the meeting point where our road
of Ascent comes into contact with the road of Descent
traversed by the Divine. But can man undertake this
stupendous task of climbing above himself? How can
he find intimations of the timeless and the true in this
gross physical existence? And without such intimations
how can he find the strength to climb to such dizzy
heights? The poet gives us a ray of hope when he says:

To seize the absolute in shapes that pass,
To feel the eternal's touch in time-made things,
This is the law of all perfection here.
A fragment here is caught of heaven's design;
Else could we never hope for greater life
And ecstasy and glory could not be.
Even in the littleness of our mortal state,
Even in this prison-house of outer form,
A brilliant passage for the infallible Flame
Is driven through gross walls of nerve and brain.

The poet tells us that even in this prison house of
gross matter can be felt the refreshing air of freedom.
One cannot and must not run away from the material
world, but discover there the secret of the Descent of
the Divine. An opening can be made through which

the Divine can commune with Man. Ashvapati undertakes the journey in order to discover this secret of the Descent of the Divine. The descent cannot be ordered; it will come, and come in unpredictable moments. The poet says:

> The enthusiasm of a divine surprise
> Pervades our life, a mystic stir is felt,
> A joyful anguish trembles in our limbs;
> A dream of beauty dances through the heart
> A thought from the eternal Mind draws near,
> Intimations cast from the Invisible
> Awaking from Infinity's sleep come down
> Symbols of That which never yet was made.

The poet tells us in the above lines that it is the divine surprise that pervades our life. Man wants to put everything into the laws of predictability, and it is this which prevents him from communing with the divine surprise which pervades his life all the time. The mind seeks the predictable in this universe, and not finding it, feels unhappy. But Divine approaches him through the doors of the Unpredictable which unfortunately he has kept all the time closed and barred. If he could open those doors then would he receive the intimations of the Divine here down on earth. These intimations come to him in symbols and allegories, in forms that are suggestive, for, like a great artist, God speaks to man in a language that is suggestive. The poet says that these are symbols of that which never yet was made. Truth can express itself only in a suggestive and a symbolical manner, for, no Form can contain the Absolute Truth. The poet speaks in the following lines about this suggestiveness in all that is manifested. He says:

> Thus we draw near to the All-Wonderful
> Following his rapture in things as sign and guide;
> Beauty is his footprint showing us where he has passed,

Love is his heartbeat's rhythm in mortal breasts,
Happiness the smile on his adorable face.

In the Manifest can be experienced the intangible
presence of the Unmanifest. And it is this intimation ·
of the Unknown which inspires man to move on until
he has been able to bring the beauty of Heaven on this
very mundane earth. Ashvapati has come to the kingdom of the Subtle Matter, the birthplace of all that we
see in the material world. He is charmed and fascinated by what he sees, for, this is his first experience of
something that is away from the gross physical. Here
he sees forms and designs of things before they enter
the distorting medium of the dense physical. In this
realm of subtle matter, he finds that:

All is a miracle of symmetrical charm,
A fantasy of perfect line and rule.

If this be the nature of the kingdom of subtle matter,
why should Ashvapati move further? Cannot subtle
matter give him the answer to find which he began his
journey? If all is a fantasy of perfect line and rule in
this realm, then why undertake a further journey into
unknown lands? The poet tells us:

A perfect picture in a perfect frame,
This faery artistry could not keep his will:
Only a moment's fine release it gave;
A careless hour was spent in a slight bliss.
Our spirit tires of being's surfaces,
Trascended is the splendour of the form;
It turns to Hidden powers and deeper states.

With all the beauty of form and pattern, Ashvapati could not remain there long, for, at best what he
saw was a perfect picture in a perfect frame. He was
in search of a Person, and so how could a picture hold
his will for long? What he found in this realm of subtle matter was a slight bliss experienced in a careless

hour. It was certainly a great change from the sordid patterns of the gross physical. He saw the perfect form, pure and undistorted. But he was seeking something deeper than a mere perfection of form. He must break down the distorting medium of the physical, but a mere perception of the Pure Form cannot give him that strength. He must needs find something more than the perfect form—more than a perfect picture in a perfect frame. He must commune with the Person and obtain a secret of creative living from Him. The poet says:

So now he looked beyond for greater light.
His soul's peak-climb abandoning in its rear
This brilliant courtyard of the House of the Days,
He left that fine material Paradise.

Sri Aurobindo describes the world of subtle matter as only a brilliant courtyard. Ashvapati must move into the inner chamber and not settle down in the court-yard, however attractive it may be. Ashvapati has to move on negating even the most charming spots, for, thus alone, by constant negation, by abandoning the real, can he hope to reach the Portal of Reality. As the poet says: "His destiny lay beyond in larger Space". And so Ashvapati leaves behind this material paradise, the House of Days, compared to the House of Nights that the gross material world is. The subtler world is just the opposite of the dense material. The subtle matter is only a counterpart of the gross physical. From the darkness of the physical, Ashvapati experienced the light of the subtle. But how could this give an answer to his deep inquiry? He must move on to the further beyond, into the realms of the larger Space, where per-chance he may find an answer to his deep inquiry.

CHAPTER VIII

A CARAVAN OF THE INEXHAUSTIBLE

It has to be borne in mind that Ashvapati's journey is a movement in consciousness, and so the descriptions of this journey given by the poet refer to states of consciousness, and not to any locations in space. This journey in consciousness has two aspects—one linear and the other vertical. It is a movement in extension as also in depth. The movement in extension is a linear movement even as the movement in depth is vertical. These two movements are otherwise known as the Occult and the Mystic. In the Occult journey one sees the extensions of the known. But in the mystic journey one comes upon the Unknown. A spiritual aspirant is attracted first by the occult vision of things. It is the psychic and super-physical that draws his attention in the initial stages of the journey. But when he finds that the Occult is unable to give answers to his deeper inquiry, he turns to the approach of Mysticism. We see in Ashvapati's journey both these aspects. In his movement from Matter to Life and from Life to Mind we see the occult aspect of his journey. Ashvapati, however, finds that even the subtlest expression of Mind is unable to satisfy him. He then halts, not finding any further area to traverse, and in this repose of silence listens to the Mystic word which for ever dispels his darkness and impels him to return to earth with Happy Tidings.

Ashvapati's experience of the Kingdom of the Subtle Matter is obviously an Occult experience where he sees the forms of the dense physical in a purer form. For a while he feels that he has come to the end of the journey, for, what more beautiful and sublime can there be than the perfect patterns of line and rule that he sees in the subtle realm of matter? But as the poet says these subtle forms cannot hold his attention for long. He decides to move away from the brilliant courtyard of the subtle matter so as to reach the Inner Chamber where alone he can find the end of his deep quest. In the courtyard he has seen the perfect picture in a perfect frame, but it is only in the Inner Chamber that he can meet the Person. Ashvapati's search is for the Person. As the poet says in the earlier canto: "To evoke a person in the impersonal Void" that is the entire purpose of creation. But to find the person one must move on to the point of the Impersonal Void. It is this which demands constant negation. This implies not merely the negation of the realm of Matter, but also of Life and Mind. These three aspects of Evolution, namely, Matter, Life and Mind relate to the physical, the Vital and the psychological fields of evolution. The gross and the subtle matter represent the Physical aspect of evolution. Ashvapati moves on from this, the brilliant courtyard, to the fields of life, simple as well as complex. The plane of Life is indeed the plane of Vital Being. It is here that we see change, toil, rest as well as restlessness. The realm of Matter is comparatively static, but the realm of Life is intensely dynamic and ceaselessly vibrant. It is change which is the fundamental characteristic of this Kingdom of Life. Life cannot be kept confined to one form for ever. It changes form after form to suit its expressional needs. The poet says "Every change prolongs the same unease". In fact it is this unease which is at the root of all change that occurs in this realm of life. And unease indicates constant struggle where success and failure alternate. The realm of life is replete with conflict, for, life feels attracted to one thing now and at the next moment it feels fascinated by its opposite. The poet says: "Life is almost in love with amorous Death". Life is a realm of eternal flux where one feels that the ground on which one stands is uncertain. The poet tells us:

> As one who meets the face of the Unknown,
> A questioner with none to give reply,
> Attracted to a problem never solved,
> Always uncertain of the ground he trod,
> Always drawn on to an inconstant goal
> He travelled through a land peopled by doubts
> In shifting confines on a quaking base.

Ashvapati has come to a land where everything is uncertain. From the static conditions of Matter he has come to the ever changing panorama of Life. This is indeed the vital nature of life. The poet says that in this region of Life, he felt that he was nearing his destination and yet everything was elusive. He saw "a far retreating horizon of mirage". In the realm of life everything seems like a mirage. The flux of life is beautifully expressed by the poet in the following lines:

> A vagrancy was there that brooked no home,
> A journey of countless paths without a close.

Ashvapati saw many paths in front of him, but all of them seemed pointing to some beyond. He felt that life demanded of him the acceptance of a state of vagrancy—and how can a vagrant think in terms of a home? In this realm of the Vital everything was ceaselessly moving—there was nothing that was steady or stationary. Here Ashvapati felt a little dizzy because of tireless wandering, for, here he saw "a movement of unquiet seas". Released from the deep involvement in matter, when life emerges into action there is a vital upsurge in it, demanding movement and adventure. It needs sensation and excitement; it is prepared to go anywhere and experiment with anything. It is a vital energy demanding ever-new avenues of expression. The poet says:

Assuming whatever shape her fancy wills,
Escaped from the restraint of settled forms
She has left the safety of the tried and the known.
Unshepherded by the fear that walks through Time,
Undaunted by Fate that dogs and chance that
                                        springs,
She accepts disaster as a common risk;
Careless of suffering, heedless of sin and fall,
She wrestles with danger and discovery
In the unexplored expanses of the Soul.

There is a law of nature that in microcosm takes place the recapitulation of the macrocosm. What happens at the level of vast cosmos and nature is repeated in the life of an individual. When we look at a little child, released from its state of inertia in which it found its steadiness in the early years, entering its stage of vitality and activity, we see that the child becomes almost a symbol of restless activity. In fact, at this stage the child displays pure vitality where physical activity has no particular goal to fulfil. The child has such tremendous vitality that it does not know what to do with it, and so it runs about with no purpose whatsoever. Here we find the child emerging from the state of matter to the state of life or vitality. What we see in the child is only a recapitulation of what nature did when it emerged from Matter into Life. It was this irresistible vitality that impelled nature to experiment with all the diverse forms of life. In this, nature lavishly spends her energies, building form after form. She seems to be a spend-thrift producing far more forms than are warranted. She is not worried about time nor about destroying what she has produced. She plays about with creation and destruction—such is the tremendous pressure of limitless vitality. Sri Aurobindo says:

Amid a tedious crawl of drab desires
She writhed, a worm mid worms in Nature's mud,

Then, Titan-statured, took all earth for food,
Ambitioned the seas for robe, for crown the stars
And shouting strode from peak to giant peak,
Clamouring for worlds to conquer and to rule.

The movement of life seems without any plan or purpose. Ashvapati has yet to discover the purpose of life, but as he moves in this realm he gets completely baffled by what he sees—movement upon movement and yet no knowing whither it moves. The seeming aimlessness of the movement of life is portrayed by the poet in the following lines:

Amid her swift untold variety
Something remained dissatisfied ever the same
And in the new, saw only a face of the old,
For every hour repeated all the rest
And every change prolonged the same unease.

To Ashvapati all movement seemed a mere repetition of the old. Even the new bore the face of the old. He has yet to discover the meaning and purpose behind the movement of life. Sri Aurobindo introduces us first to the "Fall of Life" indicating life's involvement in dense matter. Ashvapati sees this and wonders as to what all this means. Regarding this fall of life, the poet says:

A perverse savour haunts her thirsting lips:
For the grief she weeps came from her own choice,
For the pleasure yearns that racked with wounds
                                        her breast;
Aspiring to heaven she turns her steps toward hell.

The poet indeed utters the truth when he says that aspiring to heaven, life seems to be turning her steps towards hell. This is what appears as one looks at life and its happenings from the outer and rather superficial standpoint. Ashvapati is still in the comparatively lower regions. He has moved on from the realm of subtle

matter, but still he is in the lower regions of life. And
so it is not possible for him to perceive the nobler origins of life. Life arises not from sin but from the sublime
realms of the spirit. The poet says:

> Yet pure and bright from the Timeless was her birth,
> A lost world-rapture lingers in her eyes,
> Her moods are faces of the Infinite:
> Beauty and happiness are her native right,
> And endless bliss is her eternal home.

As Ashvapati moves on into higher and higher
regions of the Vital World, he begins to have distant
glimpses of the great purpose of life. He has visions
of the great peaks and summits of life. But he looks
at them like one lying deep in a well gazing at the clear
sky. Nevertheless even this distant gaze appears fascinating, and almost rapturous. The poet tells us:

> At once caught in an eternal vision's sweep
> He saw her pride and splendour of highborn zones
> And her regions crouching in the nether deeps.
> Above was a monarchy of unfallen self,
> Beneath was the gloomy trance of the abyss,
> An opposite pole or dim antipodes.

Ashvapati on his journey, through the vital realms,
sees the diverse expressions of life, heaven above and hell
below. The two are antipodes, the opposing points as the
poet says. Sri Aurobindo gives an expression to Ashvapati 's feelings when he says; "Heaven's joys might have
been earth's, if earth were pure". It is the distorting
medium of earth which transforms the joys of heaven into
the sorrows of the earth. This distorting medium, as
Ashvapati discovers later, is indeed the medium of the
mind. He sees the glories of life from a distance and
aspires to touch them. But as the poet says :

> This world of bliss he saw and felt its call,
> But found no way to enter into its joy;
> Across the conscious gulf there was no bridge.

Why does the poet speak of the "conscious gulf"? It was not a natural gulf but one that was created by the conscious workings of the human mind. It is because of these workings of the human mind that

A darker air encircled still his soul
Tied to an image of unquiet life.

It was the image of the unquiet life that pulled him down. He could not enter the land of bliss which he saw from a distance, for, there was no bridge across the gulf. Naturally Ashvapati must ponder over the question as to why there is no bridge and how can it be constructed so that Heaven and Earth may not be separated from each other with an abyss that is unbridgable. But for this, he must inquire into the very beginnings of life—how it emerged and why. The poet takes us into these beginnings when the stirring of life appeared in that which seemed a Void. Sri Aurobindo follows the line of the Upanishads in dealing with the beginnings of life. He says:

In the crude beginnings of this mortal world
Life was not nor mind's play nor hearts desire.
In that desolate grandeur, in that beauty bare,
In the deaf stillness, mid the unheeded sounds,
Heavy was the uncommunicated load
Of Godhead in a world that had no needs;
For none was there to feel or to receive.

The poet says that the Godhead felt the uncommunicated load, and, perchance, that was the beginning of life. With whom will the Godhead communicate his joys and ecstasies? There was none to feel or to receive. Sri Aurobindo says that the Godhead "hungered for the beat of yearning and response". Evolution has to be understood both at the structural as well as the spiritual level. It is the descent of the Spirit which is the cause for all structural changes. It was the yearning which induced the One to become the Many. It is in the demand of the Fullness to communicate that lies the impelling force behind creation. The Godhead could no longer bear the load of un-communicated fullness—and so the diversity of life's expressional forms came into existence. The meaning of structural changes does not lie in the structure but in the life that descends. Where Spirit meets Matter there the birth of Life takes place. Life is indeed the bridge between Spirit and Matter. But Ashvapati has yet to discover this bridge. In the lower Vital regions he sees only the unbridgeable gulf. It is in this journey for the discovery of the bridge that Ashvapati inquires into the beginnings of life—the Whence, the How and the Why of this entire creation with its teeming forms and patterns of life. The poet says that in the realm of seemingly dead matter:

> A voice was heard on the mute rolling globe,
> A murmur moaned in the unlistening Void.
> As comes a goddess to a mortal's breast
> And fills his days with her celestial clasp,
> She stooped to make her home in transient shapes;
> In matter's womb she cast the Immortal's fire.
> In the unfeeling Vast woke thought and hope.

With the touch of the Vital Breath of Life, the earth with its dull drab matter was changed beyond recognition. So far, only the material and chemical life existed, but with the Vital touch of Life there sprang into existence numerous forms of biological life. Evolution proceeds from the chemical to the biological form of life and then the psychological expression of the self-same life. In Matter, Life and Mind we see the expression of this three-fold nature of life. The poet says:

> Alive and clad with trees and herbs and flowers
> Earth's great brown body smiled towards the skies,
> Azure replied to azure in the sea's laugh;
> New unseen creatures filled the unseen depths,

Life's glory and swiftness ran in the beauty of beasts,
Man dared and thought and met with his soul the
world.

Here the poet tells us about the growth of life from
the vegetable to the animal and from there to man. In
the above lines he indicates that life began first in the
waters as is declared by science today, and as was proclaimed by the seers and sages of India when they spoke
of the first incarnation being that of Fish. It was after
that that the incarnation of Tortoise came, the animal that
lives both in land as well as water. The purely land
animal, Varaha came after that. So that according to this
concept of Avatara or Incarnation, life began first in the
waters. The entire story of the Avataras or the Incarnations is the story of Evolution, commencing from the beginnings of life in water to the arrival of the perfect man
in the person of Sri Rama. It may be noted that according to this story, Sri Krishna is the Divine Man. In
Ashvapati 's journey from Matter to Life and thence to
Mind, Sri Aurobindo relates this whole story of Evolution,
not in a prosaic manner but in language that is surcharged
with beautiful poetic imagery. The poet in just two lines
sums up the whole purpose of evolution when he says:

Our human ignorance moves towards the Truth
That Nescience may become omniscient.

The Fall of Life to which Sri Aurobindo alludes is
indeed Life's involvement in Matter. And in this involvement, Life indeed comes down to earth from its majestic
realms above. The poet describes this Fall in a beautiful
manner in the following lines:

And all her glory into littleness turned
And all her sweetness into a maimed desire.
To feed death with her works is here life's doom.

But even when life fell into matter and got involved,
she could not entirely forget her lofty origins. There was

all the time an unconscious pull towards the Heaven
even when she was in the midst of her deepest involvement in matter. It is this unconscious pull which is at
the root of all the restlessness of life seen here below on
earth. About the ceaseless yearning of life, the poet says:

> She brought into Matter's dull tenacity
> Her anguished claim to her lost sovereign right,
> Her tireless search, her vexed uneasy heart,
> Her wandering unsure steps, her cry for change.
> Like a child-soul left near the gates of Hell
> Fumbling through fog in search of Paradise.

It is this fumbling of life in search of the lost Paradise
that lies at the root of the slow process of evolution. In
this evolutionary movement of life one sees the play of the
opposites, or as the poet says:

> A contradiction found the base of life:
> The eternal, the divine Reality
> Has faced itself with its own contraries.

It is this play of the opposites which imparts vitality
and movement to this evolutionary stream. From the
vegetable kingdom of life, Ashvapati moves on to view
the vast animal world. In the words of the poet it is a
world of "great puissant creatures with a dwarfish brain".
The whole story of evolution as depicted by Sri Aurobindo is a rhythm of involvement and release. He
points to the utter involvement of the spirit in the following very expressive lines:

> Here she first crawled out from her cabin of mud
> Where she had laid inconscient, rigid, mute:
> Its narrowness and torpor held her still,
> A darkness clung to her uneffaced by Light.

The poet says that the darkness remained uneffaced
by light—such was the involvement in conditions dense
and dark. Sri Aurobindo does not deviate from the facts

revealed by science in the domain of evolution—but he imparts to these facts a plan and a purpose unimagined by science. In structure, he sees the powerful impact of the spirit. As he says:

When life broke through its half-drowse in the plant
That feels and suffers but cannot move or cry,
In beast and in winged bird and thinking man
It made of the heart's rhythm its music's beat.

The poet sees the rhythmic beat of music in the throbbing of life in its march from the mineral to the man. There can be no more graphic picture of evolution than the one that is given by Sri Aurobindo in his *Savitri*. He says:

An insect hedonism fluttered and crawled
And basked in a sunlit Nature's surface thrills,
And dragon raptures, python agonies
Crawled in the march and mire and licked the sun,
Huge armoured strengths shook the frail quaking ground,
Great puissant creatures with a dwarfish brain,
And pigmy tribes imposed their small life-drift.

There was first dwarf-humanity before man in the present form arrived. This dwarf-man was *Vamana*, the predecessor of *Parasurama* and *Rama*. The dwarf-humanity was represented by the pigmy tribes of men. But this dwarf humanity was preceded by giant creatures, described by the poet as the "huge armoured strengths". When this giant animal moved, even the earth, as it were, quaked under his pressure. Here the poet uses a very strange phrase, namely, "the hedonism of the insects". He refers to that stage of evolution when the tiny insects could engage themselves in pleasure-hunting without the danger of being attacked by superior creatures. The insects themselves constituted the superior race of creation. But then came other creatures, dragons and serpentine creatures, and then the mammals and the tiny, pigmy man. The poet says:

> In a dwarf model of humanity
> Nature now launched the extreme experience
> And master-point of her design's caprice.

The poet calls man, the master-point of life's caprice. The use of the word "caprice" is most significant. It means something that is unaccountable or unpredictable. All mutations are unaccountable and therefore unpredictable. And man is indeed a mutation of nature, but not a freak of nature. In bringing man into existence nature has launched on an extreme experience. It is a bold experiment. Will it succeed? The answer to that lies in the future—but also partly in the present, for, as man makes his choice today, so will he move towards a greater future. But with the dwarf humanity there came a very rudimentary mind, but what was its nature? The poet says:

> A mind was there that met the objective world
> As if a stranger or enemy at the door:
> Its thoughts were kneaded by the shocks of sense;
> It captured not the spirit of the form,
> It entered not the heart of what it saw;
> It looked not for the power behind the act,
> It studied not the hidden motive of things
> Nor strove to find the meaning of it all.

It was an infant mind that began to stir in the humanity that still had links with the animal. It was really an animal mind. The giant animal creatures had dwarfish brains, but the dwarf humanity had in it the stirrings of a more developed mind. But according to the poet the nature of this mind was: "Fettered to puny thoughts with no wide range". There is an animal mind which can adjust to outer environment, but its adjustment has a very limited range. As the mind develops, its range widens; and so its psychological environment becomes increasingly vast. The story of evolution tells us that it is the greater capacity of the brain which enables a creature to adjust to the fast changing physical conditions of life. The giant dinosaurs disappeared giving place to tiny creatures—but this strange phenomenon happened because the tiny creatures were superior in brain power to their giant predecessors. Nature seems to be aiming at the development of the mind, and in this process creates man as its crowning glory. But this mind had its slow beginnings. As the poet says:

A thought was there that planned, a will that strove,
But for small aims within a narrow scope.

There is hardly any difference between the mind of the higher animal and the mind of the primitive man. With the development of the mind, life does awaken to a large number of its potentialities, yet the infant mind knows not "the Immortal in its house". In fact, even the so-called mind of the modern man does not know about the presence of the Immortal in its own house. The infant mind of man, almost animal in its nature, is depicted by the poet thus:

Mind looked on nature with unknowing eyes.
Adored her boons and feared her monstrous strokes.

The Infant Humanity looked at nature with awe and fear. The mind which in the beginning is an asset soon becomes a great liability. One may ask: Why? The answer to this is given by the poet when he says:

Absorbed in the little works of its prison-house
It turned around the same unchanging points
In the same circle of interest and desire.

The movement of the mind keeps one in the prison-house where the fresh air of life cannot come. With the appearance of vital life, mind arrives in its footsteps, for,

even the undomesticated animals have rudimentary facul-
ties of the mind such as memory and anticipation. The
reasoning faculty comes much later, but even this cannot
enable man to step out of the prison. It can, at best,
rationalise one's prison-existence. In ‚Ashvapati's journey
there is a wide survey of the vast field of evolution. In
fact, the royal pilgrim, as it were, sees the entire film of
the evolutionary drama unfolded before his eyes. In the
animal and the early human stage, life was incessantly
engaged in defending itself, for, survival constituted its
main problem. The poet says:

> Isolated, cramped in the vast unknown,
> To save their small lives from surrounding Death,
> They made a tiny circle of defence
> Against the seige of the huge universe:
> They preyed upon the world and were its prey,
> But never dreamed to conquer and be free.

Here Sri Aurobindo refers to the relentless struggle
of life for its survival. This struggle begins almost with the
first beginnings of life and continues upto the point when
dangers to biological survival cease. But when it ceases,
then begins the struggle for psychological survival in
which modern man is even today completely engrossed.
In this struggle for biological survival, the development of
the brain was a great asset. As we have stated above, the
new power of the brain contained elements of memory
and anticipation. But these expressed themselves not as
intellect but as instinct. The poet tells us :

> Instinct was formed; in memory's crowded sleep
> The past lived on as in a bottomless sea;
> Inverting into half-thought the quickened sense
> She felt around for truth with fumbling hands,
> Clutched to her the little she could reach and seize
> And put aside in her subconscient cave.

It is only the half-thought that one sees here. The
animal and the primitive man are guided by instinct.

Science as it studies evolution watches the whole struggle for the survival of the fittest, but is unable to make any sense out of that struggle. Sri Aurobindo tells us that unless our whole thinking is reversed so that we see in the "Above" the meaning of what happens in the "Below", we will never be able to solve the mystery of evolution. Sri Aurobindo says:

> That strange observing Power imposed its sight.
> It forced on flux a limit and a shape,
> It gave its stream a lower narrow bank,
> Drew lines to snare the spirit's formlessness.
> It fashioned the life-mind of bird and beast,
> The answer of the reptile and the fish,
> The primitive patterns of the thoughts of man.

Sri Aurobindo speaks here of the "life-mind". This sugggests that as yet there was no individualized mind, but only the mind of nature. Instincts are indeed the movements in the mind of nature. It is this mind that guides the life-patterns of animals and primitive humanity. But there is a saving grace when the animal and the primitive man are guided by the mind of nature. Here we see the innocence of mind which gets corrupted when the individualized mind comes into existence. Man has to move away from the limits of the individualized mind to the free air of the universal mind when intuition takes the place of intellect. But that development is in the future. Evolution moves first from the mind of nature to the individualized mind where intellect is the supreme ruler. The poet tells us as to what happens when this individualized mind with intellect as its supreme ruler begins to function. He says:

> A backward scholar on logic's rickety bench
> Indoctrinated by the erring sense,
> It took appearance for the face of God,
> For casual lights the marching of the suns,

> For heaven a starry strip of doubtful blue;
> Aspects of being feigned to be the whole.

The mind, sitting on logic's rickety bench, regards the part as the Whole. It is guided by the law of "As below, so Above". It imagines the Above only in terms of the below. Our royal traveller has yet to come to the regions of the individual mind. He is still lingering in the world of animals and dwarf humanity where instinct rules in a realm that has a very limited range. Seeing this, he is unable to make any sense of the appearance and disappearance of various forms of life. He sees everywhere the struggle for survival, with no pattern of meaning emerging. The poet tells us:

> A little light in a great darkness born,
> Life knew not where it went nor whence it came.
> Around all floated still the nescient haze.

There was everywhere the haze of ignorance. How could Ashvapati remain here long? This world cannot give him the answer in search of which he had travelled thus far. He must move on. Now Ashvapati's journey is fundamentally of an Occult nature. It is only when the occult revelations do not satisfy him that there is a mystic turn in his approach. An occult journey indicates an experience of planes not cognised by the physical senses. It is a movement in what is otherwise known as the Occult world. Having moved away from the world of matter he has come to the Vital region, and is watching the happenings in the lower strata of that realm. The poet says that for ℓ Ashvapati this was "an unhappy corner in eternity". Here he saw movement of life but utterly divested of meaning. He desired to understand the happenings of this region more clearly and so as the poet says:

> He plunged his gaze into the siege of mist
> That held this ill-lit straitened continent.

When he turned his gaze intently, then he saw strange creatures inhabiting this land—goblins, imps, genii, spirits etc. They were half-animal and half-god. Here the word "god" only suggests superphysical entitites. In the astral world he came across these creatures. It is these creatures and other dis-embodied spirits that plague the minds of ignorant and passive human beings. They are interested in doing this, for it gives them a perverse delight. About their role in the life of human beings down on earth, the poet says:

> To sport with good and evil is their law;
> Luring to failure and meaningless success,
> All models they corrupt, all measures cheat,
> Make knowledge a poison, virtue a pattern dull
> And lead the endless cycles of desire
> Through semblances of sad or happy chance
> To an inescapable fatality.

Here Sri Aurobindo has spoken in unmistakable terms about the dangers of establishing contacts with these creatures. In spiritualistic seances and in lower psychism people do try to contact them and attempt to act in accordance with their instructions. The poet says that these creatures create in man a feeling of inescapable fatality. Sri Aurobindo says that under their influences men are driven to various things and they always speak "with the voices of the Night". There is something weird about them, and they utilise human beings for the fulfilment of their own strange purposes. Man ultimately suffers when he acts under their guidance, for here, as the poet says "reason is used by an irrational Force". There are all types of forces that exercise their influence on earth— they are good as well as bad. But man can call down the sublime influences only when his consciousness ceases to respond to crude and unpleasant influences that emanate from such creatures as dis-embodied spirits. But so long as he lives in the prison-house of the mind, he cannot hope to invoke the power of the Sublime Forces of Light for his own guidance. He has to transcend the realms of reason, for, as Sri Aurobindo days:

Inapt to feel the pulse and the core of things,
Our reason cannot sound life's mighty sea
And only counts its waves and scans its foam.

The mind of man wants to understand the depth of the mighty sea by counting the waves and scanning the foam. Its capacity ends there. Until he is able to go beyond the limitations of reason he is exposed to the dangers of the lower entities using him as a tool The poet says that as long as man is a slave to reason and to the outward tendencies of the mind, so long he is subject to "incurable littleness". The mind of man transforms even the most sublime into the most profane. It is due to this that, according to the poet, man's "little hour is spent in little things". As he days, under the profane influence of the mind even the best is reduced to mere "convention and routine." Man has to step out of this prison-house of the mind, and it is for this that Ashvapati has undertaken the stupendous journey. The royal pilgrim must come to a point in his travels when he can know:

The unfelt Self within who is the guide.
The unknown Self above who is the goal.

It is only when one is conscious of the unfelt Self within that he comprehends the nature of the unknown Self above. With this awakening to the unfelt self within there occurs an event which in the words of the poet is a door cut in the mud-wall of self. The wall erected by the personality for its own safety and continuity is a mud-wall of self. When one becomes aware of the unfelt self within, then immediately an opening is made in the mud-wall of human personality. To be aware of the unfelt Self within is to grow in sensitivity so that even in the tangible one is able to feel the presence of the intangible, for, the Self within is indeed the Intangible. But for this, Ashvapati must continue his ascent. It is at the summit of the ascent that the presence of the Intangible is felt. The poet says :

> The soul must soar sovereign above the form
> And climb to summits beyond mind's half-sleep.

Ashvapati in the occult astral world was still in the realm of mind's half-sleep. He saw many strange entities, and realized how man was subjecting himself to their influences because of the distortions brought about in mind's prison house.

Negating this world of spirits and dis-embodied entities, Ashvapati moves on to the higher realms of the occult world to which he had arrived. Feeling the unpleasant influences of the lower regions, he strives to contact higher expressions of life in the Vital world. These higher realms seemed outwardly better, but there was no deeper content in its living. There was allurement but no satisfaction. The outer allurement was in plenty, but as the poet says : "It seemed a realm of lives that had no base." Ashvapati saw in the influences of this higher realm of the Vital World those forces whose impacts are felt in the earth life. And these impacts are indeed the source of pleasant and happy activities down on earth. The impact of this influence was certainly better than the one emanating from the world of the dis-embodied spirits. Nature in the evolutionary movement displays a continual march to better and nobler expressions of life. The poet says :

> Her high procession moves from stage to stage,
> A progress leap from sight to greater sight,
> A process march from form to ampler form,
> A caravan of the inexhaustible.

The march of evolution is indeed the caravan of the inexhaustible, for how can the Unmanifest be expressed completely in the Manifest. Nothing can exhaust the Unmanifest—not even the noblest of forms. Evolution is indeed a play of Life and Form, of Spirit and Matter, of Purusa and Prakriti. Form desires for ever to hold Life in its net; Prakriti wants Purusa to remain under her clasp. The poet gives expression to this game in the following lines :

> To catch the boundless in a net of birth,
> To cast the spirit into the physical form,
> To lend speech and thought to the Ineffable.

Can this be done? Surely the spirit cannot be cast completely in the physical form. As the form becomes finer, as matter becomes more and more sensitive, a greater closeness comes between Life and Form, between Spirit and Matter. Is it possible for Matter to hold comletely the Spirit? Ashvapati has started his journey to find an answer to that supreme question. About Purusa and Prakriti, the poet says:

> Although she is ever in him and he in her,
> As if unaware of the eternal tie,
> Her will is to shut God into her works
> And keep him as her cherished prisoner
> That never they may part again in Time.

Can Time hold Timeless in its bondage? It cannot; but they cannot leave apart. There is a close relationship between the two. And the relationship becomes more and more intimate as evolution proceeds. The poet says that even now Prakriti has not failed completely, for, "she has lured the Eternal into the arms of Time". But even this luring has become possible because of the constant movement of the stream of evolution. Ashvapati sees in this higher Vital world, how a greater affinity comes between Life and Form, between Spirit and Matter. But he realizes that this contact is intermittent, not steady and full. Here in this realm, Ashvapati feels as if this is "a first immigration into heavenliness". He is only in an immigration tent, isolated from the main land. But though intermittent, this relationship between Purusa and Prakriti is something he had not seen so far. He begins to see some purpose in the frantic efforts of the Prakriti, of the Form or of the Matter. It is for her great lover, the Purusa, that Prakriti has been working, trying all along to "cajole with her small gifts his mightiness". She is striving to see that he remains attached to her, "lest from her arms he turn to his formless peace". The poet says that the Prakriti :

> . . . builds creation like a rainbow bridge.
> Between the original Silence and the Void.

The mind cannot understand the workings of Prakriti, for, mind sees only from the outside. When the workings of Prakriti are sought to be explained by the mind, then, as the poet says "they seem yet more inexplicable".

In this higher vital world where Ashvapati has come, there is seen everywhere the Hero's mould. The Hero becomes the ideal for the beings in this world. This Hero-worship results in the inhabitants of this realm alternating between good and evil, for, it is the hero that matters, no matter what he espouses. The sense of discrimination is clearly lacking. And so the poet says about the beings of this realm that they are:

> Warriors of Good, they serve a shining cause,
> Or are Evil's soldiers in the pay of sin.

The undiscriminating minds of these beings show forth these tendencies comparable to the swings of a pendulum. And so there may be :

> A mighty victory or a mighty fall,
> A throne in heaven or a pit in hell.

Ashvapati could not tarry in this realm where there were flashes of the presence of the Good, but it was more of a passive presence. He missed here something, and so even this world must be negated if Ashvapati is to find the answer that satisfies the need of humanity. Here in this world as the poet says there was "hunting for pleasure in the heart of pain." Man was seeking happiness but could not find it in this world of Vital Being where things alternated between Good and Evil. Life's intention in this realm is to "marry with a sky of calm a sea of bliss". But these intentions are thwarted because of the alternating currents. And so the result is instead of creating such godlike being, there comes into existence "a demi-god emerging from an ape." Ashvapati wanted to see if there was a way of escape out of the movement of this plane of vital being. But he saw that no final solution can be found in this plane, for, the new things that were made soon approximated to the old. The mind in this vital realm was unable to bring to completion its good intentions. Here mind attempted, but its attempts were "a world made ever anew, never complete". It was like piling half-attempts on lost attempts. To Ashvapati this realm appeared as "a fugitive paradise". There were potentialities of a paradise, but there were also factors that worked for purposes contrary to such a dream. Ashvapati was in search of something where, in the words of the poet:

. . . repose and action are the same
In the deep breast of God's supreme delight.

The royal traveller was in search of a condition where repose and action would be the same. They would be the two sides of the same medallion, with no interval between them. It would be the co-existence of *Nivritti* and *Pravritti*, of Infinite Rest and Infinite Motion. In this state there is no hiatus between Spirit and Matter, no unbridgeable gulf. In this co-existence of Repose and Action the very earth would become the abode of heaven. The poet says:

Then God could be visible here, here take a shape,
Disclosed would be the Spirit's identity;
Life would reveal her true immortal face.

But for this Ashvapati has a long way to go, for, at present "Life has no issue, death brings no release". Life appears to be without any purpose, there is no living issue that impels its activities. And surely death brings no release from this meaningless existence. In fact, Ashvapati feels that:

An error of the gods has made the world,
Or indifferent the Eternal watches Time.

Does the Eternal watch the movement of Time with utter indifference? Or is the Eternal involved in the very processes of Time? It is true that all is dark and dismal, no plan or purpose is visible. But in the deep consciousness of man he feels that this cannot be true. There must be a purpose towards which life moves. The poet says:

There is no end or none can yet be seen :
Although defeated, life must struggle on;
Always she sees a crown she cannot grasp;
Her eyes are fixed beyond her fallen state.
There quivers still within her breast and ours
A glory that was once and is no more,
Or there calls to us from some unfulfilled beyond
A greatness yet unreached by the halting world.
In a memory behind our mortal sense
A dream persists of larger happier air
Breathing around free hearts of Joy and love,
Forgotten by us, immortal in lost Time.

Ashvapati is obviously hungering for this happier air, and having negated the world of gross as well subtle matter, and having rejected the pleasures of the vital world, he proceeds with his journey. He is in search of the very secret of Life, and it is with that secret that he must return to his kingdom to assuage the hunger and thirst of his people. And so as the poet says, Ashvapati "turned to find that wide world-failure's cause". For this search, he must descend into the darkness of the Night, and so it is to the Call of the Night that Ashvapati responds.

CHAPTER IX

THE ALTARS OF THE TRIUMPHANT NIGHT

THERE are some who believe that Sri Aurobindo's SAVITRI cannot be classified as an Epic, for, the dictionary meaning of Epic is "a long narrative poem which tells of heroes and heroic deeds, usually of high significance to the nation involved, and embodying its early history or traditions". Can Sri Aurobindo's *Savitri* be put within the framework of this definition? It speaks of no hero and heroic deeds as are commonly understood. There are no fierce battles described where heroism is displayed, glorifying the history and tradition of any country. And yet can there be anything more heroic than the journey of Ashvapati ? This journey demanded of him such strength and valour as would have been impossible for even the greatest heroes of history to display. Ashvapati had to fight the battles for the entire human race, and these were the battles against the forces of Night. His was a herculean task such as would have cooled the enthusiasm of the bravest of the brave. And so *Savitri* has a claim to be regarded as a great epic poetry of the world, in which no one country is involved but where the destiny of the entire race is at stake. There is no doubt that Sri Aurobindo's *Savitri* is one of the greatest epics of the world.

In the study of Evolution which forms the subject matter of Ashvapati's journey there is one fact which needs to be clearly noted, and that is, that Evolution does not proceed in a straight line. Evolution at all stages displays a spiral movement where the crest and trough alternate. It marches through summits and valleys. It surely does not jump from summit to summit.

Between two summits there intervenes the valley, and so in order to reach another summit, evolutionary caravan has to move through the valley. In the evolutionary story we come across summit-periods as also the valley-periods. Surely the valleys cannot display what the summits can do. And so it would be meaningless to compare the summit of one age with the valley of another. In the valley, the sun rises much later than it does on the summit, and so the valleys are naturally enveloped in darkness. It is idle to compare the light on the summit with the darkness in the valley. The evolutionary march will move on from the valley to the next summit, perhaps higher than the summit left behind. And so it would be right for one to regard evolution as a whole, taking into account both the summit-as well as the valley-existence. In Ashvapati's journey we see both the summits and the valleys, both the light of the day as well as the darkness of the night. Ashvapati wants to know the cause of earth's failure, but for this he must peer into the darkness of the night. As he thus peered:

> He saw the fount of the world's lasting pain
> And the mouth of the black pit of Ignorance.
> The evil guarded at the roots of life
> Raised up its head and looked into his eyes.

Ashvapati after moving away from the higher vital world had now come to the realm where the forces of darkness ruled. From the light, however dim of that vital world, he had now come to the night of darkness. But even the light of the vital region was only darkness made visible. He was aspiring to reach the world of Pure Light, but before that he must pass through the valley of the night. In the earlier realm he could visualize, though faintly some Destiny; but here it was Doom that faced him. The poet says that here were the forces that "effaced the signposts of Life's pilgrimage" and

instead "erected its bronze pylons of misrule". It was
this gateway of misrule that Ashvapati saw. About
this region the poet says:

> Its power could deform divinest things.
> A wind of sorrow breathed upon this world;
> All thought with falsehood was besieged, all act
> Stamped with defect or with frustration's sign,
> All high attempt with failure or vain success,
> But none could know the reason of his fall.

When humanity moved from the region of Vital
life, where there was the surging of emotion, however
conflicting it may be to the realm of Mind, there existed this passage through the Dark Night. In fact, before each major step in evolution there comes the experience of the valley. It is as one passes through valley
after valley that one can reach the high summits of life.
The poet says:

> A darkness settled on the heavy air;
> It hunted the bright smile from Nature's lips
> And slew the native confidence in her heart
> And put fear's crooked look into her eyes.
> The lust that warps the spirit's natural good
> Replaced by a manufactured virtue and vice
> Made evil a relief from spurious good.

Surely there is nothing so annoying as the spurious
good. The poet says that in that context evil comes
as a great relief. In this world of the Dark Night both
virtues and vices were manufactured commodities. And
when virtue is manufactured then surely it is utterly
spurious. The descriptions of the Kali Yuga that one
finds in popular religious books are akin to the Civilization of the Night given in the above lines by Sri Aurobindo as also in the following lines:

> All glory of life dimmed tarnished into a doubt,
> All beauty ended in an aging face;

All power was dubbed a tyranny cursed by God
And Truth a fiction needed by the mind;
The chase of joy was now a tired hunt;
All knowledge was left a questioning Ignorance.

There were in this land creatures "whose very gaze was a calamity". Even the beauty in this region was but a snare. Sri Aurobindo describes this country in his inimitable manner. He says:

There all could enter but none stay for long.
It was a no man's land of evil air,
A crowded neighbourhood without one home,
A borderland between the world and hell.
There unreality was Nature's lord:
It was a space where nothing could be true.
A vast deception was the law of things.

This was Ashvapati's descent into night, and the night was with unrelieved darkness. Here everything was a deception and a fraud. We see such members of the human race even now, for Kali Yuga is not something chronologically separated from Satya Yuga. All Yugas co-exist, for they represent the states of consciousness. The experience of the Night which Ashvapati. y has does find its reflection here below on earth. The Dark Forces use humanity for their purposes. When they find a fertile soil in human mind, they put their seeds in such a soil so that the plant of evil may sprout in good time bearing fruits and flowers that are utterly poisonous. But the Dark Forces invariably appear in garments that are outwardly attractive, for, that is a part of their evil game. The poet says:

The Fiend was visible, but cloaked in light:
He seemed a helping angel from the skies:
He armed untruth with Scripture and the Law;
He deceived with wisdom, with virtue slew the soul
And led to perdition by the heavenward path.

His rigorous logic made the false seem true,
Truth-speaking was a strategem in that place,
Falsehood came laughing with the eyes of truth.

The poet further says regarding the land of the Night that:

Truth was exiled lest she should dare to speak
And hurt the heart of darkness with her light,
Or bring her pride of knowledge to blaspheme
The settled anarchy of established things.

No better phrase could have been used regarding the affairs in this land of darkness than the one used by the poet in the above lines where he speaks of "the settled anarchy of established things". One wonders whether the poet is referring to things that obtain in the present-day civilization. We see today Truth being exiled more and more from the affairs of men, and we see falsehood laughing with the eyes of truth. The reign of Dark Powers is always there, but sometimes they do not have the chance to express themselves easily. But there are other times when the Dark Powers have their full innings. In Hindu Mythology there is a story of Nala and Damayanti. The story says that Nala came under the influence of the Dark Powers, because, while he had washed the whole body, there was just a tiny portion of the feet which was left unwashed. And Kali of the Dark Power entered his body through that unwashed portion. The meaning of this mythological story is clear. It is when human consciousness contains even a tinge of impurity that the Dark Powers have an opening through which they can influence the man. Ashvapati in the region of the Night is watching the activities of these Dark Powers. Ashvapati saw that in this region while there was a Capital, it was without a State. The State is obviously the integrating factor. To have a capital without a state is to lack this unifying or integrating factor of life. The poet says, it was a city:

Founded upon a soil that knew not Light,
There Ego was lord upon his peacock seat
And falsehood sat by him, his mate and queen.

Here Ego was the king and Falsehood his queen.
In this city, unity was founded upon fraud and force.
Ashvapati was terribly afraid to remain in this land.
And so inwardly he uttered the Name of God so as to
guard himself against the impact of evil influences. The
poet says that the realm of Night was slightly better than
the region lying still deeper, and to which Ashvapati
now turned his gaze. It was a savage slum of Night.
Here life had fallen into the lowest depth of degradation
and demoralization. It is in this slum area of the Night
that lust was turned into a decorative art. If there
could be any hell this indeed was the most wicked hell.
The poet says:

A greater darkness waited, a worse region,
If worse can be where all is evil's extreme;
Yet to the cloaked the uncloaked is naked worst.

Describing life in this region, Sri Aurobindo says:

In this regime that soiled the being's core,
Beauty was banned, the heart's feeling dulled to sleep
And cherished in their place sensation's thrills;
A new philosophy theorised evil's rights,
Mind changed to the image of a rampant beast.

Are there no such slums of the night in our civilization? And if there are none, are we quite sure that
efforts are not being made to construct such festering
slums? Ashvapati was moving in the realm of darkness and sin, defending himself against its vile influence.
It needed great courage to be in it but not of it. Sri
Aurobindo describing the condition of the royal traveller says:

A lone discoverer in these menacing realms
Guarded like termite cities from the sun,

Oppressed mid crowd and tramp and noise and flare,
Passing from dusk to deeper dangerous dusk,
He wrestled with powers that snatched from mind
                                                its light
And smote from him their clinging influences.

Ashvapati was an utterly lonely man in this fierce
and unpleasant surroundings. But this was the price
that he had to pay in order to reach the Land of Light.
It is only the pure that can go to those heights, and
the pure have to be tested in surroundings impure and
unclean. If anything of the unclean ·clings to the consciousness, then the man is not ready to rise higher. If
the impure has a resting place in one's consciousness,
then the higher summits cannot be climbed. The poet
tells us:

    ....he endured, stilled the vain terror, bore
    The smothering coils of agony and affright;
    Then peace returned and the soul's sovereign gaze.
    To the blank horror a calm light replied:
    Immutable, undying and unborn,
    Mighty and mute the Godhead in him woke
    And faced the pain and danger of the world.
    He mastered the tides of Nature with a look:
    He met with his bare spirit the naked Hell.

Sri Aurobindo says that "None can reach heaven
who has not passed through hell". And Ashvapati
was no exception to this unalterable rule. When Ashvapati woke from the dull and stupefying atmosphere of
the Night, then he saw what ghastly and crooked things
were happening. He had regained a clear sight and so
could watch with complete objectivity the strange activities of this land. He saw that the beings in this land
could be compared to

    ....a faithless gardener of God,
    Watered with virtue the world's upas-tree.

The Upas tree is a fabulous Javanese tree which poisons vegetable and animal life for miles and miles. From this tree deadly poison is extracted. Ashvapati saw that in this land of the Night it was virtue that watered the poisonous plant. But when virtue feeds poison, is it virtue at all? There is a facade of virtue, a mere outer garment, but behind it lies something intensely evil and poisonous. Men who move about with the facade of virtue are indeed very dangerous. They deceive and mislead others. In the vicinity of such people only poisonous trees flourish, the trees that do not allow any innocent and harmless life to grow. In this land, not vice but virtue was the problem, for here it was virtue that gave shelter to vice. The Dark forces always masquerade as benign and beneficial influences. In the garb of virtue they come and demolish the very house of virtue. It is this masked behaviour which overpowers many a struggling soul, for, he is taken in by the outer appearances. The poet calls these pretenders as the Sons of Darkness. Ashvapati saw this land of utter darkness peopled by

....souls who never had tasted bliss;
Ignorant like men born blind who know not light.

It is these inhabitants of the strange land of Darkness that had created a new order, substituting the divine or the natural order. The poet says:

A new order substitutes for the divine.
A silence falls upon the spirit's heights,
From the veiled sanctuary the God retires,
Empty and cold is the chamber of the Bride,
And hushed for ever is the secret Voice;
A flame that sang in Heaven sinks quenched and mute,
In ruin ends the epic of a soul.
This is the tragedy of the inner death,
When forfeited is the divine element
And only a mind and body live to die.

The Kingdom of the Dark Powers is characterised by the denial of freedom to the human individual. The most powerful expression of this denial is the worship of a Dogma or a Creed. One of the essential freedoms is the Freedom to Think, but this has no place where dogmas and creeds rule. In any country or civilization where dogma takes the place of intellectual freedom, there, very soon, decadence starts. It is difficult to maintain intellectual freedom; sooner or later man desires to settle down in some dogma or creed. In a dogma truth is sought to be organised and put into a framework of system. But how can this be? Truth is intensely dynamic, and when it is sought to be put into the framework of a dogma then surely it escapes. As the poet says in the above lines "from the veiled sanctuary the God retires". Sri Aurobindo tells us further about this dogma of the Dark Land in the following lines:

> The doors of God they have locked with the keys
>   of creed
> And shut out by the Law his tireless Grace.
> Along all Natures' lines they have set their posts
> And intercept the caravans of Light.
> Adepts of the illusion and the masque,
> The artificers of Nature's fall and pain
> Have built their altars of triumphant Night
> In the clay temple of terrestrial life.

Ashvapati must have felt utterly depressed at the sight that lay before him in the Kingdom of the Dark Powers. He had come out of the comparatively light atmosphere of the Vital world. Even the world of the dis-embodied spirits was gay compared to what he saw in this dreadful land of the Night. The atmosphere must have been suffocating, for he saw that:

> Laughter and pleasure were banned as deadly sins:
> A questionless mind was ranked as wise content,

A dull heart's silent apathy as peace:
Sleep was not there, torpor was the sole rest,
Death came but neither respite gave nor end;
Repose was a waiting between pang and pang
This was the law of things none dreamed to change.

It was in this land that Ashvapati was moving. It demanded tremendous courage. A man of lesser inner strength would have succumbed to the wiles of this country. Ashvapati was made of a sterner stuff, and he knew what he wanted. If the Vital realm could not give him the answer, surely it was unthinkable that this country of Dark Night could take him anywhere near to what he was seeking. Ashvapati knew that he was in the darkest hell, for no darker conditions of hell could be imagined. The poet says about him:

In this infernal realm he dared to press
Even into its deepest pit and darkest core,
Perturbed its tenebrous base, dared to contest
Its ancient privileged right and absolute force:
In Night he plunged to know her dreadful heart,
In Hell he sought the root and cause of Hell.
Its anguished gulfs opened in his own breast;
He listened to the clamours of its crowded pain,
The heart-beats of its fatal loneliness.
Companionless he roamed through desolate ways.

Ashvapati was indeed companionless in this dark world. But such was his inner strength that he challenged this dreadful Empire of the Night. Undaunted, he moved on wanting to know the very cause as to why life had fallen to such deep levels of existence. The poet says that inspite of:

The ordeal he suffered of evil's absolute reign,
Yet kept intact his spirit's radiant youth.

It is this spirit's radiant youth which saved Ashvapati from being swallowed up by the forces of Dark-

ness. The descriptions of the land of Darkness given
by the poet do not refer to far-away places. In our
own civilization we find many a spot which answers to
these descriptions, and they are indeed the danger spots
of our present age. In fact, the journey of Ashvapati
has not to be regarded as a geographical movement
nor a movement in other planes. The whole concept
of planes and sub-planes has to be altered, for, these
so-called planes and sub-planes are here, and not away.
The planes are states of consciousness as also states of
matter. There are inter-spaces in all grades of matter,
and it is in these inter-spaces that finer and subtler states
of matter exist. Since that is the case, all states of matter
are to be found here, and contacts can be established
with them through different states of consciousness. The
kingdom of the Dark Powers is also here, and one comes
under its influence due to certain states of consciousness
awakening to such grades of matter. Ashvapati, because of the condition of radiant youth which he had
maintained, could remain outside the influence of the
Dark Forces. The expression "radiant youth" is most
significant. This seems to be the talisman against all
such hazards. If one could keep one's consciousness in
this state of radiant youth, then, like Ashvapati, one
can travel through all grades of matter and yet remain
untouched. The poet says about Ashvapati that:

> There in the stark identity lost by mind
> He felt the sealed sense of the insensible world
> And a mute wisdom in the unknowing Night.

To awaken to the mute wisdom in the unknowing
night is indeed to respond to the Intangible in the midst
of the tangible. It is this which alone can protect a man
against all attacks of the unpleasant and the undesirable.
This perception of the Intangible in the midst of the
tangible is portrayed by the poet in the following lines:

He saw in Night the Eternal's shadowy veil,
Knew death for a cellar of the house of life,
In destruction felt creation's hasty pace
Knew loss as the price of a celestial gain
And hell as a short cut to heaven's gates.

With this awakening of intense sensitivity, where the Intangible was perceived in the bosom of the tangible, Ashvapati experienced a new hope and a new delight. In this awakening he saw that "falsehood gave back to Truth her tortured shape". He saw:

Hell split across its huge abrupt facade
As if a magic building were undone
Night opened and vanished like a gulf of dream.

The poet says that with this opening of the night, Ashvapati woke to a great felicitous Day. Now once again evolution was moving from the Valley to the Summit, from the trough to the crest. This was the Paradise of the Life-Gods, the highest peak of the Vital region. The poet says:

All things were perfect there that flower in Time;
Beauty was there creation's native mould.

This was still the Paradise of Time, for, the poet says here was everything perfect that flowers in Time. There is the flower of the Timeless and there is one that blooms in Time. Ashvapati was still in the realms where the limitation of Time prevailed. The poet says:

In that paradise of perfect heart and sense
No lower note could break the endless charm.

After the anguish of long strife in the region of the Night, Ashvapati was at last able to rest and heave, a sign of deep relief. The whole inner make-up of Ashvapati was changed, and

His earth dowered with celestial competence
Harboured a power that needed now no more
To cross the closed customs-line of mind and flesh
And smuggle godhead into humanity.

Ashvapati felt that he could now carry to earth
the ecstasy of godhead openly, not requiring him to
smuggle it across the customs line of mind and flesh.
Ashvapati had not yet awakened to the realm of the
Mind, and so the obstacles of its customs line, if any,
did not bother him. To use the occult terminology,
he was experiencing the joys of the Astral Heaven. He
felt under the impact of this Vital· Bliss that the barriers
of flesh would no longer constitute any hurdle to him,
so that along its customs line he could safely carry the
attainments so far accomplished by him. His stay in
this Astral Heaven,

....drew from sight and sound spiritual power,
Made sense a road to reach the Intangible.

The atmosphere here in this Vital Paradise was so
different from what he had experienced in the Kingdom
of Night that he felt "its honey of felicity flow through his veins like the rivers of Paradise." His mood is
expressed beautifully by the poet thus:

The dire delight that could shatter mortal flesh,
The rapture that the gods sustain he bore.
Immortal pleasure cleaned him in its waves
And turned his strength into undying power.

But this was the paradise where man's vital desires
are fulfilled. There is something more that man craves
for, and that something is not within the power of the
Vital world to give. Ashvapati ascended the summit
of Vital Life and felt the refreshing air of the great heights. But such is the march of evolution that ,he higher
one climbs, the still higher peaks become visible. From
the Valley of the Night the highest peak visible was the

peak of Vital Paradise. But having reached this peak, he saw a still higher summit calling him and asking him to scale the further heights. The Vital Paradise was just a halting place. He can tarry awhile in its parks and palaces, but he cannot settle down in this region. Ashvapati must reach the Highest if he is to bring the Elixir of Life for the rejuvenation of the human race. As the poet says:

> This too must now be overpassed and left,
> As all must be until the Highest is gained
> In whom the world and the self grow true and one:
> Till that is reached our journeying cannot cease.

CHAPTER X

A HUGE CHAMELEON

In our study of *Savitri*, we have left behind the evolutionary stages of Matter and Life, and are now proceeding towards the realm of the Mind. It is very strange that even though modern civilization has raised its stupendous structure on the foundations of Mind, it has begun to feel sick of that mind itself. There is an attempt on the part of the modern man to move away from the Mind, and take shelter in the regions that lie below the realm of the Mind. This "below-the-mind" movement is gathering strength. We find numerous modern religious cults advocating this movement below the spheres of the mind. There is no doubt that this is something entirely against the natural stream of evolution, and as such is bound to prove utterly frustrating. Man will return from this "below-the-mind" realm completely depressed and dejected, for in that realm he cannot find any solution to the many baffling problems of his life. There has to be an upward movement, but the climb is so steep that man ordinarily shudders at the idea of scaling such heights. Ashvapati emerges from the paradise of the Vital realm, for, how can he settle down there? He is the spearhead of the advance guard of humanity, and as such he must lead humanity onwards and not backwards into the regions that lie below the mind. Humanity cannot regress into conditions below the mind, however attractive that realm may be. Modern man, sick of the mind, is trying to seek pleasures of the vital world through drugs and many other devices. All these devices tend to dull the mind. Some of them induce the mind to go to sleep. But going to sleep is no solution to the problems of life. It is true that the mind has created

113

innumerable problems which the mind is unable to solve. But the way lies not in dulling the mind but in transcending the mind. And .Ashvapati ' takes that road of going beyond the mind. But in order to go beyond the mind, one must clearly understand the realm of the mind. Without finding out as to how the mind functions, one can never hope to go beyond. The heights of the Beyond all the time call out to man. But there are very few in the human race who are able to answer to the call of the greater heights of life and nature. The poet says:

> This creature who hugs his limits to feel safe,
> These heights declined a greater adventure's call.
> A glory and sweetness of satisfied desire
> Tied up the spirit to golden posts of bliss;
> It could not house the wideness of a soul
> Which needed all infinity for its home.

Discontent is indeed the impelling force behind all progress and adventure in the life of man. Life reveals its secrets only to the adventurous, and not to the timid who for ever seek security and safety. There is a world of difference between Discontent and Dissatisfaction. Those who seek security and safety speak the language of Dissatisfaction. But it is only the adventurous that know the language of Discontent. The man of dis-satisfaction only seeks new points of adjustment where he can settle down and eventually stagnate. He wants assurances from life before he can move further. But life gives no such assurances, and so he who demands them must come to a point of stagnation. The poet in the above lines says that the creature "who hugs his limits to feel safe" can never hear the call of the great heights. There is a glory and sweetness of satisfied desires in which most people settle down. Man is not usually aware of the wideness of his soul "which needs all infinity for its home". Those who seek infinity for their home are rare individuals. But it is these that have been the great Fire Pillars of Humanity.

Ashvapati was indeed made of this stuff, and so spurned all attractions of safety and security. He would rather go into the great wilderness of life than settle down in petty comfort and ease. Ashvapati ý heard the call of the Unknown and was ready to respond to it. From the bliss of the Vital world, with its heavenly joys, he was moving towards the Mind, a supremely unknown quantity in the field of evolution. The poet gives a graphic picture of the ways of the mind in the following lines:

> Here are devised the forms of an ignorant life
> That sees the empiric fact as settled law,
> Labours for the hour and not for eternity
> And trades its gains to meet the moment's call
> The slow process of a material mind
> Which serves the body it should rule and use.
> Advancing tardily from a limping start
> Crutching hypothesis upon argument,
> Throning its theories as certitudes
> It reasons from the half-known to the unknown
> Ever constructing its frail house of thought,
> Ever undoing the web that it has spun
> A twilight sage whose shadow seems to him Self,
> Moving from minute to brief minute lives;
> A king dependent on his satellites,·
> Signs the decrees of ignorant ministers,
> A judge in half-possession of his proofs,
> A voice clamant of uncertainty's postulates,
> An architect of knowledge, not its source
> This powerful bondslave of his instruments
> Thinks his low station Nature's highest top,
> Oblivious of his share in all things made
> And haughtily humble in his own conceit.

Perhaps nowhere in world's literature of philosophy or psychology do we find such an apt description of the nature and the function of the mind as we see in the above lines of Sri Aurobindo. Each line, nay each word, in the above passage is significant. One can write a whole commentary on the subject of Human Mind based on the above passage. However, the poet in the above lines has just given us an intimation of what is in store for Ashvapati   as he moves on in this land of the Mind. Ashvapati   does not realize all at once the limitations of the Mind, for, at first he enters the Kingdom of the Little Mind. The lowest is the realm of the Physical Mind. The poet says that Ashvapati :

> ....came into a realm of early Light
> And the regency of a half-risen sun.
> Out of its rays our mind's full orb was born.

The entire orb of the mind was born only from the rays of the half-risen sun! How limited and small must the circle of mind be when it is built out of the half-risen sun? The mind in its initial stages regards ignorance as the measuring rod of knowledge; even later it is the same rod with different modifications. The beginnings of the mind are described by the poet in terms of the three dwarfs. These are the Physical Mind, the Mind of Desire and the Reasoning Mind. The Physical Mind is the mind steeped in habit. About this mind the poet says:

> Abhorring change as an audacious sin,
> Distrustful of each new discovery.

Most of us have not stepped out of the limits and tendencies of the Physical Mind, for, much of what we think and do is rooted in habit. The inertia of the mind is more tenacious than the inertia of the body. To such a mind "only what sense can grasp seems absolute". It is averse to doing any thinking, apart from what goes on by the law of inertia. The physical Mind is indeed Mind rooted in *Tamas* or inertia. Then comes the Mind of Desire where one sees the *rajasic* tendency of the mind where restless movement is the predominant factor. Speaking about the nature of this mind, the poet says:

A huge chameleon gold and blue and red
Turning to black and grey and lurid brown
Nursing the splendid passion of its hues.
Ardent to find, incapable to retain,
A brilliant instability was its mark.

But the last to arrive on the scene was the Reasoning
Mind and man has hardly outgrown it even now. The
Reason is the third of the dwarfs belonging to this land
of the Mind. The poet says that "of all these Powers the
greatest was the last" meaning the Reasoning Mind. Sri
Aurobindo describes this in the following lines:

Came Reason, the squat godhead artisan
To her narrow house upon a ridge in Time.
Adept of clear contrivance and design,
A pensive face and a close and peering eyes,
She took her firm irremovable seat,
The strongest, wisest of the troll-like Three.
Armed with her lens and measuring rod and probe.

Even to the mighty reason, the poet gives the epithet
of troll-like, meaning utterly dwarfish. But the most significant word in the above passage is "squat". The poet
likens the mind to squatters who have no legitimate right
to occupy the seat on which they are sitted. To describe
reason as a mere squatter is indeed most apt, for, it is a
pretender trying to be very objective with the lens and the
measuring rod. About Reason, the poet further says:

She strove to reduce to rules the mystic world.
Nothing she knew but all things hoped to know.
Ignorant of all but her own seeking mind
She sets the hard inventions of her brain
In a pattern of eternal fixity.

The greatest drawback of reason is that it seeks to
understand the dynamic flux of life with an approach
that is utterly static. It is in the pattern of eternal fixity

that she sees everything, and so misses the living quality of things. The poet says:

> A million faces wears her knowledge here
> And every face is turbaned with a doubt.

How can Reason speak with certainty when it deals with the flux of life as if it were fixed and static? On all that reason achieves there is the hallmark of doubt and uncertainty. Even its conclusions lead one nowhere, for, it moves endlessly in a circle, like the dog chasing its own tail. As the poet says:

> Her thought is an endless march without a goal.
> There is no summit on which she can stand
> And see in a single glance the Infinite's whole.

Life can be comprehended only as a whole, not part by part. This comprehension cannot happen in time-sequence. In one single glance is seen the Whole. Does not the experience of Love come in one single glance? Sri Aurobindo says "An inconclusive play is Reason's toil". How graphic is the following description:

> Balanced she sits on wide and empty air,
> Aloof and pure in her impartial poise.
> Absolute her judgments seem but none is sure;
> Time cancels all her verdicts in appeal.

The poet's criticism of Reason is most scathing, and how true it is! Modern man worships at the altar of Reason but does not realize that the god whom he worships is a false god. Reason may seem very pompous, but its content is utterly hollow. It poses to pass an impartial judgment on men and things, but its judgments have no validity. Reason is like an advocate who accepts every brief, for, she knows not what is right and what is wrong. The poet says:

> She travels on the roads of erring sight
> Or looks upon a set mechanical world

Constructed for her by her instruments.
As if she knew not facts are husks of truth,
The husks she keeps, the kernel throws aside.

We of this age of science talk a great deal about "facts".
We seem to be thinking that by scientific means and by
the application of reason we are gathering facts. And we
feel that only those superstructures will survive that are
raised on the groundwork of facts. But what after all
are these facts? The poet says that what we term as facts
are mere husks, and reason engaged in gathering facts keeps
the husks and throws away the kernel. The real fact is the
kernel and content of life, but reason has no means to
recognize it. Its processes are too slow and tardy to grasp
the meaning of life which is in a state of constant flux.
And so after all what can reason achieve? The poet says:

Then science and reason careless of the soul
Could iron out a tranquil uniform world,
A reasonable animal make of man
And a symmetrical fabric of his life.

The great scientist, Le comte du Nuoy, says in his memo-
rable book *The Human Destiny* that life is not symmetrical,
it is dis-symmetrical. But reason wants to put everything
into the framework of symmetry. Logical thinking itself is
symmetrical thinking. That which is living cannot be put
in the straight-jacket of symmetry. But reason revolts
against anything that violates the laws of symmetry. And
so when science and reason undertake to build a new
world, it will be based on the rules of symmetry and therefore displaying a quality of dead uniformity. As the poet
says science and reason will make of man a reasonable animal. But surely that is not the destiny of man. The peace
which science and reason will create will be the peace of
the graveyard , not the peace of a living world. But how
can Reason understand that category of experience which
has to be seen as a Whole and not part by part? The poet
says:

> For not by Reason was creation made
> And not by Reason can the Truth be seen.

In Life there are areas of experience where logic and reason, mathematics and measurement can prevail. But there are areas where these are of no avail. And the experiences that matter in the life of an individual are beyond the purview of measurement. Reason and logic at best can understand the pattern of things, but they cannot reveal the secret of the purpose of existence. The poet says:

> Our reason only a toys' artificer,
> A rule-maker in a strange stumbling game.
> The world she has made is an interim report
> Of a traveller towards half-found truth in things
> Moving twixt nescience and nescience.
> For nothing is known while aught remains concealed;
> The Truth is known only when all is seen.

The report of reason is an interim report; and it has no means at its disposal to complete the report. And so all its judgments and conclusions are based on this interim report covering half-found truths. As the poet says "Truth is known only when all is seen", but it is this seeing of the all which lies outside the field of reason and logic. Sri Aurobindo tells us further while dealing with the limitations of reason that:

> Finding her hands too small to hold vast Truth
> She breaks up knowledge into alien parts.

This is exactly what reason does—the breaking up of an experience into different parts. It examines it part by part and then creates a synthesis. The highest knowledge attained by Reason is only a synthesis. But a synthesis is something artificial, for, it is the product of comparison and contrast. It is arrived at by gathering the similarities and rejecting the dis-similarities. In synthesis, the *thing as it is* is always missed, for, the thing is examined in comparison with something else. But each living thing is incomparable and therefore unique. Reason, at best, may know the universal but not the unique. The hands of reason are too small to hold the vast Truth. And that is why one has to transcend the dwarfish trinity of the Physical Mind, the Mind of Desire and the Reasoning Mind. But is there a Mind that lies beyond this dwarfish trinity? The poet says:

.... Thought transcends the circles of mortal mind,
It is greater than its earthly instrument.

Here perhaps Sri Aurobindo uses the word "Thought" in the sense of the Sanskrit word *Manas*. The mind is the instrument of Manas, and as such functions under greater limitations than the Principle of Manas. Mind represents the crystallization of Thought. One may describe this distinction by the traditional terms of the Concrete Mind and the Abstract Mind. The Concrete is the lower even as the Abstract is the higher or what Sri Aurobindo calls the Greater. In his philosophy there are numerous subdivisions of the Mind. The four of these divisions are most important—they are the Higher Mind, the Illumined Mind, the Intuitive Mind and the Over-Mind. The Super-Mind is not a part of the Mind; it transcends all levels of the Mind and so cannot be fitted into any of the dimensional states of the Mind. In the Dwarfish Trinity of the Mind, Sri Aurobindo was concerned with the lowest levels of his mind-classification. When Ashvapati finds that even the Reasoning Mind is much too small, unable to hold Truth, he moves further into the higher realms of the Mind. He comes to the Kingdom of the Greater Mind or the spheres of the Illumined Mind. This is evident when we read the following lines of the poet:

Where Thought leaned on a vision beyond thought,
And shaped a world from the Unthinkable.

Thought beyond thought refers obviously to a realm beyond the sphere of concrete thinking. There are moments

in the life of man when he feels a touch of illumination
where things mundane seem all of a sudden pregnant with
spiritual significance. The poet says:

> A thought comes down from the ideal worlds
> And moves us to new-model even here
> Some image of their greatness and appeal

The four-fold classification of mind by Sri Aurobindo
has some relationship with the four-fold state of consciousness to be found in ancient Hindu Psychology. The four
states of consciousness are *Jagrat* or the Waking, *Svapna* or
Dreaming, *Sushupti* or Deep Sleeping and *Turiya* or the
Transcendental. Now the Higher Mind of Sri Aurobindo is the Waking state, and the highest point of the
Waking state is the Reasoning Mind. The Illumined Mind
of Sri Aurobindo is indeed the Dream state. In Dream
come certain intimations which are unable to penetrate
the Waking state because of the ceaseless choice in which
it is engaged. It is to these intimations that the poet refers
in the above lines. However in the Dream state there is the
dreamer who interprets his dream, even though unconsciously. There is no choice in the Dream state, but surely
there is interpretation. It is because of this interpretation
that we get up from the dream sometimes in a happy mood
and sometimes in a sad and a depressing mood. We are
unable to account for it because there has been no conscious interpretation. The Intuitive Mind of Sri Aurobindo is comparable to the state of *Sushupti* or Deep Sleep
where there are intimations without interpretation, for,
how can there be an interpreter in Deep Sleep? In Deep
Sleep, the Sleeper and the sleep have become one, and so
there is no interpreter who interprets the intimations that
come. These intimations remain un-named in the Deep
Sleep condition. After that comes the Over-Mind of Sri
Aurobindo which is akin to the Turiya state or the Transcendental state of consciousness. The Super-Mind of Sri
Aurobindo is *Turiyatita*, meaning beyond the transcendental.

state of the mind. That is all that one can say about
the Super-Mind, for, there are no words in the vocabulary
of the mind to describe it. Now as Ashvapati moves from
the limitation of the Reasoning Mind, he comes into the
realm of the Illumined Mind or into the Dream state of
consciousness. The poet says just in one line what the
nature of this realm is. He says: "In his little world built
of immortal dreams". In the intimations of the illumined
mind there is an effort on the part of the mind to im-
prison Truth. One feels that at last one has caught Truth
in one's net, but this is indeed the illusion of the Dream.
The poet says:

> In our thinking's close and narrow lamp-lit house
> The vanity of our shut mortal mind
> Dreams that the chains of thought have made her ours;
> But we only play with our own brilliant bonds;
> Tying her down, it is ourselves we tie.
> In our hypnosis by one luminous point
> We see not what small figure of her we hold;
> We feel not her inspiring boundlessness,
> We share not her immortal liberty.
> For still the human limits the divine.

In our dream state we may feel that we have brought
Truth within our hold, but alas, it is just a case of self-
hypnosis induced in the condition of dream. Out of the
Dream state arise Ideals and Ideations, and the mind of man
wishes to hold Truth in the framework of these ideals. But
as the poet says:

> ....Truth is wider, greater than her forms.
> A thousand icons they have made of her
> And find her in the idols they adore;
> But she remains herself and infinite.

Even a thousand icons cannot contain her; even a
thousand Names of God cannot describe His Glory, for,
Truth overflows all forms and patterns. But living in the

Dream world of the Illumined Mind, man feels for ever an irresistible call of the Ideal. From afar it beckons to him. It is this which takes the form of Aspiration. It has its birth in the intimations of the Dream state. Moved by the urge of the Ideal, Ashvapati left "known summits for the unknown peaks". That indeed is the urge that impels all spiritual travellers. In the ascent of the spiritual life each step seems marvellous, and one feels that there cannot be anything more glorious than what one sees at the moment. As the poet says:

> The heavens of the Ideal mind were seen
> In a blue lucency of dreaming space
> Like strips of brilliant sky clinging to the moon.

The heavens of the Ideal mind look like lovely kingdoms of the deathless Rose. In this kingdom of the Idea there are two streams, one of the Rose and the other of the Flame as the poet tells us in terms of his beautiful imagery. Sri Aurobindo says that

> They offered to the Traveller at their gates
> A quenchless flame or an unfading flower.

The Flower and the Flame are indeed the embodiments of the highest ideal. They symbolise Bliss and Knowledge respectively. The Flame and the Flower are the *Cit* and the *Ananda* of Hindu mysticism. But Ashvapati felt that while the world of the Ideal was intensely attractive, there existed here only a partial light. He saw in this world, ideals of variegated colours. In these colours there was an attempt at approximation towards perfection. But approximation could not satisfy him. Ideals at best can only be approximations. But once again approximations have relevance to something that is fixed and static. Ideal itself is static, how can it establish its relationship with something that is intensely dynamic, such as life is? About Ashvapati 's experience in this world of ideals, the poet says:

He through the Ideal's kingdom moved at will,
Accepted their beauty and their greatness bore,
Partook of the glories of their wonder fields,
But passed, nor stayed beneath their splendour's rule.
All there was an intense but partial light.

In the world of ideals everything shone with a partial
light. There was never a feeling of abandonment in this
region, for, how can spontaneous action arise where life is
tethered to the post of an ideal? Action in terms of an ideal
can never be free; in fact, it can be only a reaction.
Here action itself seeks an approximation to the ideal.
The poet says that here was

made a circle of bliss with married hands;
Light stood embraced with light, fire wedded fire,
But none in the other would his body lose
To find his soul in the world's single soul,
A multiplied rapture of infinity.

In this world of Ideals, there remained a duality, for,
there was no merging of the one in the other. There
was no experience of one losing himself in the other.
To find one's soul by losing it in the other was something
unknown in this realm. And so,

Onward he passed to a diviner sphere:
Above the parting of the roads of Time
Above the Silence and its thousandfold Word
In the immutable and inviolate Truth
For ever united and inseparable,
The radiant children of Eternity dwell
On the wide spirit height where all are one.

But to reach this destination, Ashvapati must move
a long way traversing many a land where he may pause
for a while but not settle down. Traversing beyond the
world of the Ideals, he came to a region "Where Silence
listened to the Cosmic Voice". He enters the realm which
the poet describes as the Self of Mind. What after all is this

Self of Mind? It is Mind in the state of being a witness to
things. It is a mind not involved in various forms of action,
but one that is a witness to all that happens. It is this
which the poet describes by saying that here Silence listened
to the cosmic Voice. It is only when the chattering of the
mind ceases, that it can listen to the Voice of the Silence
or to the Cosmic Voice. About this mind the poet says:

> It acted not but bore all thoughts and deeds
> The witness Lord of Nature's myriad acts.

Ashvapati is now coming to what Sri Aurobindo calls the
Intuitive Mind, or to the state of *Sushupti* or Deep Sleep.
When the interpreter is not there, consciousness becomes a
witness. It is from the inaction of the mind that true action is born, the action that binds not. The poet aptly describes this by saying: "In the world which sprang from it,
it took no part". About this state, Sri Aurobindo says:

> As one who builds his own imagined scenes
> And loses not himself in what he sees
> Spectator of a drama self-conceived.

In these lines the poet has given the secret of Immanence and Transcendence, the creator being in the creation
and yet above it. Standing in this new world, Ashvapati
realised that whatever the mind had collected so far was
of no significance whatsoever. Mind even when it is engaged in noblest thoughts cannot reach the heights where
Reality lives. The poet says that the thoughts,

> Never can win however high their reach
> Or overpass however keen their probe
> A doubt corroded even the means to think,
> Distrust was thrown upon Mind's instruments;
> All that it takes for reality's shining coin,
> Proved fact, fixed inference, deduction clear,
> Firm theory, assured significance,
> Appeared as frauds upon Time's credit bank
> Or assets valueless in Truth's treasury.

All the assets of the mind are utterly valueless in the treasury of Truth. It is this realization to which Ashvapati comes when he reaches the frontiers of the Intuitive Mind. To see for oneself the utter hollowness of mind's accumulations is a revolutionary act, for, it gives a new direction to one's action in life. About this hollowness of the mind, the poet says:

What it knew was an image in a broken glass,
What it saw was real but its sight untrue
All the ideas in its vast repertory
Were like the mutterings of a transient cloud
That spent itself in sound and left no trace.

The entire repertory of the mind, even its finest collection, is like an empty sound. It casts its glance on the Real but its sight is untrue. The Self of the Mind is only the threshold that leads to the Intuitive Mind. But as Ashvapati crosses the threshold, his mind sees what he has so far been doing, Now its accumulations are completely valueless. The poet tells us:

Our mind is a house haunted by the slain past,
Ideas soon mummified, ghosts of old truths,
God's spontaneities tied with formal strings
And packed into drawers of reason's trim bureau.

The bureau of reason is indeed very trim and properly pigeonholed. But it contains only mummified ideas. The poet very graphically says that God's spontaneous expressions are tied with formal strings of red-tapism. Mind no doubt is efficient, but its efficiency is with regard to things that are dead. On the threshold of the Intuitive Mind, there is only a witness — a silent spectator of things and events. But a mere witness cannot answer the deep questionings of Ashvapati . What can a mere witness say? But this witness mind is only a guardian of the gates that lead to the ecstasies of intuition. The self of Mind is only a doorway, opening into the inner chambers of consciousness. The poet says:

> A greater Spirit than the Self of Mind
> Must answer to the questioning of his soul.

The Self of Mind was only a neutral ground where one could watch the futile activities of thought. But **Ashvapati** was in search of something positive. The choice that presented itself to him was: To remain here or to escape, for, as the poet says "To be was a prison, extinction the escape". His escape lay only in the extinction of the mind. A mere passive neutrality would keep him only in the prison house, may be a better lighted courtyard of the prison. But Ashvapati wanted to escape from the prison-house of the mind. And this escape lay only along the total extinction of mind itself. We have to bear in mind that Intuition arises only where the mind is not. The mind clings to its own individualised consciousness. But it is this individualised consciousness that must disappear, for where intuition is born there one is in contact with the Universal Consciousness. This extinction of the mind is the dew-drop slipping into the sea. **Ashvapati** must find the way that leads to the slipping of the dew-drop into the sea. This is the extinction of the mind, and there alone lies his escape from the prison-house of thought. It is this urge to escape from the prison-house that enabled **Ashvapati** to discover an opening which invited him to explore a new region, unthought of by mind. The poet says:

> A covert answer to his seeking came.
> In a far shimmering background of Mind-Space
> A glowing mouth was seen, a luminous shaft;
> A recluse gate it seemed, musing on joy,
> A veiled retreat and escape to mystery.
> Away from the unsatisfied surface world
> It fled into the bosom of the unknown,
> A well, a tunnel of the depths of God.

This way led to the world's heart. Can there be a
more apt description of Intuition than the world's heart?
In intuition there is a co-existence of impersonality and
intimacy. Ashvapati had seen the seeming impersonality of
reason, but there he missed the intimate touch of a Person.
He was in search of the intimate Person, and yet a Person
completely free from the involvements of personality. About
this part of Ashvapati 's journey, the poet says:

As one drawn to his lost spiritual home
Feels now the closeness of a waiting love,
He travelled, led by a mysterious sound.

This sound that he heard had a diversity of notes. In
the realm of intuition one can say "Thus have I heard",
not "Thus have I seen". The seeing comes in the state
of the Overmind. In the intuitive realm the communicating medium is the sound. The poet says about this
sound:

A murmur, multitudinous and lone,
All sounds it was in turn, yet still the same.
A hidden call to unforeseen delight
In the summoning voice of one long-known and loved,
But nameless to the unremembering mind
It led to rapture back the truant heart.

The coming of Ashvapati thus far was indeed the
return of the truant heart, the heart that had stayed away
too long from its real home. It was like the return of
the Prodigal. In the world of Intuition there come intimations from realms beyond, but these remain nameless.
It is these intimations left unnamed that make it possible
for one to move on from the hearing of the Sound to
the seeing of the Person. If the mind names the intimation that comes through the sound then the doors of
the Overmind, where alone perception is possible, remain
closed. The Illumined Mind is prone to name its intimations, but it is the Intuitive Mind that keeps them

unnamed, and therefore retains their absolute purity. It is the naming of an experience that defiles it. Let the deity on the altar of life remain unnamed; then there comes the Miracle of Seeing. Ashvapati heard a diversity of notes. In the hearing of these sounds, he felt "the approach of the invisible Beloved." The poet says:

> Into a wonderful bodiless realm he came,
> The home of a passion without name or voice,
> A depth he felt answering to every height,
> A nook was found that could embrace all worlds,
> A point that was the conscious knot of space
> An hour eternal in the heart of Time.

This was a bodiless realm—a region without form, for, it is in the Formless that all forms can reside. In the negation of all forms of thought there arises the Purest and the Sublimest Form. In intuition lies the negation of all forms of thought. It is in the Formless that the invisible Form of the Beloved is felt. As the poet says: "A formless spirit became the soul of form". We are told that:

> All here were known by a spiritual sense:
> Thought was not there but a knowledge near and one
> Seized on all things by a moved identity,
> A sympathy of self with other selves,
> The touch of consciousness on consciousness
> And being's look on being with inmost gaze
> And heart laid bare to heart without walls of speech.

In the above lines the poet has described the condition of one who has come to intuitive insight. There is knowledge by ideation and there is knowledge by being. Here we see the latter category of knowledge. In the Waking state there are no intimations because the mind is much too occupied with its own judgement and choice. In the Dream state there are intimations but they are covered by unconscious interpretation. It is in the

Deep Sleep state that there are intimations uncovered by any interpretation. It is when intimation is left un-interpreted that there comes an Insight which characteri-zes the Intuitive Mind. In this there comes knowledge from within which after all is the nature of Intuition. Intimation, Insight and Inspiration are three different things. While the Illumined Mind and the Intuitive Mind are the fields for Intimation and Insight, it is Overmind which is the recipient of Inspiration. The Higher Mind or the Waking state represents a stage of Intellection. Ashvapati moved on from Intellection to Intimation and thence to the realm of Insight. It is this field of Intuition which he is exploring. It is of this realm that the poet speaks when he says that here the heart is laid bare to heart without the walls of speech. When there is knowledge by being then speech is super-fluous, for, one speaks to the other through a medium which is more powerful than speech. It is the being that speaks to the being. Here as the poet says there is know-ledge without the intervention of thought.

Sri Aurobindo says that in this realm Ashvapati knew things "by their soul and not their shape",

As those who have lived long made one in love
Need word nor sign for heart's reply to heart
He met and communed without bar of speech
With beings unveiled by a material frame.

This is indeed the perception that comes in the mo-ment of intuitive insight. In this experience of intuitive insight there are moments of creative interval. It is thought that covers all things with a screen of continuity, but not so the Intuition. Where intuition functions there one becomes aware of the intervals of discontinuity. As the poet says:

Here was the fashioning chamber of the worlds.
An interval was left twixt act and act,

Twixt birth and birth, twixt dream and waking
dream
A pause that gave new strength to do and be.

In intuition there comes a jump of consciousness, a break in the continuity of thought. It is thus the ground in which mutation is born. In the continuity of thought there is always the tiredness and the exhaustion arising out of the feeling of sameness. It is always in the pause that there is the renewal of strength to be and to do. Man knows no pause, no psychological pause, in his life, and that is why he does not know the secret of renewal. The pause of the soul is indeed the moment of great wonder. In the experience of intuitive insight one comes to such a pause, and the pause enables one to see what one had never seen — the Beauty and the Grandeur of Life itself. What Ashvapati saw in this pause, in this interval, was something most wonderful and indescribable. Here Ashvapati had the vision of the Supreme Mother, in her grace. He saw only the outline of a Face—the face of the Mother. The Kena Upanishad speaks of the appearance of Uma, the consort of Shiva, in the darkness of the Night. Here Sri Aurobindo speaks of the Face of the Mother outlined in that pause or the interval. Man can become complete only when the masculine and feminine aspects of consciousness merge in each other. Ashvapati was indeed in search of the feminine aspect of consciousness, for, without it the entire human race was disintegrated within and disorganised without. He was the leader of humanity, and so knew what the problem of man was. He ascended thus far, rejecting heaven and hell, for he knew that unless there comes the Vision of the Mother, of Uma, there cannot be found an answer to the question with which he started on the journey. He had a glimpse, just a faint glimpse, of the Mother. It was in this Void of the Interval that this experience comes to Ashvapati. The poet says:

A light appeared still and imperishable
Attracted to the large and luminous depths
Of the ravishing enigma of her eyes,
He saw the mystic outline of a face
Overwhelmed by her implacable light and bliss,
An atom of her illimitible self
He cast from the rent stillness of his soul
A cry of adoration and desire
And the surrender of his boundless mind
And the self-giving of his silent heart
He fell down at her feet unconscious, prone.

In such a vision comes a spontaneous surrender, and it is this which Ashvapati experienced. But it was a surrender of his boundless mind. The surrender of a dull and limited mind has no value—it has to be a boundless mind, a mind that has no frontiers. Ashvapati had brought such a mind which had refused to settle down and had thus broken boundary after boundary in which the heaven and the hell wanted to keep him. The poet says that in this glimpse of the Mother, he saw the ravishing enigma of her eyes. Enigma it certainly was, but not an enigma that frightens, but one that is ravishing to the sensitive heart and mind of Ashvapati. But what he saw was only an atom of her illimitable self, and such a vision came to him from the rent stillness of his soul. Even stillness can become a wall and a prison-house. But this happens when stillness is given a name. It is only the unnamed stillness which opens one's vision to the Vastness of Eternal Life. What could Ashvapati do under the powerful impact of this Vision? He fell down at her feet, unconscious and prone. His consciousness was unable to contain what he saw. There was a surrender, total and spontaneous. It is in such surrender that one reaches the highest point of one's consciousness, and that is the point of the Over-mind. Ashvapati had come to the very summit, the highest point to which he could move. A movement from the Intuitive Mind to the Over-mind is an unconscious movement. It is only when the mind naturally and spontaneously comes to the prone state that the high summit of the Over-mind is reached. It is when the boundless mind realizes its own limitations, and knows that it does not know, that the Light from above descends. And the boundless mind knowing its limitations is the moment of the arrival of the state of the Over-Mind. This is a state of total receptivity; it is a receptivity containing anticipation without any tinge of expectation. The mind that is receptive but free from any pre-conceived anticipation is indeed the Ground of Over-Mind. It is to this condition that Ashvapati has come, the summit of his stupendous Ascent. There was no land further from this point that he could traverse.

The poet says about Ashvapati standing on the summit of his journey of Ascent;

> After a measureless moment of the soul
> He stood in a realm of boundless silences
> Awaiting the Voice that spoke and built the worlds.
> A consciousness lay still, devoid of forms,
> Free, wordless, uncoerced by sign or rule,
> For ever content with only being and bliss;
> A sheer existence lived in its own peace
> On the single spirit's bare and infinite ground.
> Out of the sphere of Mind he had arisen,
> He had left the reign of Nature's hues and shades;
> He dwelt in his self's colourless purity.
> A state in which all ceased and all began.

The colourless purity of the self is indeed the supremely negative state of the Over-Mind. It is only in the negative soil that the positive plant can grow. The poet says that this was the state where all ceased and all began. It is the point of cessation that also was the point of creation. The Negative and the Positive are not separated by an interval. Where all ceases is the negative and where all begins is the positive. It is the co-existence

of the two that characterises the state of the Over-Mind.
Ashvapati had stepped out of the sphere of the Mind. The
state of the Over-Mind is the state of sheer existence.
This implies an existence from where all motives and all
efforts have disappeared. It is only when one comes to
this state of "sheer existence" that one can listen to the
Voice of the Silence. The poet says:

> Here came the thought that passes beyond Thought,
> Here the still Voice which our listening cannot
> > hear,
> The Knowledge by which the Knower is the Known,
> The Love in which Beloved and Lover are one.

Ashvapati has come to the experience of the non-
dual. It is a state where the Knower is the Known,
where the Lover and the Beloved are not two, where the
Creator and the Creation are a non-dual entity. There
is a condition where the perceived is the projection of the
perceiver, but there is a state where the perceived is the
expression of the perceiver. There is a difference between the projection and the expression. In projection the
perceiver seeks fulfilment through the perceived, but in
expression the perceiver communicates out of its fullness.
It is in this sense that the Lover and the Beloved are one,
or the Creator and the Creation are a non-dual entity.
The Knower is the Known, for, here the fullness of experience is being communicated through the forms of
expression. In every point of Creation, the creator abides. But this can happen only when man is free from
the projections, of the mind, when he is free from the
limiting factors of the known. The poet says:

> The known released him from its limiting chain,
> He knocked at the doors of the Unknowable
> The gazing with an immeasurable outlook
> One with self's inlook into its own pure vasts,
> He saw the splendour of the spirit's realms,
> The greatness and the wonder of its boundless works,

> The power and passion leaping from its calm,
> The rapture of its movement and its rest.

Here the poet speaks to us of the co-existence of two completely contradictory factors, the movement and the rest, the power and the passion. The rest and movement are the negative and the positive co-existing. The poet says that Ashvapati was on "the rim of two continents of slumber and trance". It is in the mid-point that one hears the Voice of Reality. Ashvapati had come to the realm where existed neither the attachment of the personal nor the cold detachment of the impersonal. The poet says:

> In that high realm where no untruth can come,
> Where all are different and all is one,
> In the Impersonal's ocean without shore
> The Person in the World-Spirit anchored rode.

When in the shoreless ocean of the Impersonal arises the Person then is the negative permeated with the presence of the Positive. When the Person is born in the ocean of the Impersonal then is the renewal of man made possible. The poet says:

> He came new-born, infant and limitless
> And grew in the wisdom of the timeless Child
> He communed with the Incommunicable
> The Gods conversed with him behind Life's veil
> Thoughts rose in him no earthly mind can hold
> Mights played that never coursed through mortal
> > nerves
> He scanned the secrets of the Over-Mind,
> He bore the rapture of the Oversoul.

The rose must re-become the bud, the pupil must regain the child-state—such indeed is the requirement of the Mystic Path. Thus alone can the secrets of the Over-mind be scanned. The child-state is the supremely negative state of consciousness. And that truly is the state of the Overmind. It is here that arise thoughts which no earthly mind can ever hold. It is only the virgin consciousness of the Overmind that can hold the rapture of the Oversoul. Ashvapati had come to the bliss of the Overmind, to the joys of Nirvana. But is this all? He had come to bliss eternal, but surely he had travelled not for enjoying the bliss for himself. The question arose in him: What about the human race for whom he had come thus far?

CHAPTER XI

THE TRANSFIGURING HOUR

THERE is one charge which is levelled against Hindu philosophical thought by Western critics and that is that it is utterly negative in its nature and content. But in this criticism the real significance of the negative is very often lost sight of. First of all, negative is not identical with passive. In fact, the two are poles asunder. Passivity arises from an inert condition of the mind, whereas Negativity demands a boundless condition of the mind. Such a mind has enormous breadth. It is to this breadth that negativity imparts the quality of depth. If the mind has not the element of boundlessness then whatever depth it acquires is utterly superficial. After all in the state of negativity the mind is emptied of all its contents. But if it has no content worth its name, then the emptying creates a condition of blankness. A passive mind is a blank mind. It has a blank look about it. Its depth is nothing more than the scratching of the surface. When such a mind empties itself it has nothing but a scratched surface to display. But a mind that has enormous breadth, one that has boundlessness as its quality, assumes great depth when its contents are emptied. When Ashvapati came to the state of the Overmind, Sri Aurobindo says that he brought with him a boundless mind, a mind that had no frontiers, a mind that had a tremendous expanse. The poet says, as we saw towards the close of the last chapter, that Ashvapati's boundless mind lay prone before the Great Vision that was vouchsafed to him. When the boundless mind lies prone then it is emptied of itself, and in such emptiness is revealed an immense depth of consciousness. Hindu philosophers

138

have not spoken about a state of passivity, but about the state of negativity. It is the negative soil which supplies the necessary depth in which the positive plant of Reality can grow. The attainment of breadth and the creation of depth are not two different things. When the mind is emptied of all that it has accumulated in the course of building up its expanse, then, in that very emptying, an immensity of depth is created. Depth will depend upon the breadth of consciousness. If the breadth is small then the depth too will be superficial, but if the breadth has a wide expanse then the depth too will be immense. If Ashvapati cannot bring to the door of Reality an immensity of depth then of what use is his coming so far? What will he carry to the struggling and suffering humanity if he goes to Reality with a vessel that is miserably shallow? He must needs go back to feed the starving humanity with food that is nourishing. But if his vessel is small, he will not be able to assuage the hunger and thirst of humanity which is anxiously await-ing his return. And so the poet says, Ashvapati brought a boundless mind, and it was such a mind that lay prone, in a state of total and spontaneous surrender.

In the spiritual literature of the world, surrender is regarded as the highest state. But surrender is not to be mistaken for submission. When surrender requires an effort then it is none other than submission. Surrender is effortless and therefore is not an act of the conscious mind. The poet says that Ashvapati became unconscious and lay prone. The act of surrender is always unconscious. If a person is conscious that he has surrendered or is su-rrendering then there is no surrender at all. But once again the surrender is not of one's possessions; it is of the very sense of possession. And so surrender of things has very little value. It is the surrender of the mind which brings one to the experience of the Divine Grace. It needs to be borne in mind that depth cannot be created; in the very emptying of the contents accumulated by the breadth of the mind that brings depth into existence. In the surrender of the mind it is this emptying that takes place. The Overmind is indeed the state of mind's surrender, and when this happens the Grace of the Supermind is received. As is the *Patra* or the Vessel, so is the receiving. But whatever is received has the same quality of Divine Grace. Ashvapati brought to the door of the Supermind a vessel that was utterly pure and enormously deep. But when will the nectar of the Supermind descend?

Standing on the great summit of the Overmind, Ashvapati saw, in retrospect, that even in the highest achievements of the mind there was something that was missing. Without that something life seemed devoid of meaning and significance. The poet says:

> The labour to know seemed a vain strife of Mind;
> All knowledge ended in the Unknowable:
> The effort to rule seemed a vain pride of Will.

And so his eyes were searching for something beyond. He had some glimpses of the beyond, but "Near it retreated; far, it called him still". It is the call of the far that had brought Ashvapati so far. But still that something was beyond his grasp. He knew this much that when that something was absent then even the greatest action seemed dull, and in its presence even the smallest action seemed divine. What was this "something" so intangible and beyond the grasp of the mind? This is what Aswapathy wanted to know. He knew this much in the words of the poet that:

> All he had been and all towards which he grew
> Must now be left behind or else transform
> Into a self of That which has no name.

Ashvapati must leave everything behind—even those things towards which he grew. And these are the ideals and aspirations nurtured by him in terms of his mind.

He is now moving towards something which has no Name. In fact, IT must remain nameless, for, the very naming will bring it within the framework of that which the mind knows. Reality must needs always remain Nameless It is in naming that the sublime is brought to the level of the ridiculous. Ashvapati had come to that summit in the course of his journey when he himself must become nameless. He must cast away all names that he 'may have 'accumulated' in the course of life's journey. It is in Name that the whole past is symbolised, for, with the uttering of the name, even silently by the mind, the entire past becomes activised. And so the poet says:

The separate self must melt or be reborn
Into a Truth beyond the mind's appeal.

It is name which is the identifying label, and so it is through the name that a separate identity is maintained. Here name does not mean something that is used for social convenience, but has to be considered as a point of psychological identification. One must use a name for recognition, but when it is used for psychological identification then does it symbolise the past, containing all the likes and dislikes, all the resistances and indulgences. Ashvapati had come to the state of the Overmind. Here he has to be divested of the garments of the mind; in fact, he has to be divested of the company of his own thoughts. He must stand alone, for, the approach to Reality is from the alone to the Alone. The poet says:

A stark companionless Reality
Answered at last to his soul's passionate search:
All person perished in its namelessness.
There was no second, it had no partner or peer:
Only itself was real to itself
The One by whom all live, who lives by none.

And so the state of the Overmind is the state of complete negation where even the name must vanish. It is

only the Nameless Being that can listen to the Nameless
Reality. The earth knows no silence comparable to the
silence of the Nameless, and into such silence of the Over-
mind Ashvapati had come. About this silence, the poet
says:

> A stillness absolute, incommunicable
> Meets the sheer self-discovery of the soul.

The discovery of the soul takes place only in such
stillness, in such Absolute Silence. We here know only
of the relative silence which comes with the cessation of
Noise. But there is an Absolute Silence which has no
relevance with noise. The poet says that this stillness
"makes unreal all that mind has known". In this silence
only "the Inconceivable is left, only the Nameless without space and time". But looking from this great Summit
of Negation, Ashvapati cries out:

> Only the everlasting No has neared
> But where is the Lover's everlasting Yes?

The Overmind is the land of complete negation, but
has Ashvapati to return to earth with this Negation?
Will he not carry something positive to the hungry humanity? Must he remain here in the Bliss of Negation?
He journeyed thus far not in order to enjoy the bliss of
Nirvana; he came with a mission to carry to the world
the joy that corrupts not. What about this mission? And
so Ashvapati says that he has neared the everlasting
No, but where indeed is the Lover's everlasting Yes? It
is not for the Overmind to give an answer in the affir-
mative. The Lover's Yes must come from the Beyond.
The riddle of the world which is an unfinished play cannot be solved by mere negation. In the heart of the
Negation must arise the Positive. As the poet says "In
absolute silence sleeps an absolute Power". Sri Aurobindo
says about Ashvapati standing on the summit of Negation that:

Even while he stood on being's naked edge
And all the passion and seeking of his soul
Faced their extinction in some featureless Vast,
The Presence he yearned for suddenly drew close.
Someone came infinite and absolute.

This was the presence of the Mother "who took to her breast Nature and world and soul". About the arrival of this Presence the poet says:

Abolishing the signless emptiness,
Breaking the vacancy and voiceless hush
Piercing the limitless Unknowable,
Into the liberty of the motionless depths
A beautiful and felicitous lustre stole
Imaged itself in a surprising beam
And built a golden passage to his heart
Touching through him all longing sentient things.

The Presence not only touched the heart of Ashvapati, but through him the entire sentient world. This was the Presence which released the royal traveller from all doubt and dismay. He forgot everything, the hard toil of the journey and the ascent which had made him almost breathless. He felt the steep climb of the journey was worth it if it ended in bringing him to the presence of the Divine Mother. The poet says :

The Formless and the Formed were joined in her.
Immensity was exceeded by a look,
A face revealed the crowded Infinite.
Incarnating inexpressibly in her limbs
The boundless joy the blind world-forces seek
Her body of beauty mooned the seas of bliss.
Alone her hands can change Time's dragon base.
Here is the mystery the Night conceals.
She is the golden bridge, the wonderful fire.
The luminous heart of the Unknown is she,
A power of silence in the depths of God;
The magnet of our difficult ascent.

If man seeks to climb higher and higher inspite of the heavy odds, it is because of the fact that she is the magnet of man's ascent. In sorrow and suffering when everything seems to be lost it is this magnet which draws man imperceptibly and yet unfailingly to greater lands of hope and cheer. As the poet says:

> All Nature dumbly calls to her alone
> To heal with her feet the aching throb of life
> And break the seals on the dumb soul of man
> And kindle her fire in the closed heart of things.

As the poet says "her clasp will turn to ecstasy our pain" such is the healing miracle that happens in her presence. But Ashvapati somehow felt inwardly guilty that he should be experiencing this joy for himself. How could he live in this land of bliss while the human beings down below on earth toiled and suffered? The poet says:

> His single freedom could not satisfy,
> Her light, her bliss he asked for earth and men.

But how will he convey this light to humanity? Can he evoke such strength from within to convey to the world the joy and the bliss of this Heaven of heavens? He must break earth's seal of ignorance and death. He realized that

> Heaven is too high for outstretched hands to seize.
> This Light comes not by struggle or by thought
> In the mind's silence the Transcendent acts
> And the hushed heart hears the unuttered Word.
> A vast surrender was his only strength.

He by his strength alone can never achieve this stupendous goal of breaking the seal of ignorance and death for the world. It is only when the mind is silent and the heart completely hushed that there can be the action of the Transcendent. For this surrender, total surrender, was the only way. It is only when the Supreme acts that the light

and joy of the heaven can be carried to the earth. Ashvapati felt too powerless to do this; and yet the Elixir of
Life which he had found must be carried to suffering humanity. He had only one desire in his heart, an impelling
desire to release humanity from the bonds of suffering
and sorrow. As the poet says:

Only he longed to draw her presence and power
Into his heart and mind and breathing frame;
Only he yearned to call for ever down
Her healing touch of love and truth and joy
Into the darkness of the suffering world.

He feels that he cannot enter the portal of Nirvana so
long as a single human being is in the throes of pain and
suffering. He was visibly torn between the Bliss of Heaven
and the Torment of Earth. The land to which he had
come was superb beyond words. What he experienced
here is given expression to by the poet in the following
words:

A Mind too mighty to be bound by Thought,
A Life too boundless for the play in space,
A Soul without borders unconvinced of Time,
He felt the extinction of the world's long pain,
He became the unborn Self that never dies,
He joined the sessions of Infinity.

About this land the poet says that "there Oneness was not
tied to monotone". Even though there was Oneness there
existed in it in a mysterious manner the Uniqueness also.
To see Oneness and Uniqueness existing together is something which the mind of man cannot understand. In the
entire creation too there is this strange phenomenon of
Uniqueness in the midst of Oneness. To be aware of
Oneness is not enough, there has to be an awareness of the
Unique as well, for, it is in the awareness of the Unique,
in the midst of the Universal, that one is able to unravel
the mystery of Creation and therefore of the Creator so.

D.–10

This was the land where the Divine Mother ruled, and one could see here,

Untired of sameness and untired of change,
Endlessly she unrolled her moving act,
A mystery drama of divine delight.

Ashvapati saw the enactment of the mystery drama in which he saw the Mother ever untired either of sameness or of change. In the whole story of Creation, the *Purusa* is ever the Formless, it is *Prakriti* that is the revealer of Forms. But the Formeless and the Form are never separated one from the other. It is only when the Form and the Formless are seen separately that one comes across the paradoxes and the contradictions of life. We try to solve the paradox by rejecting the one or the other. But it is only in seeing the play of the two, the mysterious play of the Form and the Formless, that one can unravel the meaning of the Great Mystery Drama. The Formless always speaks through the Form, the Purusa communicates only through the Prakriti. And so there is the supreme surrender of Ashvapati to the Divine Mother, for, she alone can grant his prayer to permit him to carry to the suffering humanity the bliss of heaven. The poet says that as if in response to this prayer:

Then suddenly there rose a sacred stir.
Amid the lifeless silence of the Void
In a solitude and an immensity
A sound came quivering like a loved footfall
Heard in the listening spaces of the soul.

Ashvapati heard the voice in that deep silence. The sound came quivering like a loved footfall. In the silence of complete void, when one hears the footfall and recognises it as coming from one's loved one, then one is naturally beside oneself. And the listening of the footfall is done in the spaces of the soul, for, it is not the ear that can hear nor can the eye see. This is the listening which only the soul can do. And Ashvapati hears this Voice in the silence of the Void, and the Voice says:

> O Son of Strength who climbst creations' peaks,
> No soul is thy companion in the light;
> Alone thou standest at the eternal doors,
> What thou hast won is thine, but ask no more.
> How shalt thou speak for men whose hearts are dumb,
> Or lighten the burden of the senseless globe?
> I am the Mystery beyond the reach of mind,
> I am the goal of the travail of the suns.
> Awake not the immeasurable descent,
> Speak not my secret name to hostile Time,
> Man is too weak to bear the Infinite's weight.
> Truth born too soon might break the imperfect earth.

The Voice asked Ashvapati to give up the mad idea of transforming the earth in the likeness of the heaven. It asked him to remain in the land of Bliss. It says "Leave the all-seeing Power to hew its way". The Voice tells him to give up the intention of returning to earth, for,

> How shall thy mighty spirit brook repose
> While Death is still unconquered on earth?

There is a hint given to Ashvapati that unless Death is conquered on earth, it would be idle to think in terms of carrying the Immortal Bliss to humanity. How can the feeble earth, tied to the flow of time, ever be able to bear the enormous weight of Infinity? The Voice asks Ashvapati to see reason and not ask for the impossible. It says it is too dangerous to awaken the immeasurable descent, for truth born too soon may break the imperfect earth. The Voice explains to Ashvapati that man

> ....knows not his own greatness nor his aim;
> He has forgotten why he has come and whence;
> His spirit and his members are at war;
> His heights break off too low to reach the skies,

His mass is buried in the animal, mire.
A strange antinomy is his nature's rule.
A riddle of opposites is made his field:
Freedom he asks but needs to live in bonds,
He has need of darkness to perceive some light
And need of grief to feel a little bliss;
He has need of death to find a greater life.
He seeks himself and from himself he runs
Meeting himself, he thinks it other than he
Unknowing what he does or whither he tends
He fabricates signs of the Real in Ignorance
He is compelled to be what he is not.

In the above lines the poet has indeed described most graphically the psychological state of man. What greater tragedy can there be than that man should need darkness to perceive some light? Man asks for freedom but needs to live in bonds, for, he is afraid of the freedom that he seeks. He feels that he can be secure only within bonds, and so he hugs the chains that bind him. If he really were to win the freedom that he seeks then, inwardly he would feel his security gone. Such freedom will make him intensely vulnerable. And it is this that he dreads the most. But this does not mean that there is no hope for man. The Voice only says that Ashvapati should not hasten too much the pace of Nature. The Voice says to him:

Let not the impatient Titan drive thy heart,
Ask not the imperfect fruit, the partial prize.
Only one boon, to greaten thy spirit, demand;
Only one joy, to raise thy kind, desire.
Above the blind fate and the antagonist powers
Moveless there stands a high unchanging Will;
To its omnipotence leave thy work's result.
All things shall change in God's transfiguring hour.

The Voice tells Ashvapati to leave things to the Will of God. Things will change, but such changes must be

left to the transfiguring hour itself. ،Ashvapati is told that
he must not ask for the imperfect fruit or for the partial
prize. Nature can be hastened, but not too much. It is
best to leave these mighty things to the Mighty Will itself. But Ashvapati naturally feels—how long will the
course of Nature take to bring about transformations?
And so he asks:

How shall I rest content with mortal days
And the dull measure of terrestrial things,
I who have seen behind the cosmic mask
The glory and the beauty of thy face?

Ashvapati is burning with a Divine Afflatus. How
could he be content to see humanity trudging along at the
slow speed of Time? Of what use is his journey through
lands unknown and unfamiliar, if he is to go back to
humanity and tell mankind to hold its soul in patience and
wait for the transfiguring hour for all changes to occur?
He was afire with discontent, and therefore did not feel
like returning to the suffering world with only a gospel of
patience. And so out of sheer impatience and moved by
tremendous discontent, he once again asked the Voice:

Pack with the eternal might one human hour
And with one gesture change all future time.
Let a great word be spoken from the heights
And one great act unlock the doors of Fate.

It was a strange prayer and yet most significant. After
all he was asking only for one act, only one gesture. His
demand was only for one hour—but it must be packed with
the eternal might. Ashvapati would be content to return
to earth with that single gesture of the Divine Mother. If
such a gesture were not forthcoming, with what face could
he return? The entire human race was awaiting his return
—but a return with happy tidings. How could he ask men
merely to trust the movement of time? He must carry
with him something Positive. Would not the Divine Mother

be pleased to grant that Positive Gesture to him? The voice of the Divine Mother speaks and says:

O strong forerunner, I have heard thy cry.
One shall descend and break the iron Law,
Change Nature's doom by the lone spirit's power;
Beauty shall walk celestial on earth,
Delight shall sleep in the cloud-net of her hair
A music of griefless things shall weave her charm,
The harps of the Perfect shall attune her voice,
Strength shall be with her like a conquerer's sword
And from her eyes the Eternal's bliss shall gaze.
A seed shall be sown in Death's tremendous hour,
A branch of heaven transplant to human soil,
Nature shall overleap her mortal step,
Fate shall be changed by an unchanging will.

Ashvapati stood overawed with these prophetic words. What more could he ask? He had asked for a single gesture, and his prayer has been answered. He can go back to earth and announce the happy tidings to suffering humanity. The Mother has promised to him the descent of the limitless Mind—verily the descent of the Super-Mind. Ashvapati returns and as he glides down he hears the moan and the laugh of the earth. He came to the world but a changed man, with a great promise in his heart, the promise for the perfection of earth itself. The poet says:

The Lord of Life resumed his mighty rounds
In the scant field of the ambiguous globe.

CHAPTER XII

THE CHARIOT OF THE GOLDEN BRIDE

After a long and·an arduous journey, Ashvapati returns to earth but in a mood full of hope and cheer. He has brought the answer to the great need of the world. He has come back with a promise of humanity's redemption, and that too soon. The Divine has assured him that one of the most brilliant rays of the Supreme shall come down and illumine the darkened realm of the earth. There is a rejoicing in the whole world. All are engaged in preparing for the great event. How can Nature lag behind when an event of such great magnitude is to happen by which the entire creation shall move forward to meet the Divine? The birth of Savitri was not just the birth of an individual—it was the birth of a New Age, of a new dimension of living. For such an event preparations have to be long and intense. No doubt there was the normal cycle of seasons, but then even here there were intimations of the coming event. The poet says:

....through a glamour of shifting hues of air
The seasons drew in linked significant dance
The symbol pageant of the changing year.

It is this pageant of seasons that the poet describes, and one feels that in this description of the changing seasons, he is imperceptibly indicating the arrival of that great moment. The poet says:

Across the burning langour of the soil
Paced Summer with his pomp of violent noons
And stamped his tyranny of torrid light
And the blue seal of a great burnished sky.

It is most appropriate that the poet should start the description of the seasons with the summer and the pomp of its violent noon. Before the arrival of Savitri it was indeed a severe summer for humanity. The earth was parched under the scorching heat of the sun. There was stamped everywhere the tyranny of torrid light. And then came the welcome rain. The poet tells us:

> Next through its fiery swoon or clotted knot
> Rain-tide burst in upon torn wings of heat,
> Startled with lightning air's unquiet drowse,
> Lashed with life-giving streams the torpid soil
> The cloud's unending march besieged the world
> And thunder drums announced the embattled gods.
> Day a half darkness wore as its dull dress
> Light looked into dawn's tarnished glass and met
> Its own face there, twin to a half-lit night's.
> Earth's mood now changed; she lay in lulled repose,
> The hours went by with slow contented tread.

And so on the cycle of seasons moved on bringing autumn and winter. And behind all this movement of the seasons there was the hint and the intimation of the coming great event. The poet says:

> Three thoughtful seasons passed with shining tread
> And scanning one by one the pregnant hours
> Watched for a flame that lurked in luminous depths
> The vigil of some mighty birth to come.

The seasons were keeping a vigil for the arrival of the great event. When something most significant, like the birth of Savitri happens, the whole creation assumes a festive mood. This is so not only with human beings, but with the whole nature—the trees and the flowers, the birds and the animals, the rivers and the seas, the sun and the moon—all vie with each other in celebrating the festive occasion. And the poet tells us that it was so on this occasion too, for, the birth of Savitri was an event that happens once in many centuries. When the other three seasons had prepared the ground then came the very queen of seasons, the spring. The poet says:

Then Spring, an ardent lover, leaped through leaves
And caught the earth-bride in his eager clasp.
He made her body beautiful with his kiss.
Impatient for felicity he came.
His breath was a warm summons to delight.

The arrival of spring is most appropriate for the great event of Savitri's birth to take place. Savitri was also coming to humanity with the message of the spring. In her arrival lay the hope of mankind's renewal. Indeed, Savitri's birth was to be a warm summons to delight. When the Divine descends in the heart of the human, then the human is transformed into the Divine. Such a descent is a call to total transformation; it is a call to renewal. After the birth of Savitri the world cannot be the same again. It was for this great event that Nature had adorned the earth with the colourful garments of spring. The poet says:

In this high signal moments of the gods,
Answering earth's yearning and her cry for bliss
A greatness from our other countries came.
A silence in the noise of earthly things
Immutably revealed the secret Word,
A lamp was lit, a sacred image made,
A mediating ray has touched the earth
Bridging the gulf between man's mind and God's;
Translating heaven into human shape
Its brightness linked our transience to the Unknown.

Savitri has come to translate the heaven into human shape, to bridge the gulf between God and Man. Obviously she has come in answer to the yearning of the earth carried by her best representative, King Ashvapati.

When the Divine descends into humanity, there is a tremendous limitation that it has to accept for its functioning. This is traditionally known as the Eternal Sacrifice of God. The Hindu mythology speaks of the sacrifice of Prajapati in order that ·the world may come into existence. All descent is a limitation, but the Divine cheerfully accepts this limitation so that the earth may draw nearer to heaven. The poet says about Savitri:

> A spirit of its celestial source aware
> Descended into earth's imperfect mould
> And wept not fallen to mortality,
> But looked on all with large and tranquil eyes.
> She took again her divine unfinished task;
> Once more with her fathomless heart she fronted Time,
> Again there was renewed, again revealed
> The ancient closeness by earth-vision veiled,
> The secret contact broken off in Time,
> A consanguinity of earth and heaven,
> Between the human portion toiling here
> And an as yet unborn and limitless Force.

Savitri was the representative of the Mother-Wisdom. She has come as the ambassador of Heaven upon earth. She has come from the Divine Mother to infuse mother-consciousness in man. It is this mother-consciousness which is the feminine touch so urgently needed by the masculine consciousness of humanity in its present day civilization. Without this feminine touch the mere masculine consciousness, whether in man or in woman, will tend to cause wars and dissensions in human society. Without the feminine touch the human individual will remain disintegrated in the inner nature. It is to make the human individual Whole that Savitri has come as the messenger of the heavens down on this earth. The Divine Mother goes on age after age to raise humanity to greater heights. The poet says:

> Time cannot weary her nor the Void subdue,
> The ages have not made her passion less;
> No victory she admits of Death or Fate
> Always she drives the souls to new attempt;

Always her magical infinitude
Forces to aspire the inert brute elements;
As one who has all infinity to waste,
She scatters the seed of the Eternal's strength
On a half-animate and crumbling mould.

In these lines we see the description of the task to which Savitri is called. She cannot accept any victory of death or fate, for, she has come to infuse a new life in humanity so that man may undertake a fresh attempt to move on from being a creature of mortality to an entity that has come to his own estate of Immortality. In Savitri, even during her childhood days, the signs of her coming greatness were seen. The poet says:

Even in her childish movements could be felt
The nearness of a light still kept from earth,
Feelings that only eternity could share
Thoughts natural and native to the gods.
As needing nothing but its own rapt flight
Her nature dwelt in a strong separate air
Like a strange bird with large rich-coloured breast,
That sojourns on a secret fruited bough
Lost in the emerald glory of the woods,
Or flies above divine unreachable tops.

Savitri indeed was like a bird that flew over unreachable tops, for, she was the free bird that belonged to the vastness of the sky. Even when Savitri mixed with children of her own age, there was something that was aloof and yet intimate. As the poet says:

Even when she bent to meet earth's intimacies
Her spirit kept the stature of the gods.

To keep the stature of the gods even during intimacies with men is something unimaginable, and yet Savitri was able to display this, most naturally and effortlessly. The poet says that in Savitri a new epiphany had appeared. Now an epiphany is the manifestation of the divine or the supreme.

In Savitri there appeared a strange phenomenon of the divine expressing itself in the human without any restriction whatsoever. In her case the human did not constitute a limitation on the Divine. This was so because as the poet says:

> The body that held this greatness seemed almost
> An image made of heaven's transparent light.
> Its charm recalled things seen in vision's hours,
> A golden bridge spanning a faery flood,
> A moon-touched palm tree single by a lake,
> A fiery halo over sleeping hills,
> A strange and starry head alone in Night.

The poet tells us that she was like "a moon-touched palm tree alone by a lake." This factor of aloneness is again and again brought out by the poet while describing the person of Savitri. While all around was darkness as of the night, she was the only star shining in the firmament. She no doubt moved with people and was intensely friendly to them. And yet she was far above them. Sometimes it looked that she was more at home in the company of Nature than in the company of men. Those who came in contact with her

> ....felt her with their souls and thrilled with her
> A greatness felt near yet beyond mind's grasp;
> To see her was a summons to adore.
> A being they loved whose bounds exceeded theirs
> Her measure they could not reach but bore her touch;
> Answering with the flower's answer to the sun,
> They gave themselves to her and asked no more.

Even during the childhood years, Savitri showed the true stature of her greatness. Her presence created strange, sometimes contradictory feelings in the hearts of those in whose contact she came, for, she was far above even the tallest of them. They were greatly attracted by her, for, as the poet says "Her heart's inexhaustible sweetness lured

their hearts". And yet she remained an enigma. She was
with them but somehow she was not of them. The poet
says:

> They were moved by her towards great unknown
> things,
> Faith drew them and the joy to feel themselves hers;
> They lived in her, they saw the world with her eyes.
> Some turned to her against their nature's bent;
> Divided between wonder and revolt,
> Drawn by her charm and mastered by her will,
> Possessed by her, her striving to possess.

People adored her, respected her, but were unable to
possess her. In fact, the more they tried to possess her, the
more they were possessed by her. They wanted her to come
down from her heavenly stature, so that she could be
one of them. As the poet says:

> As earth claims light for its lone separate need,
> Demanding her for their sole jealous clasp,
> They asked from her movements bounded like their
> own
> And to their smallness craved a like response;
> They hoped to bind to their heart's human needs
> Her glory and grace that had enslaved their souls.

This has indeed been the lot of all truly great. He
who towers above humanity is most often not understood at
all. Humanity demands that nothing must be outside the
range of its own measuring rod. The divine must be fitted
into the framework of the human. Savitri tried her best not
to look higher than others, but as the poet says "None
could stand up her equal and her mate". She had come
to fulfil her mission; she wanted a partner, an equal partner, in the great undertaking that she had come to accomplish. But,

> Among the many who came drawn to her,
> Nowhere she found her partner of high tasks;

> The comrade of her soul, her other self,
> Some near approached, were touched, caught fire,
>   then failed.
> Too great was her demand, too pure her force.

Savitri could fulfil her mission only if she could find her other self, the comrade of her soul. But none could dare, for,

> Her beauty and flaming strength were seen afar,
> Like lightning playing with the fallen day,
> A glory unapproachably divine

And so:

> No equal heart came close to join her heart,
> No transient earthly love assailed her calm,
> No hero passion had the strength to seize,
> No eyes demanded her replying eyes.

Savitri surely must have felt very lonely in the midst of a large number of adoring people. It was because of this that she felt perfectly at home with nature. She felt a greater kinship with the trees and the flowers, with the sea and the sky than with the human beings ʹwith whom her lot was cast. She belonged to royalty and so she had her mates drawn from royalty itself. And yet this royalty was unable to measure up to her height and her glory. The poet says:

> Whoever is too great must lonely live,
> Adored he walks in mighty solitude;
> **Vain is his labour to create his kind,**
> His only comrade is the Strength within.

In these lines the poet has described the state of all truly great throughout the ages. The great in all ages and in all lands have been supremely lonely. These have always walked in mighty solitude. Crucifixions and coronations go together. It is in the crucifixion of loneliness that they are installed as great rulers of humanity. He who is afraid of being lonely cannot know what true greatness is. The poet says that Savitri had to pass through this Valley of Loneliness before climbing the great heights of glory. He says:

> Thus was it for a while with Savitri,
> All worshipped marvellingly, none dared to claim.
> Her mind sat high pouring its golden beams,
> Her heart was a crowded temple of delight.
> A single lamp lit in perfection's house,
> A bright pure image in a priestless shrine,
> Midst those encircling lives her spirit dwelt,
> Apart in herself until her hour of fate.

The poet says that Savitri was like a "single lamp lit in perfection's house", she was like a "pure image in a priestless shrine". The image was there but no priest dare come near. Such was the blinding light that emanated from her. But the poet says that Savitri experienced this loneliness for a while. She was apart in herself until her hour of fate. It was in her hour of fate that she was to be united with her companion. But how will she find her companion? Born in royalty, will she not be bound by the traditions and the conventions of royalty? Tradition must find a suitor for her, and to him she must be married. If this happens, how could she fulfil the great mission for which she had come down to earth from the dizzy heights of heaven? After all Ashvapati must discharge his duties as a king. What would happen to the human race, if the king himself were to deviate from the strict path of duty? He must have felt greatly puzzled at the behaviour of this strange child. She attracted all to her, and yet none had the strength to claim her. What was he to do? It is in the moments of this bewilderment that Ashvapati hears a voice, a commanding Voice, which tells him:

> O Force-compelled, Fate-driven earth-born race,
> O petty adventurers in an infinite world
> And prisoners of a dwarf humanity,

How long will you tread the circling tracks of mind
Around your little self and petty things?
But not for a changeless littleness were you meant,
Not for vain repetition were you built;
Out of the Immortal's substance you were made;
Your actions can be swift revealing steps,
Your life a changeful mould for growing gods.

The Voice was like a clarion-call to Ashvapati asking
him to step out of the petty circle of existence. He must
needs break through the shell of custom and tradition, and
not be lost in vain repetition or in changeless littleness.
The king realised that Savitri could not be kept confined
within the traditions of mediocrity. How could he find a
comrade for her who was far above humanity? He felt
himself too small to guide the destiny of such an illustrious
soul as Savitri. And so he addresses her thus:

O Spirit, traveller of eternity,
Who camest from the immortal spaces here,
Armed for the splendid hazard of thy life
To set thy conquering foot on Chance and Time,
A mighty Presence still defends thy frame.
Thy fate, thy work are kept somewhere afar.
Depart where love and destiny call your charm.
Venture through the deep world to find thy mate.
For somewhere on the longing breast of earth,
Thy unknown lover waits for thee the unknown
Thy soul has strength and needs no other guide
Than one who burns within thy bosom's powers.

Ashvapati asks Savitri to find her mate, for, how
can another make a choice of the mate for one who is
so sublime and so utterly beyond the reaches of humanity? Savitri needs no other guide than the One that
directs her movements from within. She must find a
mate who measures upto her, who is

The second self for whom thy nature asks,
He who shall walk until thy body's end

A close-bound traveller pacing with thy pace,
The lyrist of thy soul's most intimate chords
Who shall give voice to what in thee is mute.

Ashvapati says that she will be in the company of
such a mate and will discover "new notes of the eternal
theme". These words of Ashvapati awakened Savitri
to a sense of her divine mission. She suddenly realised
that she had come to discharge a heavenly responsibility.
She now became free from the accustomed scenes, for,
she regarded all that as an ended play. She felt that the
secrets of an unseen world were close. The poet says
that the day ended and the "night lit the watchfires of
eternity". When the day dawned Savitri had already
left in search of her mate and comrade in whose company she would rebuild the earth nearer to heaven. The
poet says:

When the pale dawn slipped through Night's sha-
                                    dowy guard
Vainly the new-born light desired her face;
The palace woke to its own emptiness;
The sovereign of its daily joys was far;
Her moonbeam feet tinged not the lucent floors;
The beauty and divinity were gone.
Delight had fled to search the spacious world.

Savitri had gone on the quest, and as the poet says,
with her going away the palace woke to its own emptiness. She had filled the palace with her presence. Now
the sovereign of its daily joys was far far away, for, delight had fled to search the spacious world. The quest
of Savitri was indeed like the flight of the alone to
the Alone. But where will Savitri go? She had never
stepped out of the sheltered existence of the palace. She
was an utter stranger to wide open spaces of the world.
She left the palace, not knowing where she must wend
her way. She was on a quest, not merely of her mate,

but her spiritual companion, for, they two together must
build the new world. A spiritual quest is indeed a plunge into the Unknown. Such a quest cannot be undertaken with a calculating mind. It has to be an adventure, not knowing in advance where one would have to
go and what would one find. It is not a movement
of the known to the known, nor is it a movement of the
known to the unknown. The nature of this quest has
been described by the poet wherein he says: "Thy unknown lover waits for thee, the unknown". Here both
the lover and the beloved are unknown to each other.
The spiritual quest is the movement of the unknown to
the unknown. And so Savitri leaves the palace not knowing where to go, and whom to meet. The poet says:

> Across wide noons and glowing afternoons,
> She met with Nature and with human forms
> And listened to the voices of the world;
> Driven from within she followed her long road,
> Mute in the luminous cavern of her heart,
> Like a bright cloud through the resplendent day,
> Like a swift hope journeying among its dreams
> Hastened the chariot of the golden bride.

She was like a swift hope journeying among its dreams. She at first went through such areas where there
were people moving about. She passed through the
"theatres of the loud act of man". The poet describes
all those places which lay in her way. Through markets
and gardens, through temples and assembly halls, she
moved on. Leaving the cities and towns she passed through
hamlets and villages where she saw "homes of a life bent
to the soil it ploughs for sustenance of its short and passing
days". She wended her way through forests away from the
haunts of men. The poet says:

> As floats a sunbeam through a shady place,
> The golden virgin in her carven car
> Came gliding among meditation's seats.

Often in twilight mid returning troops
Of cattle thickening with their dust the shades,
When the loud day had slipped below the verge,
Arriving in a peaceful hermit grove,
She rested drawing round her like a cloak
Its spirit of patient muse and potent prayer.

The poet says that the hermit grove breathed the spirit of patient muse and potent prayer. From the din and noise of civilization, Savitri had come to a place of deep silence. She rested here awhile, for, the journey was long and arduous. Savitri moves on unknown to the unknown. And so the rest too was short-lived, for,

.... morn broke in reminding her of her quest
And from low rustic couch or mat she rose
And went impelled on her unfinished way
Like a desire that questions silent gods.

There was something within her that impelled her movement. She knew not where she was going, and yet such was the inner power that she was ready for travel through desert and forest, through hills and valleys. The poet tells us about this journey that she—

Travelled in a strange and empty land
Where desolate summits camped in a wierd heaven,
Mute sentinels beneath a drifting moon,
Or wandered in some lone tremendous wood,
Ringing for ever with the cricket's cry,
Or followed a long glistening serpent road

Through fields and pastures lapped in moveless light. In spite of all these wanderings through strange lands, Savitri seemed to be as far away from her destination as she was when she started the journey. As the poet says:

Still unaccomplished was the fateful quest;
Still she found not the one predestined face
For which she sought amid the sons of men.

Another day arose when the burning breath assailed the soil. Savitri must move on until she finds the predestined face. But how long will it take? When shall the Unknown meet the Unknown? Perhaps Savitri will suddenly come upon that predestined face as happens with all spiritual quest. The Vision comes when one expects the least. The great joy lies in this sudden arrival of the great event. The poet tells us that the "spring winds had failed; the sky was set like a bronze". Such was the unbearable heat of the day. There was nothing that indicated the arrival of the happy event. But what seemed was not true; there was something that was happening under the surface. The poet says:

> But now the destined spot and hour were close,
> Unknowing she had neared her nameless goal.
> ....nothing happens in the cosmic play
> But at its time and in its foreseen place.

CHAPTER XIII

THE MOMENT MADE ETERNAL

Sri Aurobindo says that nothing happens but at its time and in its foreseen place. Does this not indicate a philosophy of fatalism? If the place and time for everything is predestined, then where is the place for human effort? We have earlier discussed this question of Freedom and Determinism. Savitri had come to conquer Chance and Fate, as the poet says, but in terms of the above statement she too seems to be merely a plaything of chance and fate. Here the predestined time and place have to be understood in the psychological sense. The poet says that there is a psychological moment for everything, and without this moment, all efforts of man seem fruitless. It is true that true Love is always at first sight, but this does not necessarily mean the physical first sight. Two people may have known each other for years, and yet the Flame of Love may remain unkindled. But suddenly, some unpredictable factor comes which brings to them an experience of the first psychological sight. They see each other for the first time, because of the screen of mind's projections having been rent asunder due to some unknown cause. Now the psychological moment depends upon no external factors—it is ruled entirely by subjective conditions. If one may speak about the predetermination of the psychological moment, then it must be with reference to the state of the mind and not the state of outer conditions. All events are determined by the internal factors of the mind. A person may come to a spot at a particular hour of chronological time, but he may experience nothing. The same spot and the same hour may at another time reveal the greatest mystery of

165

life. This is so because at one time the mind is closed and insensitive, and at another time it is completely open and therefore intensely sensitive. With regard to the destined spot to which Savitri came, there is a reference to psychological factors, ·and this is made plain by the following lines of the poet. He says:

> To a space she came of soft and delicate air
> That seemed a sanctuary of youth and joy:
> A highland world of free and green delight
> Where spring and summer lay together and strove
> In indolent and amicable debate,
> Inarmed, disputing with laughter who should rule.

How can summer and spring lie together in the physical sense? The poet here speaks of that mathematical line which has length but no breadth, or of a mathematical point which has position but no magnitude. He refers to that psychological state where summer and spring are lying indolently together, debating with laughter as to who should rule. It is a psychological moment which can be experienced but which cannot be defined. The intangible interval between summer and spring is something which only a sensitive heart can know. The poet indicates that it was difficult to know where Spring ended and Summer began. It is in this interval between summer and spring that the true state of love comes into existence. Savitri's birth was in the festive hour of spring; her first experience of love was also in the festival of spring. In the arrival of spring there is a hesitancy where nature displays her feminine modesty. It is to this that the poet refers in the following lines:

> Pale waters ran like glimmering threads of pearl.
> A sigh was straying among happy leaves;
> Cool-perfumed with slow pleasure-burdened feet,
> Faint stumbling breezes faltered among flowers.

The spring was coming with faltering steps with a sigh of joy straying among the happy leaves. The psychological moment of love was behaving like this hesitant spring. In this hesitancy is reflected the mood of the lovers. In their hearts the summer and spring were holding a pleasant debate as to who should rule. The spot to which Savitri had come in the course of her journey was in perfect harmony with her psychological mood. Here nature was completely unspoilt. The poet says, on this spot:

Earth couched here alone with her great lover
                                                            Heaven,
In her luxurious ecstasy of joy
She squandered the love-music of her notes
Wasted the passionate pattern of her blooms
And festival riot of her scents and hues.
Man, the deep-browed artificer, had not come
To lay his hand on happy inconscient things,
Thought was not there nor the measurer strong-
                                                            eyed toil,
Life had not learned its discord with its aim.

The poet says that man had not come yet to disturb the harmony of nature. When man comes; then life is in discord with its aim. But the sylvan surroundings to which Savitri had come was untouched by man, it was unspoilt because thought had not entered its precincts. The poet says that in this beauty of nature were

...disclosed to her the mystic courts,
The lurking doors of beauty and surprise
The wings that murmur in the golden house,
The temple of sweetness and the fiery aisle.
A stranger on the sorrowful roads of Time
Immortal under the yoke of death and fate,
Love in the wilderness met Savitri.

What a strange paradox that Savitri, the daughter of Ashvapati , the great king of Madra, should meet love in wilderness ! Or perhaps it is most appropriate that

Savitri should meet her mate and companion in the beauties of wilderness, away from the haunts of men. But on this day of days, Savitri was somehow beside herself. She was lost in wild beauties of nature. The poet says:

> All she remembered on this day of Fate,
> The road that hazarded not the solemn depths,
> But turned away to flee to human homes.

All that she knew was that the road took a sudden turn, away from the depths of the forest, towards a human home, a humble cottage where in the midst of wilderness some human beings lived. The poet says:

> Here first she met on the uncertain earth
> The one for whom her heart had come so far.

Here on this uncertain earth, Savitri saw Satyavan for the first time. Her heart had travelled so far to meet him. But what did he look like? The poet says:

> As might a soul on Nature's background limned
> Stand out for a moment in a house of dream
> Created by the ardent breath of life,
> So he appeared against the forest verge
> Inset twixt green relief and golden ray
> Erect and lofty like a spear of God
> His figure led the splendour of the morn.
> Freedom's imperious beauty curved his limbs,
> The joy of life was on his open face,
> His look was a wide daybreak of the gods
> Built like a moving statue of delight,
> He illumined the border of the forest page.

On the page of the forest he was like an illumined border. A moving statue of delight, erect and lofty like a spear of God—that is how Savitri saw him. She felt that this remarkable figure was just a part of nature, for, he was so completely one with the beauties of the forest that it was impossible to regard him as something different from nature itself. The poet says he was

A foster-child of beauty and solitude,
Heir to the centuries of the lonely wise,
A brother of the sunshine and the sky.

Sri Aurobindo says that on that day somehow Satyavan had turned from his accustomed path, and he saw that some unknown force had "laid the spell of destiny at his feet". It was indeed a spell of destiny, for, how could he, even in his wildest dreams, ever think of seeing such a divine spectacle as the person of Savitri, and that too in this land of wilderness? Savitri would perhaps have moved on regarding Satyavan as a part of the beauty of nature. She had passed by many beautiful spots. She would have moved away from this spot too, even though this was surpassingly beautiful. But as the poet says: "A look, a turn decides our ill-poised fate". Sometimes just a look becomes a turning point. Savitri had come to such a turning point, for, as the poet says:

Her vision settled, caught and all was changed
And saw in him the genius of the spot,
A symbol figure standing mid earth's scenes
A king of life outlined in delicate air
Yet this was but a moment's reverie:
For suddenly her heart looked out at him:
All in a moment was surprised and seized,
A mystic tumult from her depths arose,
Life ran to gaze from every gate of sense.

Such was the godlike form of Satyavan that Savitri wanted to look at him not merely with the eyes but with the other senses too. How could one sense completely absorb that magnificent form? Savitri saw that Satyavan certainly could measure up to her. Savitri was not in search of a husband—her quest was for a companion in whose company a new world may be built. The Grace

of Savitri must combine with the Dignity of Satyavan,
and she saw Satyavan as a genius of the spot and as
a king of life outlined in delicate air. And so:

> Her soul flung wide its doors to this new sun.
> An alchemy worked, the transmutation came.
> ....trembling with the mystic shock her heart
> Moved in her breast and cried out like a bird
> Who hears his mate upon a neighbouring bough.

Even Savitri was dazed at what she saw. There
was a spontaneous response, though unuttered. She recognised instantly in Satyavan her comrade of Eternity.
A great spiritual affinity was felt. As the poet says:

> In the nameless light of two approaching eyes
> A swift and fated turning of her days.

She came to the great turning of her life. Such
was the overpowering effect that in the words of the poet
"the chariot stood like an arrested wind". The chariot
had a speed of the wind. If the wind were to be suddenly
arrested in the midst of its movement, then that indeed
would be the most apt description of the chariot of Savitri suddenly coming to a halt. But Satyavan's surprise
too was as overpowering as that of Savitri. For,

> ....Satyavan looked out from his soul's doors
> And felt the enchantment of her liquid voice,
> The haunting miracle of a perfect face.
> He turned to the vision like a sea to the moon,
> His life was taken into another's life
> An unknown imperious force drew him to her
> Gaze met close gaze and clung in sight's embrace.

Satyavan's feelings were as intense as those of Savitri.
He realized that a turning point in his life too had come.
All of a sudden for him the earth had changed into
heaven. In Savitri he recognised his twin-soul that had
journeyed through time to meet him. He says to himself:

Although as unknown beings we seem to meet,
Our lives are not aliens nor as strangers join,
Moved to each other by a causeless force.
The soul can recognise its answering soul
Across dividing Time, and on Life's roads
Absorbed wrapped traveller, turning it recovers
Familiar splendours in an unknown face.

If Savitri and Satyavan together are to build a New
world then they must first be united in true and abiding
love. The task of building a new world is indeed most
arduous, but if they are united in love then no obstacle
will be too great, no hardship insurmountable. Savitri
had come down to fulfil a mission, but the mission had
to be accomplished on earth. She had undertaken to
bridge Heaven and Earth, but before it is done outwardly
there must first be the meeting of the earth and the
heaven in her own life. Love is the only power that
can redeem the earth. As the poet says:

To live, to love are signs of infinite things,
Love is a glory from eternity's spheres.
Abased, disfigured, mocked by baser mights
That steal his name and shape and ecstasy,
He is still the Godhead by which all can change.

Without Love all changes, whether in the individual
or in the society, are utterly meaningless. Love is the
only alchemy that can change the baser metals into gold.
It alone possesses the secret of transmutation. And there
is no man in whom lies not the sweet fragrance of love.
The poet says:

Love dwells in us like an unopened flower
Awaiting a rapid moment of the soul
He lingers for a sign that he can know
And, when it comes, wakes blindly to a voice,
A look, a touch, the meaning of a face.

Both Savitri and Satyavan saw the signs, and recognised them. Both had travelled distant areas in time
and had now met after a long journey. The poet tells
us,

> Amazed by a joy for which they had waited long,
> The lovers met upon their different paths
> Travellers across the limitless plains of Time
> The mist was torn that lay between two lives
> Attracted as in heaven star by star,
> They wondered at each other and rejoiced
> And wove affinity in a silent gaze.
> A moment passed that was eternity's ray,
> An hour began, the matrix of new Time.

It was a momentous hour for both of them. They
wove affinity in a silent gaze. It was in meaningful
silence that their eyes met. The mist that had separated
them had vanished. It is true that they met on the
roads of Time, but they brought with them the bliss of
eternity. They met as one unknown meeting the other
unknown. But soon they realized that they had known
each other from the beginning of time. When the mist
vanished they looked into each other's eyes. But it was
Satyavan who broke this silence, and addressed thus his
soul-mate, Savitri:

> O thou who com'st to me out of Time's silences,
> Yet thy voice has wakened my heart to an un-
>   known bliss,
> Immortal or mortal only in thy frame,
> For more than earth speaks to me from thy soul
> And more than earth surrounds me in thy gaze,
> How are thou named among the sons of men?
> Whence hast thou dawned filling my spirit's days,
> Brighter than summer, brighter than my flowers,
> Into the lonely borders of my life,
> O sunlight moulded like a golden maid?

While Satyavan addresses these words to Savitri, he does not know whether she has within her divine splendour any place for human emotions. Sri Aurobindo's portrayal of Savitri is indeed most remarkable. He has depicted her as divine and yet has endowed her with all the best human sentiments and emotions. She is divine and yet supremely human. Satyavan has yet to discover this. His first glimpse of Savitri has filled him with an overawe due to the superb divinity which she displayed. And so Satyavan speaks ·to Savitri in the following vein:

So now my mind could dream and my heart fear
That from some wonder-couch beyond our air,
Risen in a wide morning of the gods
Thou drov'st thy horses from the Thunderer's worlds.
Although to heaven thy beauty seems allied,
Much rather would my thoughts rejoice to know
That mortal sweetness smiles between thy lips
And thy heart can beat beneath a human gaze.

Satyavan naturally wants to know whether he is speaking to one who is only a representative of the gods, but also one in whom human emotions throb. As the representative of the Divine she would remain very far, worthy of adoration and worship. It is only as a human being that she would seem close to his aspiration and dreams. Satyavan is unable to know, and so at last he says to Savitri:

If our time-vexed affections thou canst feel
Earth's ease of simple things can satisfy,
If thy glance can dwell content on earthly soil
And this celestial summary of delight,
Thy golden body, dally with fatigue
Oppressing with its grace our terrain,
Descend. Let thy journey cease, come down to us.

Satyavan invites Savitri to descend and enter his simple cottage so as to rest awhile. He says that

Bare, simple is the sylvan hermit-life
Yet is it clad with the jewelry of earth.
Apparelled are the morns in gold and green;
Sunlight and shadow tapestry the walls
To make a resting chamber fit for thee.

Satyavan was inviting Savitri to the simple hermit
life, but a life made rich with the touch of nature itself. He was feeling hesitant to invite her, for she looked
a princess not of earthly realms but of the divine regions.
And yet he felt that after all Savitri would respond to
feelings of human love. Having heard Satyavan, Savitri paused "as if hearing still his voice, unwilling to break
the charm". And then she spoke:

.........I am Savitri,
Princess of Madra. Who art thou? What name
Musical on earth expresses thee to men?
Why is thy dwelling in the pathless wood
Far from the deeds thy glorious youth demands,
Surrounded by enormous silences,
In Nature's green unhuman loneliness?

Then does Satyavan tell the whole story how he
and his parents took shelter in these forests. His
father, Dyumatsena,   was king of Shalva. But his associates deprived him of his kingdom by crooked means.
He was rendered blind. It was in that plight that his
parents and he made the forest their dwelling. But Satyavan was not apologetic about his humble dwellings,
for, he says:

I reigned in a kingdom of a nobler kind
Than men can build upon dull Matter's soil
I met the frankness of the primal earth,
I enjoyed the intimacy of infant God,
I lay in the wide bare embrace of heaven,
The sunlight's radiant blessing clasped my brow,
The moonbeam's silver ecstasy at night
Kissed my dim lids to sleep. Earth's morns were mine

Satyavan relates to Savitri all the details of his life lived in the open spaces of nature. He lived here a simple and yet intensely rich life. Savitri listens to him with rapt attention; in fact, she drinks every word that he utters. When Satyavan had finished his description of life in nature, Savitri replied to him saying:

Speak more to me, speak more, O Satyavan,
Speak of thyself and all thou art within;
I would know thee as if we had ever lived
Together in the chamber of our souls.
....thou art he my spirit has sought
Amidst earth's thronging visages and forms
Across the golden spaces of my life.

What could Satyavan say to these sweet words of Savitri? He does reply, but as the poet says it is "like a replying harp to the insistent calling of the flute". He wanted to say much but words failed him as they do when the heart is filled with love. Satyavan said:

O golden princess, perfect Savitri,
More I would tell than failing words can speak
Of all that thou has meant to me, unknown,
All that the lightning flash of love reveals.
In one great hour of the unveiling gods
Even a brief nearness has reshaped my life.
For now I know that all I lived and was
Moved towards this moment of my heart's rebirth
For now another realm draws near with thee
And now diviner voices fill my ear,
A strange new world swims to me in thy gaze
My mind transfigures to a rapturous seer
....Air, soil and stream
Wear bridal raiment to be fit for thee
And sunlight grows a shadow of thy hue
Because of change within me by thy look;
Come nearer to me from thy car of light.

O my bright beauty's princess, Savitri,
Enter my life, thy chamber and thy shrine,

Satyavan asks Savitri to enter his life which will be
both her chamber as well as shrine. He asks Savitri, both
divine and human, to enter his life. For Savitri the divine
his life will be a shrine, and for Savitri the human his
life will be a chamber of unending love. Savitri was
greatly moved by these words of Satyavan, and she said:

O Satyavan, I have heard thee and I know;
I know that thou and only thou art he.

It was with these words that she descended from her
chariot. It was a great moment. In the words of the poet
"One human moment was eternal made". Savitri came
down but as the poet says with a soft and faltering haste.
There was haste to be united with Satyavan, but in that
haste there was hesitancy and a natural modesty. The
poet tells us:

She bowed and touched his feet with worshipping
hands,
She made her life his world for him to tread
And made her body the room for his delight,
Her beating heart a remembrancer of bliss.
He gathered all Savitri into his clasp
Around her his embrace became the sign
Of a locked closeness through slow intimate years.
In a wide moment of two souls that meet
She felt her being flow into him as in waves
A river pours into a mighty sea.
Her consciousness was a wave of him alone
And all her separate self was lost in his.

This was indeed the union of the Eternal Lord and
the Spouse. It was a union of Heaven and Earth. The
poet says:

As the finite opens to the Infinite.
Thus were they in each other lost awhile
Then drawing back from their long ecstasy's trance
Came into a new self and a new world,
Each now was a part of the other's unity.

Savitri and Satyavan as the united Two will now usher in a new age. In the words of the poet, "Amid the choral whisperings of the leaves, Love's twain had joined together and grew one". Satyavan showed to Savitri her future home in this forest hermitage. Savitri said to him that she must rush back to her father's place and break the happy news to the parents. Her wanderings have come to a close. But while she must go to her father, she says:

My heart shall stay here on this forest verge
And close to this thatched roof while I am far.
For soon I shall return nor even again
Oneness must sever its recovered bliss;
Or fate sunder our lives while life is ours.

And so Savitri goes posthaste to her father's place to tell him that her journey is over and that she has made the choice. Soon must she return to Satyavan and live in the new home on the verge of the forest. All along the route, back to her father's place in the country of Madra, Savitri was musing in her mind about the great turning point that had come in her life. She thought of

A nave of trees enshrined the hermit thatch,
The new deep covert of her felicity,
Preferred to heaven her soul's temple and home.
This now remained with her, her heart's constant
scene.

D.-12

CHAPTER XIV

THE IRREVOCABLE DECREE

In the whole of Hindu Mythology, there is no one as colourful as Narada, the celestial singer. He is a tireless wanderer ceaselessly moving between heaven and earth, acting as a liaison between gods and men. He carries the message of men to gods, and brings to men whatever the gods may have to say. He is thus the greatest busy-body of Hindu Mythology. He is known as one of the mind-born sons of Brahma. And being mind-born he is endowed with many qualities of the mind. When carrying messages from gods to men and vice versa, there is much of the mind that he puts in these messages. He is thus an adept at creating conflict of the opposites. In fact, Narada symbolises mind in its active and alert condition. Such a mind enjoys a play of the opposites, and Narada certainly enjoys this play the most. He has a knack of appearing at all important and interesting occasions, be they in heaven or on earth. By initiating the play of the opposites, he unconsciously enables all concerned to seek a way away from the opposites. It is left to Narada to help in formulating a problem whether of men or of gods. And all problems have to be formulated in terms of the opposites. It is only when the opposites are well formulated that the problem becomes clear for the mind to understand. Narada is not a creator of problems, he is the formulator of problems.

While Savitri was wending her way to her father's palace in Madra, the poet says:

In silent bounds bordering the mortal's plane
Crossing a wide expanse of brilliant peace

Narada the heavenly sage from Paradise
Came chanting through the large and lustrous air.

Narada is known as Devarshi in Hindu mythology, for, he was a great seer to whom future was like an open book. Because of this he was much sought after both in heaven as well as on earth. The poet says that Narada came singing as was his wont, with veena in his hand. He came chanting through the large and lustrous air. Narada was welcome everywhere both for the news he always brought, and, for the future which he revealed. And so he was received with great warmth and veneration in Ashvapati 's palace by the King and the Queen. His moods differed according to the planes through which he was passing. As he entered the atmosphere of the earth, his mood changed from what it was in the subtler realms. There were both rapture and pathos in his voice. As the poet says he did not now sing of the "light that never wanes" nor of everlasting bliss nor of deathless love. Instead he spoke of Ignorance and Fate, he sang of "darkness yearning towards the eternal light" and of inscrutable fate that brought its results. Just when Narada and the King and Queen of Madra Desha were engaged in deep philosophical discussions, Savitri walked in. It was not the same Savitri who had gone out on her quest; this was different Savitri shining with the halo of Love. The poet says:

As of her swift heart hastening, Savitri
Her radiant tread glimmered across the floor.
A happy wonder in her fathomless gaze
Changed by the halo of her love she came
Her eyes rich with a shining mist of joy
As one who comes from a heavenly embassy.

The poet says that "she stood before her mighty father's throne". Narada was awestruck at seeing this beauty, and so he flung on her his vast immortal look. No longer was Savitri a playful girl; she had grown into a beautiful

maiden. She was like spring poised towards summer,
morning making towards the noon. Her girlhood had
grown into womanhood of surpassing beauty. Narada
was a much travelled man and had seen many things on
earth and in heaven. He was a connoisseur of art and
beauty, and as such easily recognised Beauty in man and
nature. And so seeing Savitri, Narada said:

> Who is this that comes, the bride,
> The flame-born?
> From what green glimmer of glades
> Bringst thou this glory of enchanted eyes?
> ....if my thought could trust this shimmering gaze
> It would say: thou hast not drunk from an earthly cup,
> Reveal, O winged with light, whence thou hast flown
> Hastening bright hued through the green-tangled earth
> Thy body rhythmical with the spring-bird's call.
> The empty roses of thy hands are filled
> Only with their own beauty and the thrill
> Of a remembered clasp....
> O thou who hast come to this great perilous world
> Now only seen through the splendour of thy dreams,
> Where hardly love and beauty can live safe,
> Thyself a being dangerously great.

Savitri was indeed dangerously great, and she also
lived dangerously. She had known no pain or suffering
and looked at the world through the screen of her dreams.
Narada said that in this world love and beauty cannot live
with a feeling of safety. He hinted at what was going to
come. The celestial singer says:

> If thy heart could live locked in the ideal's gold,
> As high, as happy might thy waking be
> If for all time doom could be left to sleep.

Narada would very much like the doom to remain
asleep for all time. The poet says that Narada spoke
but held his knowledge back from words. He had a fore-

knowledge of what was going to happen, but how could
he dare to utter those cruel words just when Savitri had
come radiant with love and joy? But Ashvapati saw that
something was passing through the mind of Narada to
which he had not given an expression. He marked "an
ominous shadow left behind his words". Ashvapati wants
to cover up his fears, and so says to Narada:

> Behold this image cast by light and love
> A stanza of the ardour of the gods
> Her body like a brimmed pitcher of delight
> As if to seize earth's truth of hidden bliss.
> Even as her body, such is she within.
> Behold her, singer with the prescient gaze,
> And let thy blessing chant that this fair child
> Shall pour the nectar of a sorrowless life
> Around her from her lucid heart of love
> Heal with her bliss the tired breast of earth
> And cast like a happy snare felicity
> Or must fire always test the great of soul?
> Once let unwounded pass a mortal life.

Ashvapati has within his heart conflicting emotions.
He feels that doom surely cannot touch so fair a human
being as Savitri. And yet he asks the question: Must fire
always test the great of soul? Human history bears witness to the fact that all truly great have had to pass through
the fire-test always, with hardly an exception. And so Ashvapati, as it were, prays to Narada that at least once let a
mortal life pass unwounded? Cannot Narada give that
assurance for such an innocent person as Savitri? But
Narada sat silent and did not give any reply to the
pointed question of Ashvapati. Instead, as if he did not
know, Narada asked Ashvapati:

> On what high mission went her hastening wheels?
> Whence came she with this glory in her heart
> And Paradise made visible in her eyes?

Ashvapati' himself did not know with what glad tidings had Savitri returned from her great quest. And so he asked her, in the presence of Narada, "Whom hast thou chosen, kingliest among men?". The poet says:

And Savitri answered with her still calm voice
As one who speaks beneath the eyes of Fate:
"The son of Dyumatsena, Satyavan,
I have met on the wild forest's lonely verge.
My father, I have chosen. This is done".

Savitri speaks with a complete finality in her voice, for she says "This is done"., meaning there can be no further discussion about this. Hearing these words, "all sat silent for a space". But then Ashvapati recollected himself and said in measured tones to Savitri:

Well hast thou done and I approve thy choice.
If this is all, then all is surely well;
If there is more, then all can still be well.
Whether it seem good or evil to men's eyes,
Only for good the secret Will can work.
Our destiny is written in double terms:
Through Nature's contraries we draw near God;
Out of the darkness we still grow to light
Death is our road to Immortality.

Ashvapati is trying to silence the forebodings of his own heart by these explanations. He feels that after all everything must turn out good in the ultimate sense. Death is a seeming tragedy for it opens doors to Immortality. Obviously Ashvapati was trying to turn his eyes away from what seemed ordained to doom and tragedy. At this stage Narada was about to speak, but Ashvapati prevented him from speaking, and said:

O singer of the ultimate ecstasy,
Lend not a dangerous vision to the blind,
Because by native right thou hast seen clear
Impose not on the mortal's tremulous breast

The dire ordeal that foreknowledge brings;
To light one step in front is all his hope,
And only for a little strength he asks
To meet the riddle of his shrouded fate.
If thou canst loose her grip then only speak.

Ashvapati does not want Narada to break the spell
of joy by talking of some unalterable fate. He tells Narada
that "if thou canst loose her grip, then only speak". If
Narada cannot loosen the grip of Fate, then of what use
his speaking about the unpleasant future? Ashvapati
is so much disturbed within that he does not want Narada
to give expression to that disturbance by speaking about
the unalterable future. The king says:

Our mind perhaps deceives us with its words
And gives the name of doom to our own choice.

Ashvapati says that much of man's misery arises
because of the naming process of the mind. It is when to
one's own choice, the name "doom" is given that man
shudders from it. Is not "doom" only a name given by
the mind to a particular situation? He says that perhaps
what we term Fate is only the blindness of our own will.
Ashvapati tries to cover up his mental fears with a
diversity of explanations and justifications. But while the
King is doing this, the Queen feels greatly alarmed, and,
so she tells Narada:

O seer, thy bright arrival has been timed
To this high moment of a happy life.
Then let the speech benign of griefless spheres
Confirm this blithe conjunction of two stars
And sanction joy with thy celestial voice
....let thy blessing put the immortals' seal
On these bright lives' unstained felicity
If wings of Evil brood above that house,
Then also speak, that we may turn aside
And rescue our lives from hazard of wayside doom
And chance entanglement of an alien fate.

While Ashvapati was trying to hush up the whole matter lest Narada introduce some unpleasant factor from his foreknowledge, the Queen could not reconcile herself to this hushing up. She wanted to know from Narada what the exact situation in terms of his future-reading was. But Narada too was trying to evade the issue, for, he said:

A future knowledge is an added pain
A torturing burden and a fruitless light
On the enormous scene that Fate has built.

But the Queen was insistent to know what Narada had in his mind, for, how could she rest when evil forebodings are there? She must know exactly what the matter was. And so once again the Queen asks Narada:

What stealthy doom has crept across her path
Emerging from the dark forest's sullen heart
What evil thing stood smiling by the way
And wore the beauty of Shalva boy?
Perhaps he came an enemy from her past
Armed with a hidden force of ancient wrongs,
Himself unknowing, and seized her unknown
Even a stranger's anguish rends my heart,
And this, O Narada, is my well-loved child.
Hide not from us our doom, if doom is ours.
This is the worst, an unknown face of Fate
To know is best, however hard to bear.

The Queen rightly says that it is better to know what the Fate has ordained than to have an unknown fear lurking all the time. The Queen feels that if they could know what Fate lies in store, then, perchance, they may persuade Savitri to make another choice, and not rush into the arms of the cruel fate. Seeing the insistent demand of the Queen, Narada said:

The truth thou hast claimed; I give to thee the truth.
A marvel of the meeting earth and the heavens

Is he whom Savitri has chosen mid men,
His figure is the front of Nature's march
His single being excels the works of Time
A sapphire cutting from the sleep of heaven,
Delightful is the soul of Satyavan
A ray out of the rapturous infinite
As brilliant as a lonely moon in heaven
Gentle like the sweet bud that spring desires,
Pure like a stream that kisses silent banks,
Time's joy borrowed out of eternity,
A star of splendour or a rose of bliss,
His strength is like a tower built to reach heaven,
A godhead quarried from the stones of life.

Narada goes on describing the exquisite qualities of
Satyavan. He is a gem among men, and Savitri's choice
is indeed free from all blemish. In fact she could not
have made a better choice, for, none other could measure
up to her glory and greatness. But Narada says:

....earth could not keep too long from heaven
A treasure thus unique loaned by the gods,
A being so rare, of so divine a make!
In one brief year when this bright hour flies back
And perches careless on a branch of Time,
This sovereign glory ends heaven lent to earth,
This splendour vanishes from the mortal's sky:
Heaven's greatness came but was too great to stay;
Twelve swift-winged months are given to him and her:
This day returning Satyavan must die.

Savitri and Satyavan were given not merely twelve
months, but twelve swift-winged months. Satyavan has
been loaned by heaven to earth, and so the loan has to be
returned. Earth cannot keep him too long. This brilliant
emissary from heaven must return to heaven. These words
of Narada were indeed unbearable to the Queen. Why
should they be given the gift of Savitri, if their loved child
is to face such cruel decree of fate? The Queen says:

....Vain then can be Heaven's grace!
Heaven mocks us with the brilliance of its gifts;
For Death is the cupbearer of the wine
Of too brief joy held up to mortal lips
For a passionate moment by the careless gods.

For the Queen, the gift of Savitri is indeed a great
mockery perpetuated by the careless gods. The gods sent
the wine but also sent Death as the cupbearer. Must
heaven thus insult the earth by such cruel mockery? The
Queen said:

But I reject the grace and the mockery,
Mounting thy car go forth, O Savitri
And travel once more through the peopled lands
Alas in the green gladness of the woods
Thy heart has stooped to a misleading call
Choose once again and leave this fated head;
Death is the gardener of this wonder-tree,
A little joy would buy too bitter an end;
Plead not thy choice, for death has made it vain.

Must Savitri make another choice in order to defeat
the ways of Fate? Must she reject Satyavan so that her
hour of earthly joy may be prolonged? What must Savitri
do? But Savitri leaves no doubt in the minds of her
parents or in the mind of Narada, for, she says with a
voice that was calm and the face fixed like steel:

Once my heart chose and chooses not again
The word I have spoken can never be erased
It is written in the record book of God
My heart has sealed its troth to Satyavan
Its signature adverse Fate cannot efface
Death's grip can break our bodies, not our souls;
If death take him, I too know how to die
I am stronger than death and greater than my fate
Fate's law may change, but not my Spirit's will.

The Queen heard these words of love, but remained unconvinced. She felt this was just the outburst of young love. She felt that Savitri was rushing headlong into a self-chosen doom. She feels that Savitri must still be weaned away from the path of self-chosen sorrow. How could she permit her beloved daughter to knowingly plunge into the life of sorrow and death. And so she addresses her daughter and says:

O child in the magnificence of thy soul,
Dwelling on the border of a greater world
And dazzled by thy superhuman thoughts
Thou lendst eternity to a mortal hope.
Who is the lover and who is the friend?
All passes here, nothing remains the same.
None is for any on this transient globe.
He whom thou lovest now, a stranger came
And into a far strangeness shall depart
Thou who art human, think not like a god
For man below the god, above the brute,
Is given the calm reason as his guide.
The middle path is made for thinking man
To choose his steps by reason's vigilant light
To choose his path among the many paths
Hewn out of infinite possibility
Only when thou hast climbed above thy mind
And liv'st in the calm vastness of the One,
Can love be eternal in the eternal bliss,
And Love divine replace the human tie.

It is in vain that the Queen asks Savitri to follow the path of reason. Savitri belonged to realms beyond reason. Reason follows the path of safety and security. It calculates, it can never abandon. Reason can never take risks, but life offers its choicest treasures only to one who can risk everything. Savitri was made of that stuff which is never afraid to risk—to risk even ·her own life. And so these words of the Queen fell on deaf ears. Perhaps she did not know

of what stuff her daughter was made. And so Savitri
replied with steadfast eyes, without even a flicker. She
said:

> My will is part of the eternal will
> My fate is what my spirit's strength can make
> My fate is what my spirit's strength can bear.
> I have discovered my glad reality
> Beyond my body in another's being,
> I have found the deep unchanging soul of love;
> The riches of a thousand fortunate years
> Are a poverty.
> I treasure the rich occasion of my birth
> In sunlight and a dream of emerald ways,
> I shall walk with him like gods in Paradise
> If for a year, that year is all my life,
> And yet I know this is not all my fate;
> For I know now why my spirit came on earth
> I have looked at him from my immortal Self:
> I have seen God smile at me in Satyavan
> I have seen the Eternal in a human face.

The King, the Queen and Narada heard these words
of Savitri uttered from the innermost strength of her soul.
What could they say? In the words of the poet:

> Then none could answer to her words. Silent
> They sat and looked into the eyes of Fate.

CHAPTER XV

THE UNCOMPANIONED STAR

From the very beginning of time man is perplexed to find a solution to the problem of suffering. What intrigues him the most is—why should the good and the merciful suffer? By what canon of justice are the virtuous made to pass through the valley of sorrow? Man wants really to know whether justice rules the world, and whether there is only justice, or is there a place for grace? Where does justice end and when does grace begin? When Narada, Ashvapati and the ·Queen heard the irrevocable verdict of Savitri with regard to her choice of Satyavan, it was the Queen who could not reconcile herself to the dictate of Fate. Ashvapati knew that Savitri was not just an ordinary human being and that she had come to fulfil a great mission. And so in a way he had reconciled to the firm decision of Savitri. For Narada there was no question of being reconciled to the dictate of Fate, for, he knew much more than he had revealed to the royal couple. But it was the Queen who was greatly disturbed and wanted Narada to give her satisfactory answers so that she may find some consolation. And so she puts question after question to Narada regarding some of the fundamental problems of man's life, more particularly the problem of sorrow and suffering. The poet says:

A silence sealed the irrevocable decree,
Or so it seemed; yet from the silence rose
One voice that questioned changeless destiny.
A mother's heart had heard the fateful speech
That rang like a sanction to the call of death
And came like a chill close to life and hope.

All the three had heard the fateful speech of Savitri, but it was the mother that felt restless after what Savitri had said. She could not say to Savitri, for, after all Savitri must be free to make her choice. But then why should cruel fate lead Savitri to this choice? The Queen could not understand this. As the poet says: "She shared, she bore, the common lot of men". In her heart were the common emotions of men and women. And so she turned to the still immobile seer, Narada. Passionate like sorrow she questioned him saying:

> O seer, in the earth's strange twi-natured life
> By what pitiless adverse Necessity
> Or what cold freak of a Creator's will,
> By what random accident or governed Chance
> That shaped a rule out of fortuitous steps,
> Made destiny from an hour's emotion, came
> The direr mystery of grief and pain?
> Is it thy God who made this cruel law?
> Or some disastrous Power has marred his work
> And he stands helpless to defend or save?

The Queen tells Narada that either his God is utterly cruel or completely helpless. Narada must answer which of the two is the fact. She says that the ways of his God seem absolutely inscrutable. There does not seem to be any rhyme or reason in the way he seems to be administering his vast universe. The Queen says:

> A fatal seed was sown in life's false start
> When evil twinned with good on earthly soil.
> Then first appeared the malady of mind
> Its pang of thought, its quest for the aim of life.

Man suffers indeed from the malady of the mind. It is with this that the problem of good and evil arises. It is mind that makes choices out of its ignorance. The Queen says that there has been a false start given to life on earth. Man is endowed with mind, and, yet this mind

is incapable of dealing with the situations of life. This
has made the plight of man sorry. The Queen draws the
attention of Narada to the tragic paradoxes of life. She says:

Life is a marvel missed, an art gone wry,
A seeker in a dark obscure place,
An ill-armed warrior facing dreadful odds,
An imperfect worker given a baffling task,
An ignorant judge of problems Ignorance made
Its heavenward flights reach closed and keyless gates
Its glorious outbursts peter out in mire
Error is the comrade of our mortal thought
And falsehood lurks in the deep bosom of truth.

The Queen says that man has been given seeming free-.
dom to choose, but he has no ability to choose. He has
been given a curious instrument, the mind, which is unable even to see anything perfectly. A choice made by
such an instrument has no validity. The Queen says:

He walks by his own choice into hell's trap,
This mortal creature is his own worst foe,
His science is an artificer of doom,
He ransacks earth for means to harm his kind,
He slays his happiness and others' good.

The Queen is deeply disturbed by recent happenings and this has induced her to ask the most fundamental
questions pertaining to life. So deeply is she moved
that even in the very framing of her question there is
perceptible a tinge of bitter sarcasm. She asks Narada:

All is an episode in a meaningless tale.
Why is it all and wherefore are we here?
If to some being of eternal bliss
It is our spirit's destiny to return
Or some still impersonal height of endless calm,
Since That we are and out of That we came,
Whence rose the strange and sterile interlude
Lasting in vain through interminable Time?

This is a very pertinent question which has been raised.
From where does this interlude of time come, and why?
If from the Eternal man has come and to the Eternal he
returns, then why this interval of interminable time?
Why has man fallen from his Eternal realm, who caused
this fall, and could not this fall have been prevented?
The question is:

> .....Who persuaded it to fall from bliss
> And forfeit its immortal privilege?
> Who laid on it the ceaseless will to live?
> A wanderer in this beautiful sorrowful world
> And bear its load of joy and grief and love?
> Or if no being watches the works of Time,
> What hard impersonal Necessity
> Compels the vain toil of brief living things?
> Perhaps the soul we feel is only a dream,
> Eternal self a fiction sensed in trance.

These are very provocative words uttered by the
Queen. They constitute a challenge such as Narada probably had never faced in all his wanderings. For the Queen these are not mere intellectual questions; they are
real ones, for, the destiny that faces Savitri has completely shattered the very foundations of her living. The
poet says:

> Then after a silence Narada made reply
> Tuning his lips to earthly sound he spoke:
> "Was then the sun a dream because there is night?
> Hidden in the mortal's heart the Eternal lives
> A darkness stands between thyself and him
> Thou canst not hear or feel the marvellous Guest;
> Thou canst not see the beatific sun:
> O queen, thy thought is a light of the Ignorance
> Where ignorance is, there suffering too must come.

Narada says that the shell of ignorance has to be
broken, for, it is ignorance that does not allow one to

see that the Eternal is enshrined in the bosom of Time.
Man turns his back to light and says that it is dark. But
how shall man awake from this ignorance? It is here that
pain or suffering comes in. Narada says:

> Pain is the hammer of the gods to break
> A dead resistance in the mortal's heart
> His slow inertia as of living stone.
> If the heart were not forced to want and weep,
> His soul would have lain down content, at ease
> And never thought to exceed the human start
> And never learned to climb towards the sun.
> Pain is the hand of Nature sculpturing men
> To greatness: an inspired labour chisels
> With heavenly cruelty an unwilling mould
> Although the shaping god's tremendous touch
> Is torture unbearable to mortal nerves,
> The fiery spirit grows in strength within
> And feels a joy in every titan pang
> He who would save himself lives bare and calm,
> He who would save the race must share its pain.

Narada is trying to impress upon the mind of the
Queen that pain and suffering are the great helpers of
humanity. There is a saying that the more the marble
wastes, the more the statue grows. It is pain that brings
out the statue hidden in the stone. The arrival of pain
is not the doing of some alien power on whom God
has no control. Pain is God's own instrument for chisell-
ing the statue out of the rough stone of life. Narada
says that this is so even more in the case of one who aspires
to lead humanity. One who is destined to be the leader
of men must bear even harder hammer-blows so that the
beautiful statue may come out in all its glory. Narada
says:

> ....when God's messenger comes to help the world
> And lead the soul of earth to higher things,
> He too must carry the yoke he came to unloose

He too must bear the pang that he would heal
How shall he cure the ills he never felt?

Here Narada refers to the role of those who are the
leaders of men, those who usher in a new age. The lot
of all such people has been crucifixion in one form or another. They must pass through the fires of hell if they
are to be the bringers of heaven on earth. As Narada
says: "How shall he cure the ills he never felt?" He
has to bear not only his own individual cross; he must
also carry the cross of all humanity. The celestial singer
tells the Queen:

The sorrow of all living things shall come
And knock at his doors and live within his house;
The weeping of the centuries visits his eyes,
The poison of the world has stained his throat,
He dies that the world may be new-born and live.

He who becomes the leader of men must drink the
cup of poison to the full. When the great churning of
the ocean took place, gods and men fought with each other
for nectar; but none was ready to drink the poison. It
was left to Shiva who is known in Hindu mythology as
Nilakantha, for, his throat is stained by the poison that
he drank in order to save both gods and men. This
verily is the lot of all who strive to lead humanity along
a new path. Narada says:

Hard is the world-redeemer's heavy task;
This world itself becomes his adversary,
His enemies are the beings he came to save;
This world is in love with its own ignorance,
Its darkness turns away from the saviour light,
It gives the cross in payment for the crown.

There have been those who were burnt at stake for
uttering truths which were unpalatable to the powers-that
-be. As Narada says the task of the world-redeemer is
very hard because the world itself becomes his adversary.

It was Jesus who had to say "Save me from my friends".
The world-saviours find that those whom they serve become their enemies. Narada very significantly says that
the world is in love with its own ignorance, and so who-
soever tries to dispel world's ignorance is regarded by
the humn race as a traitor. Savitri has come to earth
to redeem the world. How can she escape the fate that
has greeted her predecessors? In the history of the world
we find attempts made by spiritual people to escape from
the world and enter the state of Nirvana. But how will
this escape save humanity, and if it does not, of what
use is that spiritual enlightenment? Narada says:

> An exit is shown, a road of hard escape
> From the sorrow and the darkness and the chain;
> But how shall a few escaped release the world?
> The human mass lingers beneath the yoke.
> Escape, however high, redeems not life
> Life that is left behind on a fallen earth.

Sri Aurobindo has never espoused the spirituality of
escape. In fact, his philosophy negates the two negations
of the materialist as well as of the ascetic. For him there
is neither the denial of the Spirit nor of matter. According to him the true spiritual man is not one who escapes
into Nirvana but one who establishes Nirvana on earth.
And so he visualises that mission for Savitri. If Savitri
wanted to escape into the bliss of Nirvana, there was
no need for her to come down on earth. Her descent had only one meaning—and that is to bring down
into the darkness of the earth the Light of Heaven, to show
to the mortal the path of Immortality. The ordinary
run of humanity thinks not in such terms, but then Savitri was different. As Narada says:

> Man turns aside or chooses easier paths.

But the one who comes down to redeem humanity
"keeps to the one high and difficult road." This demands

tremendous strength, and so one who does not feel this
inner strength had better leave this path alone. Narada
tells the Queen:

> For this he must go down into the pit,
> For this he must invade the dolorous Vasts.
> Imperishable and wise and infinite,
> He still must travel Hell the world to save,

Narada tells the Queen that sorrow and suffering
are not the stuff of which the world is made. The Creator is neither cruel nor is he helpless. The whole creation is impregnated with joy. It is the ignorance of man
that does not enable him to see this joy which permeates
the world. He says:

> Bliss is the secret stuff of all that lives:
> Even pain and grief are garbs of world-delight
> It hides behind thy sorrow and thy cry
> This troubled world thou hast chosen for thy home;
> Thou art thyself the author of thy pain.

Narada tells us that sorrow and pain are the projections of the mind. When the mind gives a name to a
situation, then do pain and suffering come into existence.
He says to the Queen that "thou art thyself the author
of thy pain". In fact, when man blames the creator for
injustice and pain created by him in his creation, he forgets that he has not even once looked at the world created
by the creator; he has looked only at what he himself
has projected on the world of Reality. It is only when
the projecting activity of the mind ceases that man can
look at the world which the creator has created. Narada
says:

> There are pitched desire's tents, grief's headquarters,
> A vast disguise conceals the Eternal's bliss.

Just as the Isavasya Upanishad says that the face of
Reality has been covered over by the golden veil, cast

by mind itself, similarly Narada says that desire has pitched its tents and these have become the headquarters of grief. It is these tents of desire that have concealed the bliss of the Eternal. He says:

....What the spirit sees, creates a truth;
And what the soul imagines is made a world.

Here there is made a distinction between the Spirit and the Soul. The soul is the psyche or the ego born of time; while the Spirit is the Timeless Being. The whole world is a projection of ego, and this is all that we see, and yet blame the Creator for bringing it into existence. It is desire which is the headquarters of grief, and this desire is the indwelling content of the mind. It is only when the mind is divested of its content that there arises the possibility for man to see the world as it is, to view the Creation as the Creator made it. Ashvapati has been quietly listening to this discourse of Narada, and a doubt arises in his mind, and so he says:

....What is fate if not the spirit's will
After long time fulfilled by cosmic Force?
I deemed a mighty Power had come with her
Is not that Power the high compeer of Fate?

Ashvapati feels a little bewildered about this discussion about Fate. He says that Savitri is herself the incarnation of a great power, and if so, how can Fate affect her? Ashvapati wants to know whether the Power that Savitri brings with her is a compeer of Fate, and, if it is, how can she become subject to the movement of Fate? She should be above the workings of fate, and, yet, how is it that she is being assailed by the forces of fate? Narada replies to Ashvapati and says:

A greatness in thy daughter's soul resides
That can transform herself and all around
But must cross on stones of suffering to its goal

Although designed like a nectar cup of heaven,
Of heavenly ether made, she sought this air
She too must share the human need of grief
And all her cause of joy transmute to pain.

It is difficult for Ashvapati to quite see what Narada
has been hinting. Is not Savitri a brilliant delegate from
heaven? If so, is she to obey the rules of the earth?
He went on a long journey and brought back this
gift from heaven. The gift was not for himself; it was
for the redemption of the whole human race. But if Savitri
has to face this dictate of Fate, what happens to her
great Mission of saving humanity and of ushering in a new
age of bliss and immortality? How can Savitri give the
message of Immortality to men if she has to face the cruel
fate where Satyavan dies? Narada says:

This world was not built with random bricks of chance,
A blind god is not destiny's architect;
A conscious power has drawn the plan of life
There is a meaning in each curve and line.
It is an architecture high and grand
By many named and nameless masons built
In which unseeing hands obey the Unseen,
And of its master-builders she is one.

Narada says to Ashvapati and his Queen that Savitri knows what she is doing. It is difficult for others to
understand the deep impelling force that dwells in her.
If one knows that she is not just a human being, but one
inspired by the Divine Power, then one must not judge
her actions by the usual standards of man. And so Narada
tells the Queen:

....strive no more to change the secret will;
Time's accidents are steps in its vast scheme.
Bring not thy brief and helpless human tears
Across the fathomless moments of a heart
That knows its single will and God's as one.

He tells the parents of Savitri that they must never·
forget that their daughter has come down to achieve something which man has been unable to do singlehanded.
She has tremendous strength within her so that she can
embrace a hostile destiny and yet come out unscathed.
Narada says :

Her lonely strength facing the Universe,
Affronting fate, asks not man's help nor god's:
Sometimes one life is charged with earth's destiny;
It cries not for succour from the time-bound powers.
Alone she is equal to her mighty task.
Intervene not in a strife too great for thee,
A struggle too deep for mortal thought to sound.

It was Narada who had broken the unhappy foreknowledge about Satyavan's death. But when he said
this, he had not unveiled the entire story of Fate. Perhaps he too wanted to know what inner strength inspired
Savitri. When he talked of Satyavan's death after one
year, Narada probably wanted to find out how deep was
Savitri's love; whether her love would be able to stand
the cruel face of fate. Having realized of what stuff Savitri
was made, Narada was able to assure the parents that
they should not worry about her, for she can all alone
stand up to the mighty task. And so Narada says:

As a star, uncompanioned, moves in heaven,
Unastonished by the immensities of space,
Travelling infinity by its own light,
The great are strongest when they stand alone.

Narada here tells Ashvapati and her Queen something that is to be seen in the lives of all mystics and saints. And that is the state of complete Aloneness. The
great mystic rises to his highest when he stands alone, stripped of everything. And it is this which is the greatest
hour of trial for the mystic or the saint. The last words
of Jesus when he was on the cross were: "O God, my

God, why hast thou forsaken me?" One feels that even
God does not stand by the mystic in his great hour of
trial. This feeling comes because the man of God must
stand alone where even God cannot help him. Narada
hints at this when he says to Savitri's parents that a moment will come when she must be utterly alone, for that is
the law of spiritual life; it has indeed to be a flight of
the alone to the Alone. Narada says:

> A day may come when she must stand unhelped
> On a dangerous brink of the world's doom and hers,
> Carrying the world's future on her lonely breast,
> Carrying the human hope in a heart left sole,
> To conquer or fail on a last desperate verge
> Alone with death and close to extinction's edge,
> She must cross alone a perilous bridge in Time
> And reach an apex of world-destiny
> Where all is won or all is lost for man.
> Alone she must conquer or alone must fall
> No human aid can reach her in that hour,
> No armoured God stand shining at her side.

Savitri has come down to fulfil a great mission, and
she has to do it all alone. It is in this aloneness that
she will rise to her great spiritual stature; she will come
into her own. Her inner strength must come out to the
full. And this can happen only when she realizes that
no one can save her, neither man nor God. It is in this
realization that one touches the source of some inexhaustible energy. But if one clings to that hope that some mysterious power shall come, then one is not alone. Even
the hope that some power will save has to be completely
negated. It is in the state of Aloneness that there can
be a true surrender, for, it is the surrender to the Unknown.
Savitri must come to that experience of Aloneness, for,
it is only with the staff of Nothingness that one can enter
the realm of the Unknown. This will be Savitri's great
hour of triumph—or it may be her great hour of failure.

In this hour will be tested the true spiritual strength of Savitri. And so Narada says to the Queen:

O Queen, stand back from that stupendous scene:
Come not between her and her hour of Fate.
Her hour must come and none can intervene
Think not to turn her from her heaven-sent task.
Thou hast no place in that tremendous strife,
Intrude not twixt her spirit and its force,
But leave her to her mighty self and Fate.

What could the Queen say in the face of these momentous words? She was silent, and leaving her in that silence, Narada left on his journey heavenwards. The poet describes the moment of Narada's departure in the following beautiful lines:

He spoke and ceased and left the earthly scene,
He turned towards his far-off blissful home,
A brilliant arrow pointing straight to heaven,
The luminous body of the eternal seer
Assailed the purple glory of the noon,
And disappeared like a receding star
Vanishing into the light of the Unseen;
But still a cry was heard in the infinite
And still to the listening soul on mortal earth
A high and far imperishable voice
Chanted the anthem of eternal love.

Narada departed for his heavenly home—but left behind the strains of divine music which sang of the eternal love of Savitri and Satyavan.

CHAPTER XVI

A HIDDEN KING

There is a widely prevalent misconception among the minds of most people regarding the behaviour of a spiritual man. There is a general belief that the spiritual man must be completely free from all display of emotions. He has to be austere and therefore cannot afford to show any emotional interest in anything. We come across such so-called spiritual people who are emotionally squeezed out and are indifferent to what happens round about. These people move about as emotional skeletons whose feelings are completely dead. Here impersonality is regarded as identical with indifference and sternness. When nothing moves a person then is he regarded as firmly established in spirituality. There are people who are afraid to give vent to any emotion lest they would fall from the high pedestal of spiritual life. But such emotional deadness is far from true impersonality. In fact, it is only the man of real impersonality who can be deeply interested in every person. Every person feels a nearness to such an individual of true impersonality. Impersonality is not a lack of interest in persons; it only means that the interest is not centred just in one person. The sun is impersonal and yet it is interested in ripening a bunch of grapes in a small corner of the earth. Impersonality arises when there is neither indifference nor interference. One who is afraid of being involved in personal relationships is far from being impersonal. In such so-called impersonality there is already an involvement in some one person. Impersonality is regarded as something spiritual or divine and personal feelings are regarded as worldly and mundane. But in true spirituality there is a beautiful co-existence of the Impersonal and the Personal.

It is the uniqueness of Sri Aurobindo that in his characterisation of Savitri he has shown a fine existence of
the Divine and the Human. Savitri is supremely divine
and yet at the same time she is intensely human. And this
indeed is the characteristic of one who is truly spiritual.
In Savitri there is a beautiful rhythm of the Divine and
the human, and this rhythm is seen at its best when she
begins her life in the hermitage of Satyavan. With the
departure of Narada, the whole episode arising from the
choice of Satyavan ended, and so Savitri soon started for
her home in the forest. The poet says:

> Once more she sat behind loud hastening hooves
> A speed of armoured squadrons and a voice
> Far-heard of chariots bore her from her home.
> Once more was near the fair and fated place,
> The borders gleaming with the groves' delight,
> Where first she met the face of Satyavan,
> And he saw like one waking into a dream
> Some timeless beauty and reality.

The chariot of Savitri was moving fast as if the horses,
too, understood the feelings throbbing in her heart. Very
soon the past receded and the future neared. She had left
behind the faces she had known for many a year. Her mind
was naturally crowded with memories of what she was
leaving behind. She was moving away from her life in
palaces and parks and was heading towards the simple
life of a hermitage. Ashvapati had naturally sent many
faithful servants from the palace to escort Savitri to her new
home. The poet says:

> They saw low thatched roofs of a hermitage
> Huddled beneath a patch of azure blue
> In a sunlit clearing that seemed the outbreak
> Of a glad smile in the forest's monstrous heart,
> A rude refuge of the thought and will of man
> Watched by the crowding giants of the wood

> Arrived in that rough-hewn homestead they gave,
> Questioning no more the strangeness of her fate,
> Their pride and loved one to the great blind king,
> A regal pillar of fallen mightiness.

The escorts of Savitri handed over their charge, their pride and loved one to King Dyumatsena and to the "stately care worn woman, once a queen". She now lived only for her son. The poet says:

> Adoring wisdom and beauty like a young god's
> She saw him loved by heaven as by herself
> She rejoiced in his brightness and believed in his fate
> And knew not of the evil drawing near.

Having handed over their priceless charge to the King and the Queen, the escorts who had come from Ashvapati 's palace bade farewell to Savitri. Their parting was naturally painful as all such partings are. The poet describes their departure thus:

> Like men who lengthen out departure's pain
> Unwilling to separate sorrowful clinging hands
> Unwilling to see for the last time a face
> Heavy with the sorrow of a coming day
> And wondering at the carelessness of Fate
> Who breaks with idle hands her supreme works
> They parted from her, with pain-fraught burdened
>   hearts,
> They left her to her rapture and her doom
> In the tremendous forest's savage charge.

But for Savitri this was the home she loved, for, here was Satyavan with whom now she will live, putting behind her that which was once her abode. Of what use are parks and palaces if there be not her Satyavan? The poet says:

> She abode with Satyavan in the wild woods
> Priceless she deemed her joy so close to death
> Apart with love she lived for love alone.

As if self-poised above the march of days,
Her immobile spirit watched the haste of time.

While Savitri lived with Satyavan and his parents, she alone was aware of the tragic prophesy conveyed to her by Narada. None in the house knew about it, and she dare not give even a hint about it, lest the atmosphere of joy be changed into sorrow. The sad foreknowledge remained in her breast unknown by others. And so while outwardly Savitri was all joy and happiness, inwardly she had to nurse a great tragedy. She had to live a double life, while to others she gave joy , for herself she kept the count of the sad moment. The poet says: "She watched the haste of time." The movement of time indeed seemed to her a great haste. Why cannot time move with a slower speed? Time was, of course, moving at its normal speed, but Savitri's mind naturally saw in it great haste. Savitri passed her days in a manner so as to give happiness to all. In fact, she was indeed happy with her Satyavan. The poet says:

Day was a purple pageant and a hymn
A wave of the laughter of light from morn to eve
His absence was a dream of memory
His presence was the empire of a god.

Satyavan was away for many hours during the day in the forest cutting wood. When he was away Savitri lived in a dream of happy memory; but when he returned she felt that she was verily in an empire of a god. Savitri and Satyavan lived in moments of intense happiness. It was difficult to say who loved the other more. It was:

A fusing of the joys of earth and heaven,
A tremulous blaze of nuptial rapture passed,
A rushing of two spirits to be one,
A burning of two bodies in one flame.

Seasons passed, from summer came the depressing months when the sky was overcast with heavy clouds. On a rainy day when "rain fled sobbing over the dripping leaves and the storm became the forest's titan voice" and when were heard "the fugitive pattering of footsteps of the showers" then, as it were, the "grief of all the world came near to her". It usually happens that when the sky is overcast and it is threatening to rain, all seems sad and sombre. On such days the innermost sorrow in the heart of Savitri came to the surface, and she felt sad and depressed. The poet says:

> Night's darkness seemed her future's ominous face
> The shadow of her lover's doom arose
> And fear laid hands upon her mortal heart;
> She reckoned the insufficient days between
> Dreadful to her were the footsteps of the hours
> Grief came, a passionate stranger to her gate
> Banished when in his arms, out of her sleep;
> It rose at morn to look into her face.

In the midst of the moments of happiness there was for her, cast all the time, the shadow of the fateful prophesy. She must have been terribly torn between joy and sorrow. And the poignancy of all that lay in the fact that she had to keep the sorrow concealed in her heart. She could not share it with any one, and the unshared sorrow always causes tremendous strain. She must have been living in great strain, and yet she had to wear a mask of joy all the time. So adept had she become at mask-wearing that none had any inkling as to what lay behind that mask. The poet says:

> The more she plunged into love that anguish grew;
> Her deepest grief from sweetest gulfs arose.
> Remembrance was a poignant pang, she felt
> Each day a golden leaf torn cruelly out
> From her too slender book of love and joy.

Her book of love was indeed very slender, and if each day a leaf is torn, how quickly will the pages go? When she was alone in her inner chamber, she paced the floor in bitter anguish. According to the poet: "Her eyes stared blind into the future's night". She saw people moving about, but she felt that she and they were moving in two different worlds, although physically close by. The torment in her heart must have been terrible. That, in spite of all this, she could keep a smiling face and make every one happy was indeed a great achievement of the spirit. She in her dreadful knowledge was alone. None knew, not even Satyavan, what was going on in the depths of her heart. She was busy with the daily routine and with the household chores. Every one admired the grace and efficiency with which she did her work. But the poet says:

> Her graceful daily acts were now a mask
> She was still to them the child they knew and loved,
> The sorrowing woman they saw not within;
> No change was in her beautiful motions seen,
> A worshipped empress all once vied to serve,
> She made herself the diligent serf of all
> In all her acts a strange divinity shone
> Into a simplest movement she could bring
> A oneness with earth's glowing robe of light
> A lifting up of common acts by love.

Here we see the great Miracle of Love shown by Savitri in her daily routine, otherwise so dull and drab. With the touch of love even the dull drudgery was changed into something intensely divine. All who saw her greatly admired her. The princess of yesterday was able to become a willing servant of all. She never made any one feel that she was engaged in acts of sacrifice.

But while this was her natural way of doing things, there were moments when the thought of the impending doom became much too oppressive to allow her to do her normal activities. The poet says:

But when her grief to the surface pressed too close
These things, once gracious adjuncts of her joy,
Seemed meaningless to her, a gleaming shell
Or were a round, mechanical and void
Her body's actions shared not by her will.

There was thus a divided life which Savitri had to
live. But all throughout one sees the expression of her
human qualities. She remained a human being in spite
of her divine heritage. And Savitri became all the more
lovable because of these human traits. If she had been
just divine, then she would have looked too perfect to
fit into the imperfections of the world. The poet describes
her human qualities very graphically. He says:

Always behind this strange divided life
Her spirit, like a sea of living fire
Possessed her lover and to his body clung
One locked embrace to guard its threatened mate.
All night she woke through the slow silent hours,
Brooding on the treasure of his bosom and face
Hung o'er the sleep-bound beauty of his brow
Or laid her burning cheek upon his feet.
Waking at morn her lips endlessly clung to his,
Unwilling ever to separate again
Or lose that honeyed drain of lingering joy
Unwilling to loose his body from her breast,
The warm inadequate signs that love must use,
Intolerant of the poverty of Time;
Her passion catching at the fugitive hours
Willed the expense of centuries in one day.

Savitri was indeed impatient of the poverty of time
and she wanted to spend in love, in one day, what would
have been legitimate for a century. Such was the irresi-
tible passion that seized Savitri. One year was too short
a period, and her love was such that it needed centuries
to express itself fully. How could she wait when the year
was running out? The poet says:

After all was given she demanded still
Even by his strong embrace unsatisfied,
She longed to cry, "O tender Satyavan,
O lover of my soul, give more, give more
Of love while yet thou canst, to her thou lov'st
Imprint thyself on every nerve to keep
That thrills to thee the message of my heart.
For soon we part and who shall know how long."

She uttered these words to herself. How could she
say this to Satyavan? To him she expressed only in the
language of gestures. The poet tells us that "too well
she loved to speak a fateful word and lay her burden on
his happy head". But Satyavan who was intensely sensitive got some imperceptible hints from the behaviour of
Savitri. He did not know why Savitri was behaving as
if she was racing with time. He felt something strange
in the behaviour of Savitri.

And so Satyavan:

All of his speeding days that he could spare
From labour in the forest hewing wood
And hunting food in the wild sylvan glades
And service to his father's sightless life,
He gave to her and helped to increase the hours
By the nearness of his presence and his clasp
And lavish softness of heart-seeking words
And the close beating felt of heart on heart.

The poet says that Satyavan was trying to increase
the hours. Savitri, indeed, above everything else, needed
this increase of hours in the midst of the speeding days.
Her main complaint was with time, for, she wanted time
to have a stop. But, instead it was speeding fast, bringing the two lovers nearer and nearer to the hour of the
fateful doom. But in spite of all that Satyavan did to
increase the hours, Savitri,

D.-14

.....saw the desert of her coming days
Imaged in every solitary hour.

Sometimes Savitri thought as to why she could not
follow Satyavan on the funeral pyre.   She took a delight
in that thought and toyed with the idea when she was
alone.   The poet says:

> ...with a vain imaginary bliss
> Of fiery union through death's door of escape,
> She dreamed of her body robed in funeral flame.

She took unconscious delight in this imagery where
she, as it were, is robed in funeral flame along with Satyavan.   Would that not be the best for her since in this
fiery union they could never be separated?   But how could
she indulge even in this form of happiness?   The poet
says:

> She knew she must not clutch that happiness
> To die with him and follow, seizing his robe
> Into the sweet or terrible Beyond.
> For those sad parents still would need her here
> To help the empty remnant of their day.

And so even this escape into happiness was not open
to her.   If Satyavan is gone, his parents would need her
all the more to fill their empty remnant days.   And so
the fateful doom will draw near, and she must see Satyavan going away from her.   She cannot even follow him
into the sweet or the terrible Beyond.   She must stay behind to serve the poor parents in their days of utter emptiness.   The poet says:

> Thus in the silent chamber of her soul
> Cloistering her love to live with secret grief,
> She dwelt like a dumb priest with hidden gods
> Unappeased by the wordless offering of her days.

Even her gods were not appeased.   What could she
offer except the wordless offerings?   In this worship of

the gods her life was the altar and she herself was the sacrifice. And so the days passed by rapidly, unmindful of her intense problem. But the nearer the day of the doom came, the more intense her love for Satyavan grew. She felt that nothing could separate them. The poet says:

> For when he wandered in the forest, oft
> Her conscious spirit walked with him and knew
> His actions as if in herself he moved.

She was all the time with Satyavan even when bodily she was far away from him. Her love for him had comp-letely united her to him so that even his forest wander-ings seemed to him as if he moved in herself. Having no way of escape left she became more resolute in her spirit. She would now meet any adversary. As the poet says:

> Her spirit stretched measureless in strength divine
> An anvil for the blows of Fate and Time.

Let fate and time strike as hard as they liked, she was ready to receive their blows. She must win her victory over fate and time, and she was preparing her-self to face the battle, however fierce it may be. In the meantime the days were passing speedily. The poet says:

> The year now paused upon the brink of change
> ....her grief's heavy sky shut in her heart
> A still self hid behind but gave no light
> No voice came down from the forgotten heights
> Only in the privacy of its brooding pain
> Her human heart spoke to the body's fate.
> Repressing in her bosom its load of grief
> She sat staring at the dumb tread of Time.

As Savitri thus stood motionless, staring at the dumb tread of time, she heard a voice, a deep and a command-ing voice. Even her mind was motionless as the Voice spoke. It said:

Why camest thou to this dumb deathbound earth,
This ignorant life beneath indifferent skies
Tied like a sacrifice on the altar of Time,
O spirit, O immortal energy
If 'twas to nurse grief in a helpless heart
Or with hard tearless eyes await thy doom?
Arise, O soul, and vanquish Time and Death.

But Savitri thinks as to why she should do this?
Has the power of heaven helped her? If the Divine Forces
have left her high and dry, why should she bother to engage herself in the fierce struggle against Time and Death?
She replies to the Voice:

My strength is taken from me and given to Death,
Why should I lift my hands to the shut heavens
Or struggle with mute inevitable Fate
Or hope in vain to uplift an ignorant race?
Is there a God whom any cry can move?
He sits in peace and leaves the mortal's strength
Impotent against his calm omnipotent Law
What need have I, what need has Satyavan
To avoid the black meshed net, the dismal door,
Or call a mightier Light into life's closed room
A greater Law into man's little world?

Savitri seems to be very bitter against the Forces of
Heaven for not raising even a little finger in defence of
her lover. If the Divine Forces cannot save Satyavan
from the cruel clutches of Fate, then why should she
call on those powers? Then what will Savitri do? She
tells the Voice in no mistakable terms:

This surely is best......
....follow close behind my lover's steps
And pass through night from twilight to the sun
Across the tenebrous river that divides
The adjoining parishes of earth and heaven.
Then could we lie inarmed breast upon breast,

Untroubled by thought, untroubled by our hearts
Forgetting man and life and time and its hours
Forgetting eternity's call, forgetting God.

Savitri speaks with a sense of defiance. If she was
sent to earth by Heaven, then what has heaven done to
help her against the onslaughts of cruel fate? Has heaven
looked after her? She feels that it would be much better
to forget even God, and lie arm in arm with Satyavan
across the tenebrous river that divides earth and heaven.
But the Voice must awaken Savitri to her great mission,
and so it says to Savitri:

Is this enough, O spirit?
And what shall thy soul say when it wakes and
                                             knows
The work was left undone for which it came?
Is this then the report that I must make,
My head bowed with shame before the Eternal's
                                             seat—
His power he kindled in thy body has failed
His labourer returns, her task undone?

With these words Savitri suddenly woke up to the
needs of the great mission that she had undertaken. She
realized that she had missed something, that in being
intensely human, she had forgotten her Divine splendour
within. How to get back to the lost vision of the spirit?
Then does Savitri address the Voice thus:

I am thy portion here, charged with thy work,
As thou myself seated for ever above,
Speak to my depths, O great and deathless Voice,
Command, for I am here to do thy will.

The Voice tells Savitri to go in search of her soul.
She must rediscover her soul by rending asunder veil after
veil which has been cast over her vision. It says: "Cast
from thee sense that veils thy spirit's sight." But where
must she go to re-discover her soul? The Voice tells her

"in the enormous emptiness of thy mind" wilt thou re-
discover the soul. It says: "Conquer thy heart's throbs,
let thy heart beat in God". It is only when one is emptied of oneself that one can be filled with the energy of
God. This path of utter emptiness does the Voice indicate to her if she is to find her soul and be in contact
with the inexhaustible energy of God. The Voice says
that this is indeed the only way to conquer Death. The
poet says:

> Then Savitri by her doomed husband sat
> Still rigid in her golden motionless pose,
> A statue of the fire of the inner sun.
> Impassive mid the movement and the cry,
> Witness of the thoughts of mind, the moods of life,
> She looked into herself and sought for her soul.

Savitri sits in a reflective mood, in search of her soul.
She finds that a dream discloses to her the cosmic past.
She sees the movement of evolving life. She witnesses
the slow growth from matter to life, and how mind takes
its birth. With the birth of mind there comes into existence a consciousness in the Inconscient world. When
the mind comes, it takes charge of everything and desires
to guide the course of events. What was so far left to
Nature is now usurped by the mind. The poet says that
with this coming in of the mind, things change completely.
The new situation:

> Leaves the vicegerent mind a seeming king.
> In his floating house upon the sea of Time
> This regent sits at work and never rests;
> He is a puppet of the dance of Time,
> He is driven by the hours, the moment's call.
> This mind no silence knows nor dreamless sleep.
> It toils like a machine and cannot stop.

This mind has no rest. There are countless callers
from life's happenings demanding its attention. In the

house of mind, the poor servant has to respond to every knock. He has to bring in life's visitors and report each call to his master. Even in the tracts of sleep is there scant repose. This mind functions at various levels, for it is like an iceberg. It is more below the surface than above it. There are forces that lie in the subliminal areas from where they spring up with tremendous force. It is this which makes mind a stranger to repose and relaxation. The poet says:

> A whole mysterious world is locked within.
> Unknown to himself lives a hidden king
> Behind rich tapestries in great secret rooms.

The urges of the sublminal remain hidden behind the rich tapestries of the conscious mind. The ugly and the sordid nature of subconscious is not perceptible because of the rich coverings provided by the conscious layer of the mind. It is because of this that man's mind is subject to conflicting urges. The dream of the cosmic past tells Savitri:

> Man's house of life holds not the gods alone
> There are occult Shadows, there are tenebrous Powers,
> Inhabitants of life's ominous nether rooms;
> Man harbours dangerous forces in his house,
> The dreadful powers held down within the depths
> Become his masters or his ministers,
> Grey forces like a thin miasma creep,
> Stealing through chinks in his closed mansion's doors,
> Discolouring the walls of upper mind
> In which he lives his fair and specious life
> And leave behind a stench of sin and death.

The upper mind is the posh and attractive drawing room of life where respectability is the order of the day. It is here that every one tries to be prim and proper in terms of the rules of respectability. But the underground inhabitants of the mind steal through chinks in

the closed mansion's doors, and having come, they dis-
colour the walls of the upper mind. Even when these
underground entities depart they leave behind a stench
of sin and death. There is a constant conflict between
the conscious and sub-conscious layers of the mind. The
subconscious contains impelling desires, suppressed by the
conscious mind. But in turn, the subconscious succeeds
in suppressing the conscious. The poet says:

> Impotent to quell his terrible prisoners,
> Appalled the householder helpless sits above;
> Taken from him his house is his no more;
> Their vast contagion grips sometimes man's world,
> An awful insurgence overpowers man's soul,
> In house and house the huge uprising grows
> Hell's companies are loosed to do their work.

The mind always engages itself in the play of the
opposites. This movement of the opposites is the only
movement it knows and relishes. Thus its virtues and vices
are the opposites of each other; they have no positive
content. Even the God of the mind is the magnification
of man. To the mind, man glorified is God. It knows
of no qualitative changes, for, it measures everything in
terms of quantity. Thus it is that the evil can always
masquerade as good in the domain of the mind. The
poet tells us:

> It imitates the Godhead it denies
> Puts on his figure and assumes his face.

But then what is the way out? The entire story
of the mind is what Savitri sees as she looks into herself
in her attempt to re-discover her soul. The ways of the
mind are indeed very strange and extremely clever. But
the mind is not all. There is something higher if only
man would lend his ear to it. The poet says:

> All the world's possibilities in man
> Are waiting, as the tree waits in its seed;

The unborn gods hide in his house of Life.
The daemons of the unknown overshadow his mind
Cas   g their dreams into live moulds of thought,
The moulds in which his mind builds out its world.
His mind creates around him its universe.

We live in the universe created by the mind. If we
aspire to contact something that transcends the mind, then
we must needs know our minds and watch its behaviour
patterns as also its motivating urge. The mind lives in the
past and seeks its nourishment in the past. It thinks only
in terms of a mere modification of the past. It is tied
to its own traditions and is unable to step out of the circle
it has drawn for its movements. The poet says:

Our past still lives in our unconscious selves,
And by the weight of its hidden influences
Is shaped our future's self-discovery.
Our dead past round our future's ankles clings
And drags back the new nature's glorious stride,
Or from its buried corpse old ghosts arise,
Old thoughts, old longings, dead passions live again
Recur in sleep or move the waking man
To deeds that suddenly start and o'erleap
His head of reason and his guardian will.

In this and the following passages we find Sri Aurobindo revealing to us the secrets of the mind. In the
evolutionary movement man has come to the development
of the mind. But mind has created innumerable problems
which it is unable to solve. There must be a movement
above the mind where alone the discovery of the soul can
take place. But for this, one must clearly understand
the ways of the mind. The poet says:

An old self lurks in the new self we are,
Hardly we escape from what we once had been
In the dim gleam of habit's passages,
In the subconscient's darkling corridors,

All things are carried by the porter nerves
And nothing checked by the subterranean mind,
Unstudied by the guardians of the doors
And passed by a blind instinctive memory,
The old gang dismissed, old cancelled passports serve,
Nothing is wholly dead that once has lived.

The old gang is dismissed but the old cancelled passports serve, which means that the patterns have changed
but the content remains the same. The gang of the old
patterns is dismissed, but since the cancelled passports
can still serve, the old gang can come back in new garbs.
This is how our mind functions living in its own prison
house of content to redecorate the prison walls. But while
this is the story of the mind, this is not all. As the poet
tells us:

This is not all we are or all our world;
Our greater self of knowledge waits for us,
It sees from summits beyond thinking mind.

The history of humanity tells us that there have been
great fire-pillars of mankind who have gone beyond the
limitations of the mind and have seen a realm vaster than
the puny human mind can imagine. There have been
men who have grown beyond the limiting spheres of the
mind. The poet says:

Thus man in his little house made of earth's dust
Grew towards an unseen heaven of thought and
                                                    dream
Looking into the vast vistas of his mind
On a small globe dotting infinity.
At last climbing a long and narrow stair,
He stood alone on a high roof of things
And saw the light of a spiritual sun.

This is the possibility that is in front of all men, for
what was achieved by one man can be achieved by the

entire humanity. Savitri has come down to show to man
the path that takes him beyond the restrictive domain
of the mind. But how is this to be done, for, it is in
doing this that she will re-discover her soul. And unless
she re-discovers her soul, she cannot conquer Fate and
Time. The poet says:

> Amid the cosmic workings of the Gods
> It marked her the centre of a wide-drawn scheme,
> Dreamed in the passion of her far-seeing spirit
> To mould humanity into God's own shape
> And lead this great blind struggling world to light
> Or a new world discover or create.
> Earth must transform herself and equal heaven
> Or Heaven descend into earth's mortal state.
> But for such vast spiritual change to be,
> Out of the mystic cavern in man's heart
> The heavenly Psyche must put off her veil.

For this great destiny to fulfil itself, Savitri must put
away the veil which covers her heavenly psyche. And so
the Voice indicates to her that,

> Time, life and death were passing incidents
> Obstructing with their transient view her sight,
> Her sight that must break through and liberate
>   the god
> Imprisoned in the visionless mortal man.
> The inferior nature born into ignorance
> Still took too large a place, it veiled her self
> And must be pushed aside to find her soul.

And so Savitri undertakes the journey for the discovery of her soul, for, in that discovery alone she will
find the necessary strength to challenge the King of Death
and secure for man the heavenly boon of Immortality.

CHAPTER XVII

THE PURITY OF EMPTINESS

WHEN faced with the dire prospects of Satyavan's death, as prophesied by Narada, Savitri is asked to seek out her soul as otherwise it may not be possible for her to meet the challenge of Death. What is indeed meant by seeking out the soul? Is soul an ideal or an image formed by the mind of man? Is it something that is noblest within the realm of mind's knowledge? Is seeking out the soul identical with taking up of a particular mental attitude? None of these questions covers the essential nature of the soul. In true sense of spiritual understanding, soul is something that is Unborn. The Bhagavad Gita makes this clear in the Second Discourse wherein it says that the Soul is Unborn and Eternal. Now Eternal is not everlasting. It is Timeless. And so the Soul is Timeless and therefore Unborn. That which is born is governed by the processes of Time, and Time has a beginning and therefore an end. The soul has neither a beginning nor an end, for, it is Unborn. When Savitri is asked to go out in search of her soul, she is instructed to establish her communion with the Unborn. If she is to face the challenge of Time then she has to know the Timeless. She must journey into the Timeless state, and from there bring the necessary strength to face the challenge of Time and Fate. She had descended into the realms of Time, and perchance she had lost her contact with the Timeless. The Voice that instructed her said that she would be able to fulfil her mission if she would re-establish her contact with the Timeless. Now that which is Unborn cannot be reached by the mind; that which is Timeless is outside the jurisdiction of the human mind. It is only

220

where mind ends that there begins the entering into the light of the Unborn and the Timeless. It is because of this that the poet has discussed so much and at such length the ways of the mind and the limitations inherent in the approaches of the Mind. In order to transcend the mind one must know the limitations of the mind. Savitri must transcend the realms of the mind in order to face the challenge of Time and Fate. But how will she transcend the mind if she does not know its ways? And so Savitri becomes aware of the clever devices and subterfuges of the mind. What happens when this awareness comes? The poet says:

> At first out of the busy hum of mind
> As if from a loud thronged market into a cave
> By an inward moment's magic she had come
> A stark hushed emptiness became her self
> Her mind unvisited by the voice of thought
> Stared at a void deep's dumb infinity.

When the mind is unvisited by thought then surely it becomes Mindless. To render mind, mindless, is one of the approaches of Yoga to which Savitri had turned. There are certain outward resemblances between the travels of Ashvapati and Savitri's journey in search of the Soul. But these are very superficial, for, Savitri's journey is in depth while Ashvapati's travels were in extense. In order to seek out the Soul, Savitri must pass through the various layers of consciousness, not for getting any superphysical or occult powers, but for growing into a sensitivity so that she may be able to respond to the Unborn and the Intangible. The Soul is not invisible, it is Unborn and therefore can be discovered only in its intangible intimations. When, in the manifest, one awakens to the intangible intimations of the Unmanifest then is one brought to the discovery of the Soul. For this, Savitri must pass through the void of the mind. The poet says:

All fled away from her and left her blank.
But when she came back to her self of thought
Once more she was a human thing on earth:
A lump of matter, a house of closed sight.

To come back to a condition where the mind is visited by thoughts is to come to a house of closed sight. And so Savitri must move on and not look back at the realm of the mind. As she moves on, she hears a Voice which says:

For man thou seekest, not for thyself alone.
Only if God assumes the human mind
And puts on mortal ignorance for his cloak
And makes himself the Dwarf with triple stride
Can he help man to grow into the God.

Here Sri Aurobindo tells us that mind can be a powerful instrument only if it becomes a means of communication in the hands of the Divine. It is Divine that must descend and use the instruments of man. And so it is necessary that man must first discover the Divine. Then he can come back as the Dwarf with the triple stride or Vamana, for, even as the Dwarf he will be able to lead humanity to the vastness of God. Savitri is asked to discover her soul because that is the only Divine base from where she can act, and act effectively, to meet the challenge of Fate. And so she must explore the inner countries of her being. As she is moving and journeying, she comes to a gate and gently knocks. The poet says:

She knocked and pressed against the ebony gate:
The living portal groaned with sullen hinge,
Heavily reluctant it complained inert
Against the tyranny of the spirit's touch:
A formidable voice cried from within:
"Back, creature of earth, lest tortured and torn thou
die".

Savitri heard a hissing sound which came from the serpent of the threshold that was guarding the entrance to the inner worlds. But Savitri was unshaken and so quietly entered the inner realm. As she moved within, the poet says "all was there but nothing in its place". At every turn of her movement, the different elements of the inner worlds invited her to settle down in their realms saying there cannot be anything further. Thus did the senses invite her to make their realms her abode, for, indeed there was no Soul other than they. But Savitri was moving from Appearance to Reality, and she must negate appearance after appearance. In the realm of the senses all was there but nothing in its place, for, there was disorder everywhere. It was a realm where there was "a chaos of disordered impulses". How can there be any light or any joy in this disorderly state. She moved away from the world of the senses, and, so, for the time being all "grew still and empty". All the sense-impulses were left behind. She was comparatively free, and moved on. She heard the whisperings saying:

But how shall come the glory and the flame,
If mind is cast away into the abyss?

Moving inwards from the realm of the senses, she came to the kingdom of the Mind. The poet says:

Here was a quiet country of fixed mind,
Here life no more was all nor passion's voice
A cry of sense had sunk into a hush
Soul was not there, nor spirit, but mind alone;
Mind claimed to be the spirit and the soul.

Savitri finds that the mind arrogates to itself the role of the soul. She was in search of the Soul, but the mind detained her and said that there was no other realm of the Soul except the domain of the mind. The Voice of the Mind speaks to Savitri thus:

Traveller or pilgrim of the inner world,
Fortunate art thou to reach our brilliant air
Flaming with thought's supreme finality.
O aspirant to the perfect way of life,
Here find it; rest from search and live at peace.
Ours is the home of cosmic certainty.
Here is the truth, God's harmony is here
Register thy name in the book of the elite;
Admitted by the sanction of the few
Adopt thy station of knowledge, thy post in mind,
Thy ticket of order draw in Life's bureau
And praise thy fate that made thee one of ours.
This is the end and there is no beyond.

Savitri hears this persuasive voice of the Mind which
says that finality resides only in its realm. It wants to
convince Savitri that the mind is the end and that there
can be nothing beyond. In this voice of the mind we hear
the voice of the modern civilization with its scientific and
technological achievements. It also attempts to speak
with a finality. But to this Voice of the Mind, Savitri
gives a fitting reply. The poet says:

But to the too satisfied and confident sage
Savitri replied casting into his world
Sight's deep release, the heart's questioning inner
                                                Voice;
For here the heart spoke not, only clear daylight
Of intellect reigned here, limiting, cold, precise.

In the world of the mind there was only the daylight of clear intellect. In such daylight there is scorching
heat, for, there are no shadows where one can rest awhile.
And so to the Voice of the Mind, Savitri says:

Happy are they who in this chaos of things,
This coming and going of the feet of Time,
Can find the single Truth, the eternal Law:
Untouched they live by hope and doubt and fear.

Happy are men anchored on fixed belief
In this uncertain and ambiguous world,
Or who have planted in the heart's rich soil
One small grain of spiritual certitude.
Happiest who stand on faith as on a rock.
But I must pass leaving the ended search;
Truth's rounded outcome firm, immutable
And this harmonic building of world-fact,
This ordered knowledge of apparent things;
Here I can stay not, for I seek my soul.

Savitri brushes aside all the achievements of the world
of the mind in one sentence when she says that it is all
"ordered knowledge of apparent things". Science truly
is nothing but the ordered knowledge of apparent things.
This is so with regard to all branches of mind's activity.
Those who lived in this contented world of the mind were
greatly surprised at this reply of Savitri. While many
in this realm laughed and mocked at Savitri, there were
some who wondered with awe, and looked at Savitri, un-
believing that there could be one who could challenge
the assumptions of the mind. The poet says:

Another with mystic and unsatisfied eyes
Who loved his slain belief and mourned its death:
"Is there one left who seeks for a Beyond?
Can still the path be found, opened the gate?"

This one individual of the mind wanted to know
whether any path beyond the mind can be found? Will
the gate beyond the mind be opened? He thought Savitri was attempting the impossible. There are many in
the realm of the mind whose beliefs have been slain, and
yet hug to those beliefs, for, they know not where else
to go. The poet says:

So she fared on across her silent self.
To a road she came thronged with an ardent crowd
Who sped brilliant, fire-footed, sunlight-eyed

D.–15

Pressing to reach the world's mysterious wall
And pass through masked doorways into outer mind.

As she stepped out of the realm of the mind, she met a curious crowd. It consisted of those people who had escaped the watch of the conscious mind and belonged to the nether regions of mind's consciousness. But she met also those who aspired to go beyond the mind but were unable to find the way. They were dis-satisfied with the ways of the mind, but they did not know where to go. These were noble-minded people who found the answer of the mind unsatisfactory. These were the people who were desirous of helping humanity but did not know anything beyond the realms of the mind. They were longing to hasten so that they may save God's world. Full of noble sentiments, discontented with the ways of the mind but unable to go any further–these formed the crowd in which Savitri mingled. But as the poet says:

.... she reined back the high passion in her heart
She knew that first she must discover her soul.

Savitri too was full of passion to save the world, and would have returned with the ardent and noble crowd. But she realized that she could do nothing to save the earth unless she had first discovered her soul. The poet says:

Only who save themselves can others save.
In contrary sense she faced life's riddling truth;
They carrying the light to suffering men
Hurried with eager feet to the outer world;
Her eyes were turned towards the eternal source.

Savitri was moving in the contrary direction, for, while others were hurrying down to earth to save humanity, she was moving towards the eternal source. Of what use her returning to earth without the discovery of the soul? Savitri cried out and received an amazing answer which said:

O Savitri, from thy hidden soul we come.
O human copy and disguise of God
Who seekst the deity thou keepest hid
And livest by the Truth thou hast not known
Follow the world's winding highway to its source
There in the silence few have ever reached
Thou shalt see the Fire burning on the bare stone
And the deep cavern of thy secret soul.

And so Savitri moved on as she was directed, for, she must discover her soul if she is to face the challenge of Fate and Time on earth below. The poet says:

Then Savitri following the great winding road
Came where it dwindled into a narrow path,
Trod only by rare wounded pilgrim-feet.
There was no sound to break the brooding hush:
One felt the silent nearness of the soul.

And so Savitri moves on traversing the winding highway where it dwindles into a narrow path. This path has been trod only by rare pilgrims, for, from here begins the great ascent leading to the deep cavern of the secret soul. The poet says:

Here from a low and prone and listless ground
The passion of the first ascent began
A moon-bright face in a sombre cloud of hair,
A Woman sat in a pale lustrous robe.
A rugged and ragged soil was her bare seat
Beneath her feet a sharp and wounding stone.

Who was this Woman whom Savitri met just at the turn of the ascent? She was as it were pity incarnate; she looked like "a spirit touched by the grief of all that lives'. Describing her the poet says:

The Mother of the seven sorrows bore
The seven stabs that pierced her bleeding heart;
The beauty of sadness lingered on her face

Her eyes were dim with the ancient stain of tears.
Her heart was riven with the world's agony
An anguished music trailed in her rapt voice,
Absorbed in a deep compassion's ecstasy.

In search of her soul, Savitri first meets the Madonna of Suffering or Compassion. The poet says that there was beauty of sadness on her face—it was not her sadness, but the sadness of all that lives. He who nurses his own sadness can never shine with that beauty of sadness. If one looks at the images of the Buddha, one finds that there is sadness in his eyes. Such is indeed the Image of Christ. This Mother of Suffering and Compassion had her eyes dim with the ancient stain of tears. As Savitri approaches her, she says:

O Savitri, I am thy secret soul.
To share the suffering of the world I came;
I am the soul of all who wailing writhe
Under the ruthless harrow of the Gods.
I am woman, nurse and slave and beaten beast,
I tend the hands that gave me cruel blows,
I am the courted queen, the pampered doll,
I am in all that suffers and that cries.

This Woman of Suffering gives a healing balm to all that suffer and are afflicted. It is because of her presence that it becomes easier to bear the pangs of suffering. Her power to suffer and endure is endless. The Woman says to Savitri:

I have borne the calm indifference of Heaven,
Watched Nature's cruelty to suffering things
While God passed silent by nor turned to help.
Yet have I cried not out against his will,
Yet have I not accused his cosmic Law;
A patient prayer has risen from my breast:
I carry the fire that never can be quenched
And the compassion that supports the suns.

My God who never came to me till now:
His voice I hear that ever says "I come"
I know that one day he shall come at last.

earch of her soul when Savitri emerges from the
realm of the Mind, her first meeting is with this Madonna of Compassion, the Woman of Suffering. This is extremely suggestive. If Savitri aspires to save humanity
and show to men a new way, then she must first be filled
with great compassion. If her heart does not move with
the sufferings of humanity, and if she is not able to contain within herself the misery of all, then it would be
idle for her to think and dream about world's redemption.
How true this is for all who aspire to serve mankind!
As soon as the Woman of Suffering stopped, there arose
the voice of the Man of Sorrows. This man complained
against the suffering of men and yet unconsciously enjoyed his
suffering—in fact, he worshipped suffering. This Man says:

I am the Man of Sorrows, I am he
Who is nailed on the wide cross of the universe
To enjoy my agony God built the earth
My passion he has made his drama's theme.
I am the seeker who can never find,
I am the fighter who can never win,
I am the runner who never touched his goal,
I know my fate will ever be the same.

There are many who perversely hug their suffering.
They regard suffering as the stamp of spirituality. They
adore suffering, and in an unconscious manner want the
sympathy of others to be evoked for themselves. They
relish the sense of self-pity. The Man of Sorrows says:

I have loved but none has loved me since my birth;
There is a dull consent in my sluggish heart,
A fierce satisfaction with my special pangs
As if they made me taller than my kind

Only by suffering can I excel.
I suffer and toil and weep; I moan and hate.

Savitri saw that the Man of Sorrows had a mind that was closed against any change. He drew perverse delight in his own suffering, and so she made no reply to him but turned to the Woman of Suffering and Compassion. She said:

Madonna of suffering, Mother of grief divine
Thou art a portion of my soul put forth
To bear the unbearable sorrow of the world
But thine is the power to solace, not to save.
One day I will return, a bringer of strength
Thy love shall be the bond of human kind.
Compassion the bright king of Nature's acts;
Misery shall pass abolished from the earth
The world shall be freed from the anger of the Beast;
There shall be peace and joy for ever more.

Savitri then moved further on her upward route, where finer perfume breathed from slender trees. Here she saw a Woman in gold and purple sheen, armed with the trident and the thunderbolt with "her feet upon a couchant lion's back, a formidable smile curved round her lips". This was the Mother of Might, the Madonna of Strength. She spoke to Savitri thus:

O Savitri, I am thy secret soul
I have come down into the human world
I stand upon earth's paths of danger and grief
And help the unfortunate and save the doomed
My ear is leaned to the cry of the oppressed
I topple down the thrones of tyrant kings
I wear the face of Kali when I kill
I trample the corpses of the demon hordes.

Sri Aurobindo has described the work of Kali in most expressive terms in the entire passage dealing with the Madonna of Strength. The role of Kali is much misunder-

stood; she is considered fierce and fearsome. But she is
both Durga and Lakshmi, the goddess of the proud and
strong as also the goddess of the fair and fortunate. The
Mother of Might says that the seal of God is on her task
and she awaits the coming of God to meet the soul of
the world. Savitri has met and conversed with the Mother of Sympathy; now she meets the Mother of Strength.
To discover the soul is indeed to discover one's source
of sympathy as also one's source of strength. When the
Mother of Might had finished, then was heard the voice
of the Dwarf-titan. He believes that he is the claimant
to the throne of heaven. He represents the ego of this
great world of desire. Just as the Man of Sorrows was
concerned only with his own sorrow and not with that
of the world, the Dwarf-titan is also one who is immersed
in dwelling upon his own strength and his so-called
inalienable rights. Savitri heard him but replied not.
Instead she turned to the Madonna of Strength and said:

> Madonna of might, Mother of works and force,
> Thou art a portion of my soul put forth
> To help mankind and help the travail of Time;
> Thou hast given men strength, wisdom thou couldst
> > not give.
> One day I will return, a bringer of light,
> Then I will give to thee the mirror of God
> Thou shalt see self and world as by him they
> > are seen
> Reflected in the bright pool of thy soul.

To the Woman of Sorrow, Savitri said that she needed
strength; To the Woman of Might she said that she needed Wisdom. Saying this Savitri moves on ascending her
spirit's upward route. Here she saw:

> A Woman sat in clear and crystal light
> Heaven had unveiled its lustre in her eyes
> Her smile could persuade a dead lacerated heart
> To live again and feel the hands of calm.

This was the Woman of Light, the Madonna of Serenity. The face of this Woman was a bright sun and her feet were like moonbeams. In her floating voice was heard low music. She said to Savitri:

> O Savitri, I am thy secret soul
> I have come down to the wounded desolate earth
> To heal her pangs and lull her heart to rest,
> I am peace that steals into man's war-worn breast
> Amid the reign of Hell his acts create
> A hostel where Heaven's messengers can lodge,
> I am charity with the kindly hands that bless,
> I am silence mid the noisy tramp of life
> I bring back hope to the despairing heart
> I give peace to the humble and the great
> And shed my grace on the foolish and the wise.
> I shall save earth, if earth consents to be saved.
> Then Love shall at last unwounded tread earth's soil,
> Man's mind shall admit the sovereignty of Truth
> And body bear the immense descent of God.

When the Woman of Light had finished, then arose the voice of the Man of Knowledge, of the sense-shackled human mind. This man mistakes the knowledge of the mind as the wisdom of the soul. He knows the process but "that which moves all" is hidden from his view. About him the poet says:

> ....only reason and sense he feels as sure
> They only are his trusted witnesses.
> Thus is he baulked, his splendid effort vain;
> His knowledge scans bright pebbles on the shore
> Of the huge ocean of his ignorance.

This Man of knowledge says about himself:

> I am the all-discovering Thought of man,
> I am a god fettered by Matter and sense,
> I have mapped the heavens and analysed the stars,
> Described the orbits through the grooves of Space.
> Measured the miles that separate the suns

Computed their longevity in Time;
The Tree of evolution I have sketched,
Each branch and twig and leaf in its own place
I have detected plasm and cell and gene
The protozoa traced, man's ancestors
The humble originals from whom he rose;
I know how he was born and how he dies;
Only what end he serves I know not yet
I can foresee the acts of Matter's force
But not the march of the destiny of man.

This man of head-learning says that "his philoso-
phies are reasoned guess". For him all is a speculation
or a dream. He believes that man can never transmute
the very stuff of which he is made and therefore all concepts of man becoming divine are idle dreams. His was
head-learning devoid of soul-wisdom. Savitri heard him
but made no reply. She turned to the Madonna of Light, the Woman of Wisdom, and said:

Madonna of Light, Mother of joy and peace
Thou art a portion of my self put forth,
To raise the spirit to its forgotten heights,
And wake the soul by touches of the heavens;
But not by showering heaven's golden rain
Upon the intellect's hard and rocky soil
Can the tree of Paradise flower on earthly ground,
The mind of man will think it earth's own gleam.

Savitri says that the mere pouring in of the heaven's
rain on earth will not do, for, in the mind of man only
a bright shadow of God can come. The mind will never
know God directly; it deals with shadows and regards
them as substances. And so Savitri says to this Woman
of light:

His hunger for the eternal thou must nurse
And fill his yearning heart with heaven's fire
And bring God down into his body and life.

One day I shall return, His hands in mine
And thou shalt see the face of the Absolute;
Then shall the holy marriage be achieved,
Then shall the divine family be born,
There shall be light and peace in all the worlds.

And so Savitri in her upward journey, in search of
her soul, has met the Madonna of Sympathy, of Strength
and of Serenity. To each of them she has given an assurance that on her return she will show them what they
each need. Savitri has yet to move further, but she is
in possession of the secrets of Sympathy, of Strength and
of Serenity. These three she will need when she goes
down to help humanity. But she still needs something
without which Sympathy and Strength and Serenity would be of no avail. It is in search of this that she moves
on. The poet says:

Onward she passed seeking the soul's mystic cave:
At first she stepped into a night of God
In a simple purity of emptiness
Her mind knelt down before the unknowable.

CHAPTER XVIII

A POINT IN THE UNKNOWABLE

IN the vast Bhakti literature of India, which is rich both in content as well as variety, there has gone on an interminable discussion as to whether the worship of God with attributes is better or the worship of God without attributes. The first is known as Saguna and the latter as Nirguna. They are also Known as *Sākāra* and *Nirākāra*, meaning, with Form and without Form. Now from one standpoint this discussion is irrelevant because the Form and the Formless are not opposed to each other. Saguna and Nirguna are not the opposites. Can one say that Expression and Experience are opposed to each other? Are the Manifest and the Unmanifest opposed to each other? Is Creator opposed to his Creation? In fact, the Form becomes alive only when there is in it the touch of the Formless. Once again the Formless has no significance if it cannot express in Forms. It is true that no one form can ever contain the Formless in its completeness. And so there has to be form after form for the manifestation of the Formless. Even so, in the best and the noblest of forms, the Formless can be expressed only partially. The Formless is the Whole, while the Form is the Part. But surely there can be no opposition between the Whole and the Part. It may be that when the Form is not aligned to the Formless then the Form will have no livingness in it. In that case it will be just an Image but not a Symbol. It is said that life is in a state of constant flux. Why is it so? In this flux one sees the death and the rebirth of forms. Forms must die in order that the Formless may express itself in new forms. This constant death of forms is the flux of life. But to say that in this flux there is only the death of forms is to state a half-truth. The flux contains not merely the death of old forms but also the birth of new forms. Thus in life there is a mysterious co-existence of birth and death. Where this co-existence is not, there livingness of form ceases. The manifested universe can retain its livingness only in this rhythm of birth and death, where the Formless expresses itself in ever-changing forms.

In our story of Savitri we have come to that point where Savitri is asked to go in search of her Soul if she is to meet the challenge of Time and Fate. In this search, so far Savitri has met the expressions of the Soul, not Soul itself. She has met the Form but has not yet come to the discovery of the Formless. She has met the triple form of the Soul—Sympathy, Strength and Serenity. The three ·Madonnas are the three expressions of the Soul. That is why, while meeting these three, Savitri said: "Thou art a portion of my self put forth". They represent only a portion of herself. They do not represent the Wholeness that the soul is. She has yet to go in search of that Wholeness. Savitri has told each of the Madonnas that when she returns, she will complete their work which until then must remain incomplete. Now this Wholeness is not arrived at by putting the parts together. It is a movement in a different dimension altogether. From the Part to the Whole is not a movement in extension; it is indeed a movement in expansion. Savitri has to continue her journey, for, she must come to the experience of the Formless so that on her return she may impart to the Forms a new meaning. The poet says that as she moved on:

A sacred darkness brooded now within,
The world was a deep darkness great and nude
This blank felt more than all that Time has borne
This dark knew dumbly, immensely the Unknown
But all was Formless, voiceless, infinite.

Crossing a fathomless impersonal Night
Silent she moved, empty and absolute.

When one refers to the Formless, the difficulty is:
How to indicate it? Any description of the Formless is itself
a form. The Formless is like a mathematical point which has position but no magnitude. The Formless cannot
be described; it can only be experienced. And so this
state to which Savitri is moving is something that defies
description. And yet it has to be described. The experience of the Formless is a knowledge not by ideation but
by being. It is this which Savitri experienced in the region to which she had come. The poet says:

All this she saw and inly felt and knew
Not by some thought of mind but by the self
A light not born of sun or moon nor fire
A light that dwelt within and saw within
Shedding an intimate visibility
Made secrecy more revealing than the word
She felt herself made one with all she saw
A sealed identity within her woke
She knew herself the Beloved of the Supreme.

The soul can be known not by ideation but by direct experience. It is strange that we know ourselves today indirectly. We know ourselves only as images formed and projected by the Mind. To discover the soul is
to know ourselves directly, without any mediation of the
mind. Savitri must know herself directly if she is to meet
the challenge of Time. To know oneself is to discover
one's Timeless Being. And it is on this search that Savitri has gone. The poet says that in this state to which
Savitri had now come, she finds

In the last chamber on a golden seat
One sat whose shape no vision could define
Only one felt the world's unattainable fount
A Power of which she was a straying Force,

An invisible Beauty, goal of the world's desire
A Sun of which all knowledge is a beam
A Greatness without whom no life could be
Thence all departed into silent self
And all became Formless and pure and bare.

Savitri is now coming to the last point of her journey. It was when all became formless and pure and bare that through a tunnel dug in the last rock

She came out where there shone a deathless sun.
A house was there all made of flame and light
And crossing a wall of doorless living fire
There suddenly she met her secret soul.

The poet says that she suddenly met her secret soul. All spiritual realizations are sudden. One cannot meet one's secret soul with advance preparation. One comes upon it; one cannot go to it. Savitri crossed a wall of doorless living fire. There was no door through which one could go. But what is the nature of this secret soul whom Savitri suddenly saw and experienced? The poet says:

A being stood immortal in transience,
Deathless dallying with momentary things
The spirit's conscious representative
God's delegate in our humanity
Comrade of the universe, the Transcendent's ray
She had come into the mortal body's room
To play at ball with Time and Circumstance
All things she saw as a masquerade of Truth
Disguised in the costumes of Ignorance

Savitri saw the real nature of her secret soul. While deathless it was willing to dally with the momentary things. Her secret soul was there presentative of the Spirit, the Brahman of the Upanishads, and shared its nature. She was like a delegate of the Spirit sent to humanity, and as such it must put on the vestures required for the human race. The Spirit sends out its ray for illuminating the darkened paths of man, and it is this ray which indeed is the soul. The poet says:

> As a mother feels and shares her children's lives
> She puts forth a small portion of herself
> A being no bigger than the thumb of man
> Into a hidden region of the heart
> To face the pang and to forget the bliss
> To share the suffering and endure earth's wounds.

Here Sri Aurobindo evidently draws the simile of the soul found in the Kathopanishad where the soul is described as no larger than the thumb and seated in the heart of man. One of the most daring concepts found in the Vedanta philosophy is the qualitative identity between Brahman and Atman. The nature of Brahman resides in the Atman so say the Upanishads. The poet speaks of this identity which Savitri felt as she came to the close of her spiritual journey. The poet says:

> Here in this chamber of flame and light they met
> They looked upon each other, knew themselves
> The secret deity and its human part,
> The calm immortal and the struggling soul.
> Then with a magic transformation's speed
> They rushed into each other and grew one.

When the Spirit and the Soul realize their oneness then is the spiritual journey over, for, this is the moment of highest communion. From the bliss of communion one may return to earth to communicate the joys of this supreme oneness. And so the poet says:

> Once more she was human upon earthly soil
> In the muttering night amid the rain-swept woods
> And the rude cottage where she sat in trance
> But now the half-opened lotus bud of her heart
> Had bloomed and stood disclosed to the earthly ray
> There was no wall severing the soul and mind

No mystic fence guarding from the claims of life
In its deep lotus home her being sat
As if on concentration's marble seat
Calling the mighty Mother of the worlds
To make this earthly tenement her house.

Now in Savitri all underwent a high celestial change.
In this transformation every act of Savitri became an act
of God. The transformation was so complete that in the
person of Savitri "a firm ground was made for Heaven's
descending might". In this achievement, as the poet says:

A first perfection's stage is reached at last:
Out of the wood and stone of our nature's stuff
A temple is shaped where the high gods could live.

Man has indeed to create such a temple out of his
own life so that the high gods may live there, and create
conditions for man's ascent into the Divine. Man must
become an instrument of the Divine, and that indeed is
the meaning of creating a temple. If this is done then as
the poet says:

One man's perfection still can save the world.
There is won a new proximity to the skies,
A first betrothal of the Earth to Heaven,
A deep concordat between Truth and Life,
A Camp of God is pitched in human time.

Even if one human being creates out of his life a temple worthy for the high gods to live then he becomes a
living nucleus for the transformation of entire humanity.
One who has become an instrument works not merely with
his own strength; the strength of the Divine is added unto
him. In fact, he does not work, it is the Divine that works
through him, and that is why, as the poet says, "one man's
perfection still can save the world". Man, becoming an
instrument of the Divine, regains his lost significance. He
becomes intensely significant, capable of transforming the

entire human race, for, he is a "camp of God pitched in human time".

With this great discovery Savitri returns to her home. Physically she had been all the time in the hermitage, but now psychologically she returns to her family surroundings. However it is a different Savitri that has returned. The influence of inner perfection was felt around her. The poet says:

Although her kingdom of marvellous change within
Remained unspoken in her secret breast
All that lived round her felt its magic's charm,
The trees' rustling voices told it to the winds,
Flowers spoke in ardent hues and unknown joy,
The birds' carolling became a canticle,
The beasts forgot their strife and lived at ease;
Absorbed in wide communion with the Unseen,
The mild ascetics of the wood received
A sudden greatening of their lonely muse.

The entire creation rejoiced at the return of Savitri. Although Savitri had to keep her secret within herself, the trees and the flowers, the birds and the beasts could not contain themselves. They expressed their joy freely. The ascetics, too, felt a great change coming over their spiritual practices. Even though Savitri did not speak about her inner change, her acts of daily life proclaimed the joyous tidings. The poet says:

Even the smallest, meanest work became
A sweet or glad and glorious sacrament,
An offering to the self of the great world,
Or a service to the One in each and all.

For Savitri even Satyavan looked different. Above his head she saw not now Fate's dark and lethal orb. A greater intensity of love was felt by both in each other's company. Savitri had returned from the realms Divine but this had not made her ardour of love less intense. The poet tells us:

D.–16

Even in distance closer than her thoughts,
Body to body near, soul near to soul
Moving as if by a common breath and will
They were tied in the single circling of their days
Together by love's unseen atmosphere,
Inseparable like the earth and sky.

But still Savitri's trials were not yet over. Her first test of love came when Narada spoke about the dire fate. She had just returned from her second trial in which she had to journey into strange continents of her inner being in search of her soul. But on her return from this arduous journey, as she was sitting alone brooding over the inner joys of her realization, "an abyss yawned suddenly beneath her heart". Some unknown fear seized her, and there came to her "a denser darkness than the Night could bear". The poet says:

A voice to the dumb anguish of the heart
Conveyed a stark sense of unspoken words
In her own depths she heard the unuttered thought
That made unreal the world and all life meant
"Who art thou who claim'st thy crown of separate
birth
The illusion of thy soul's reality
And personal godhead on an ignorant globe
In the animal body of imperfect man?"

This is the voice of Death that Savitri hears in her moment of great joy just when she had returned from her triumphal journey. She is just settling down in her family surroundings after the elevating experience of soul-discovery. And Death speaks to her in a very stern voice. It says:

I have created all, all I devour
I am Death and the dark terrible Mother of life
I am Kali black and naked in the world
I am Maya and the universe is my cheat

I lay waste human happiness with my breath
O soul, inventor of man's thoughts and hopes
Thyself the invention of the moments' stream
Illusion's centre or subtle apex point
At last know thyself, from vain existence cease.

These were ·terrible words and they naturally shook
Savitri from the very depths of her being.

A barren silence weighed upon her heart
Her kingdom of delight was there no more.

But soon she heard the reassuring voice of heaven, "the
voice of Light after the voice of Night". But while this
Voice gave her an assurance, it warned her, and it was indeed a strange warning. The Voice told her of the great
danger to which she was exposed, and this was all due to
her own doing. The Voice said:

O Soul, bare not thy kingdom to the foe;
Consent to hide thy royalty of bliss,
Lest Time and Fate find out its avenues
And beat with thunderous knock upon thy gates,
Hide whilst thou canst thy treasure of separate self,
Fear not to be nothing that thou mayst be all;
Assent to the emptiness of the Supreme
That all in thee may reach its absolute:
Accept to be small and human on the earth.

Savitri must not regard her joy as her own. Let her not
establish her ownership over it. It is this sense of possession even over the joys that one has experienced that
opens out avenues for Time and Fate to walk in. Savitri
must forget the treasure of the separate self. She must become nothing, and willingly accept to be small. Not making the joys of heaven as her own, she must assent to the
emptiness of the Supreme. She must be divested even of
the experience of joy that she has had so that it does not
become her own. If she wishes to establish an ownership
on that experience of joy then she will soon be marked

out by the Forces of Darkness for their fierce attack.
Savitri is once again reminded here that she has come down
to help the struggling humanity. The feeling of joy with
which she is endowed is not for herself but for the entire
human race. And so even in the moments of personal
triumph she must not become oblivious of the sufferings
of men. She is told:

> Thou must bear the sorrow that thou claim'st to heal,
> The day-bringer must walk in darkest night.

If she wants the day-bringer to come, then there must
be all-pervading darkness of the night. Let her not break this
darkness with the joys of personal triumph. Besides, she
must know that she has to take the whole humanity with
her. If mankind feels that she is too far and too high, how
will it be able to reach her? The saviour of the world must
know that he remains within the reach of common humanity. The voice says:

> If far he walks above mortality's head
> How shall the mortal reach that too high path?
> If one of theirs they see scale heaven's peaks,
> Men then can hope to learn that titan climb;
> God must be born on earth and be as man,
> That man being human may grow even as God.

He who becomes a Saviour of man must reduce
himself to a state of nothingness. He must cease to be so
that God may live. Savitri was filled with a sense of intense
personal joy, and it was this that attracted the attention
of Death. The Lord of Time could not countenance such
a personal triumph, and so he came to humble her. The
Heavenly Voice tells Savitri:

> Banish all thought from thee and be God's void,
> Then shalt thou uncover the Unknowable,
> Consent to be nothing and none, dissolve Time's work;
> Cast off thy mind, step back from form and name;
> Annul thyself that only God may be.

She is told that she must dissolve Time's work. What indeed is meant by Time's work? The sense of ego, the acquired nature of man is Time's work. It is the product of Time. It must be dissolved, and in its dissolution there must take place the stepping back from form and name. Savitri must become nameless. She must know what existence can be without an identity. Savitri must annul herself so that God may be. It is interesting to note that she was not asked to annul herself when she was in the throes of suffering. It is in her moments of intense joy that she is asked to annul herself. Let joy remain, but the experiencer of the joy must vanish. The annulment of self in moments of suffering leaves behind a sense of frustration and of depletion of one's energies. But when the annulment of the enjoyer comes in the moment of joy, then there exists tremendous energy with which one can face the challenges of life. Renunciation not in the moment of sorrow but at the peak of joy—this is what the Heavenly Voice asks Savitri to understand. Surely this is a very hard trial —to annul oneself in the very moment of joy. But how is Savitri going to annul herself, how is she going to banish all thought and become God's void? The poet says:

> Thus spoke the mighty and uplifting Voice,
> And Savitri heard; she bowed her head and mused
> Plunging her deep regard into herself
> In her soul's privacy in the silent Night
> Aloof and standing back detached and calm
> A witness of the drama of herself
> A student of her own interior scene
> And heard in the crowded thoroughfares of mind
> The unceasing tread and passage of her thoughts
> All she allowed to rise that chose to stir
> All she beheld that surges from man's depths
> ....her gaze pursued the birth of thought.

Sri Aurobindo tells us that Savitri became aware of the entire stream of thought. She heard in the crowded

thoroughfares of mind the unceasing tread and passage
of her own thoughts. She allowed every thought to rise
which wanted to come up without suppressing it. In fact,
her gaze was fixed in order to find out the birth of thought.
She wanted to know from where did thought arise, how
did it arise, and why did it arise. It is only by thus observ-
ing the stream of thought that she could see the banish-
ment of all thoughts. Thus alone can she become God's
Void. The Voice significantly asks her to become God's
Void. Now God's Void demands a total negativity of consciousness. It is not to be mistaken for the passivity of consciousness. In a passive mind the thought may cease but
the thinker remains. In the negative state there is neither
the thought nor the thinker. And this alone is the annulment of self. The poet says:

> In that absolute stillness bare and formidable,
> There was glimpsed an all-negating Void
> There was no person there behind the act
> No mind that chose or passed the fitting word
> A pure perception was the only power
> That stood behind her action and her sight.

There was in this state a Void, a pure perception in
which there was neither the perceiver nor the perceived.
The whole world seemed a mere dream. The poet says, in
this Void, this Oneness which had no second,

> ....faced her as some vast Nought's immensity
> An endless No to all that seems to be,
> An endless Yes to things ever unconceived,
> And all that is unimagined and unthought,
> An eternal Zero or untotalled Aught
> A consciousness that saw without a seer
> The Truth where knowledge is not nor knower nor
> known.

The poet says that a "a formless liberation came on
her." She was no more a Person in a World; she had

escaped into infinity". The poet has entitled this Canto as "Nirvana and the Discovery of the All-negating Absolute". Savitri comes to this state as she moves into those inward conditions to which the Heavenly Voice had hinted. The poet says that she was now

> A vanishing vestige like a violet trace,
> A faint record merely of a self now past,
> She was a point in the unknowable,
> A memory of being still was there
> And kept her separate from nothingness;
> She was in That but still became not That.

The poet says that there was a memory of being but only just as a faint record of a self now past. This memory record has to be there, but it is a memory divested of all its psychological content. But why then should there remain a mere record of memory? Life presents us at all levels with the phenomenon of Discontinuity in the midst of Continuity. This faint record of memory supplies the base of continuity. But it is only a continuity of form, for, the content is new. Here the poet speaks of being in That but not becoming That. The identity is lost but not the individuality. The dew-drop slips into the sea, but in that there is a remarkable happening where the sea itself enters the dew-drop. Nirvana is not annihilation. One is reminded here of the words of Edwin Arnold in his *Light of Asia* wherein he says:

> If any teach Nirvana is to cease,
> Say unto such they lie;
> If any teach Nirvana is to live,
> Say unto such they err.

Nirvana is neither existence nor non-existence. It is a mystery that can be solved only by one who comes to the experience of Nirvana. Savitri had glimpses of this Nirvana. The poet says:

In infinite Nothingness was the ultimate sign
Or else the Real was the Unknowable.
A lonely Absolute negated all;
It effaced the ignorant world from its solitude
And drowned the soul in its everlasting peace.

The Unknown is not the Unknowable, for, in the infinite Nothingness is seen the ultimate sign. If this sign had not been there then the Real would have remained the Unknowable.

Savitri has come to the experience of the lonely Absolute which negated all. But it is only when all is negated that the affirmation of the Supreme comes. Savitri had come out triumphant in this second trial of hers, a trial in which she herself stands annulled so that only God may be.

CHAPTER XIX

ETERNITY LOOKED ON TIME

The Bhagavad Gita says that not even for one moment can man remain without performing action. To live is to act, and therefore action cannot be divorced from living. If that be the case then surely man must discover a right base for all his actions. It is action that is the cause of man's suffering, but since he cannot remain without performing action, it is necessary that he should find out a base from where he can act rightly. Such a base has been given by Hindu psychologists in a formula that is extremely simple and yet at the same time most profound. This formula has been repeated again and again by various thinkers in the field of Hindu psychology. It is given in the Upanishads, it is propounded in the Bhagavad Gita, and it is also to be found in the Yoga Sutras of Patanjali. The formula is *Abhyasa* and *Vairagya*, Practice and Dispassion. These two have to be together, not one after the other with a time interval. The idea of their co-existence is brought out in the Upanishads where the illustration of the Two Birds is given. The Two birds are sitting on the same tree and also on the same branch of the tree; they look exactly alike. Now one of them is eating the fruit of that tree, while the other is watching. To be a participant and yet at the same time to be a witness of one's action—this is the secret of this formula. In other words, it says that Action must be performed in the background of Inaction. This formula tells us that when any action emerges from the state of inner repose then that action can never be wrong. A repose gives depth to one's actions. In the background of repose; even ordinary actions show forth remarkable qualities of grace and dignity. In such repose the mind is completely quiet. In fact, repose is a condition where the thinker or the actor is absent. An action without an actor can never generate suffering for man. In this condition the individual is just an instrument in the hands of a greater entity. It is the presence of the actor that vitiates all actions. It is the actor that creates agitations in the mind. But when the mind is at rest, in a state of repose, then the actor is made inoperative. When this happens all actions become truly spiritual.

In the course of Savitri's second trial, she is asked to banish all thoughts from the mind so that she may become God's void. It is the annulment of herself that is demanded, for, it is only in that condition that she can face the challenge of Time and Fate. Savitri comes to this state of Void, of total Nothingness. But she continues to live in her home and is engaged in the normal activities of the household. One sees, however, a new quality in all that she does. But those who were round about her saw that she was doing the same things that she did before. They did not see any change. As the poet says:

Accustomed only to read outward signs,
None saw aught new in her, none divined her state,
They saw a person where was only God's vast
A still being or a mighty nothingness.

We always judge a person from outer signs, and therefore very often misjudge him. We think that a spiritual man is one whose patterns of behaviour must be different. If he too shows forth the same patterns then how is he different ? But the difference is not in the patterns of action but in the content of action. No one realized that Savitri had undergone a fundamental transformation within. But they saw her only from the outside and so—

To all she was the same perfect Savitri,
Life showed to all the same familiar face,
Her acts followed the old unaltered round,

She spoke the words that she was wont to speak
And did the things that she had always done.

It was only Savitri who knew what an inside revolution had taken place in her. She did the same things but she acted from a different base. The poet describes this base when he says:

A vacant consciousness watched from within
Empty of all but bare Reality;
An impersonal emptiness walked and spoke in her,
Her mortal ego perished in God's night.

And yet in spite of all this she had not lost her intensity of love. Her actions were the same, so was her speech. The only thing that had changed was the state of her mind. No more did she carry a ruffled consciousness; no more was her mind agitated. And no more did she feel that it was she who was going to meet the challenge of Death. A Power greater than she would deal with the problems of Time and Fate. She had surrendered herself to that Power. The poet says:

Her being a circle without circumference
There was no person there, no centred mind
There was no motion in this inner world
All was still and even infinity
In her the Unseen, the Unknown waited his hour.

The poet says there was in her consciousness no centred mind. Mind certainly was there, but it was a mind without a centre. We move about with centred minds, and a centred mind creates its own circumference. We are caught in this circumference and for ever are its slave. Savitri's consciousness was a circle without a circumference. This seems utterly paradoxical, perhaps meaningless. If there is no circumference then how can there be a circle at all? We know of a circle with a fixed centre, but if there could be a circle with its centre everywhere then surely there would be no circumference to such a circle. For Savitri, there was no fixed centre because there had taken place the annulment of the self. The centre of our life's circle is the self. But when that vanishes there is no fixed centre. Such an individual can make the whole creation as his centre. In other words, he can act from anywhere, needing no permanent or fixed centre. It is such a man without a fixed centre who alone can become an instrument of the Divine. He who has a fixed centre puts down a condition for the Divine to act; but a man without fixed centre lays down no conditions for the action of the Divine. The meaning of total surrender obviously lies in the elimination of all fixed centres of consciousness. The poet says:

> ....now she sat by sleeping Satyavan
> Awake within, and the enormous Night
> Surrounded her with the Unknowable's vast.

It was while she was sitting by the side of Satyavan that she saw a vision. In this all negations were negated and she experienced the positive nature of Reality itself. The positive experience can come only in the ground of the negative. Savitri had gone through the experience of total negativity, and so she was vouchsafed a vision of the Positive Reality. But this vision demands that one strays not from the negative ground. In this vision,

> ....all now became
> An evidence of one stupendous truth,
> A Truth in which negation had no place,
> A stark and absolute Reality
> All had a substance of Eternity
> ....it was Timelessness and Time
> It was the Bliss of formlessness and form
> She passed beyond Time into eternity
> Slipped out of space and became the Infinite,
> Her spirit saw the world as living God
> It saw the One and knew that all was He.

What can be the experience of the Positive in the ground of the Negative is described by the poet in words that are incomparable. So far he had talked of Savitri's transformation in terms of the negative; now he speaks of the experience of the Positive. But in this Positive, it is not she who stands. She still supplies the negative ground, but the Positive appears there in all its glory. Savitri realizes that there are in this Vision not two but One. In the experience of negativity, she the **dew-drop** had slipped into the sea; but in this positive experience she finds that the sea itself has entered the **dew-drop**. The dew-drop and the sea are not two, but have merged into One. She is the sea; for where is the Sea other than herself? Savitri has come to the highest spiritual experience. As the poet says:

> She was thought and the passion of the world's heart,
> She was the godhead hid in the heart of man,
> She was the climbing of his soul to God;
> The cosmos flowered in her, she was its bed
> She was Time and the dreams of God in Time;
> She was Space and the wideness of his days;
> From this she rose where Time and Space were not,
> Infinity was her movement's natural space
> Eternity looked out from her on Time.

But for coming to this positive spiritual experience, Savitri had to pay a great price. And the price was her complete annulment. If the **dew-drop** is afraid to slip into the sea then it can never have the positive experience of the Sea entering its very being. Now the great sea of life had entered the being of Savitri. Let the challenge of Time and Fate come. Savitri is now ready to look Death in the face.

CHAPTER XX

A SILENCE WITHOUT FORM OR NAME

It was indeed an astounding feat of creative genius on the part of Sri Aurobindo when he portrayed the character of Savitri in his monumental epic. Even in the moments of her great Divine attainments, the poet has not allowed her to forget her human affinities. There is a divine afflatus in her, and yet it is not the fire that burns; rather it is the fire that gives warmth. If the person of divine attainments forgets his relationship with man, then of what use is that experience of Nirvana? But Nirvana cannot be negated by one who has never climbed the heights of spiritual experience. The Buddha gave up Nirvana not while sitting in his palace as Siddhartha, the Prince. He went up the steep climb of spiritual experience and knew for himself what the Bliss of Nirvana was. The man who says that for him it is the service of the human race that matters, not the joys of Nirvana, speaks from a state of spiritual inertia. Let him climb up and see for himself what Nirvana is. It is easy to give up the bliss of Nirvana without knowing what it is. To know and yet not to enter its gates, unless he has brought the whole human race with him, is what constitutes the Great Renunciation of the Buddha. To know the heights of spiritual life and yet to be able to probe the depths of human suffering, it is this which alone can save humanity. In the characterisation of Savitri we see the co-existence of these seemingly contradictory poles. She has climbed the stupendous heights of spiritual life and yet has not broken her contact with the lowest of the human race. Having known for herself the Immortality of the Spirit, she is willing to cross swords with the Lord of Death himself,

not for her sake but for the sake of the human race. The
Divine and the Human are like light and shade in the
beautiful character of Savitri. She is perfectly at home
with the Divine, and she is equally at home with the
Human. She knows the Bliss of Nirvana but she also
knows the pangs of suffering. In Savitri we see a new quality of spiritual life, for, she negates neither the Spirit nor
the World. She is indeed a bridge between Heaven and
Earth.

But for fulfilling her great mission she must face another trial of her life. It is a trial for her because while she
is Divine, she is at the same time intensely human. The
trial comes on the fateful Dawn. The poet says:

> Now it was here in this great golden dawn,
> By her still sleeping husband lain she gazed
> Into her past as one about to die
> Looks back upon the sunlit fields of life
> Where he too ran and sported with the rest.
> All she had been and done she lived again.
> The whole year in a swift and eddying race
> Of memories swept through her and fled away
> Into the irrecoverable past.

Savitri's mind was crowded with innumerable memories
of the past one year. The poet says that the year fled away
into the irrecoverable past. On that fateful morning,
Savitri woke up early, and soon finished her normal household work. She bowed down to the great goddess "simply
carved by Satyavan on a forest stone". Then she came to
the pale queen, her mother-in-law. She had gone to her
with a request. Her problem was how to word her request. The poet says:

> She spoke but with guarded lips and tranquil face
> Lest some stray word or some betraying look
> Should let pass into the mother's unknowing breast,
> Slaying all happiness and need to live,

A dire foreknowledge of the grief to come.
Only the needed utterance passage found:
All else she pressed back into her anguished heart
And forced upon her speech an outward peace:

What an inner conflict Savitri must have felt on that
fateful **dawn**! And yet she was so considerate. Not even a
stray word or a betraying look must pass out from her lest
the mother get some inkling of what was going to happen.
She did not even suggest remotely that something dire
was to occur, for, that would slay all her happiness and her
need to live too may vanish. And so with utmost hesitancy
and with tremendous considerateness, Savitri placed her
request before the mother. She said:

One year that I have lived with Satyavan
Here on the emerald edge of the vast woods,
In the iron ring of the enormous peaks
Under the blue rifts of the forest sky,
I have not gone into the silences
Of this great woodland that enringed my thoughts
With mystery, nor in its green miracles
Wandered, but this small clearing was my world.
Now has a strong desire seized all my heart
To go with Satyavan holding his hand
Into the life he has loved and touch
Herbs he has trod and know the forest flowers
And hear at ease the birds and the scurrying life
That starts and ceases, rich far rustle of boughs
And all the mystic whispering of the woods.
Release me now and let my heart have rest.

Savitri puts her request in such a manner that the
mother would not have even a remote inkling that something was amiss. She says that during the whole year she
has not even once entered those spots where Satyavan
has been spending all his days. She would like to see
those spots and touch those things which he has touched.
Her request was made in a very natural manner. Besides,

Savitri had so endeared herself to all that this simple request would be granted by the mother with utmost willingness. The mother replies:

....do as thy wise mind desires,
O calm child-sovereign with the eyes that rule.
I hold thee for a strong goddess who has come
Pitying our barren days; so dost thou serve
Even as a slave might, yet art thou beyond
All that thou doest, all our minds conceive,
Like the strong sun that serves earth from above.

And so they went together for the first time into the silence and the beauty of the woods. The poet says:

Then the doomed husband and the woman who knew
Went with linked hands into that solemn world
Where beauty and grandeur and unspoken dream,
Where Nature's mystic silence could be felt
Communing with the secrecy of God.

The doomed husband and the woman who knew walked hand in hand looking at the beauties of nature. The poem says that beside her Satyavan walked full of joy because she moved with him through the green haunts. Satyavan must have felt overjoyed, for, this was the first day when they were walking together and moving into those spots where he had worked all alone these many days. Satyavan with great enthusiasm showed to Savitri all that he knew about the forest trees and flowers, of the birds and their singing, of the thick clinging creepers, red and green. He spoke of all the things he loved. He pointed out to the birds crying to their beloveds and receiving replies from distant boughs. He showed to her everything, even the smallest thing with which he was associated in the forest. The poet says:

....Deeply she listened, but to hear
The voice that soon would cease from tender words
And treasure its sweet cadences beloved

D.17

For lonely memory when none by her walked
And the beloved voice could speak no more.
Of death, not life she thought or life's lone end.
Sometimes her eyes looked round as if their orbs
Might see the dim and dreadful god's approach.

While they were walking and while Savitri was in a
deeply reflective mood, Satyavan stopped as he wanted to
finish his usual work as soon as possible. After the normal
work done, he and Savitri would move about in the forest,
just aimlessly walk and drink the beauty of the forest or
sit somewhere and talk and look into each other's eyes.
The poet says:

Wordless but near she watched, no turn to lose
Of the bright face and body which she loved.

Savitri did not want to miss anything. She wished
to look at the face and the body of Satyavan from every
side. She watched him turn his body to look at something. But she was interested in him, and so watched him
watching other things. For, as the poet says:

Her life was now in seconds, not in hours,
And every moment she economised
Like a pale merchant leaned above his store,
The miser of his poor remaining gold.

Savitri economised on every moment. She wanted to
extract as much as a moment could give, and even more.
She was like a merchant whose store had become deplet-
ed, and so make the most of what remained. To Savitri
every moment, nay, even fraction of a moment was precious. She could not fritter it away, for, there were not
many moments that were now given to her. She knew
what would happen and that too soon. But Satyavan was
completely oblivious of what was going on in Savitri's
mind. For, as the poet says:

But Satyavan wielded a joyous axe.
He sang high snatches of a sage's chant

That pealed of conquered death and demons slain,
And sometimes paused to cry to her sweet speech
Of love and mockery tenderer than love.

Satyavan was in gay mood, for Savitri was with him
and watching him. He sang and joked and wielded his
axe to cut wood as was his wont. While doing the work
he spoke and sang. And Savitri,

....like a pantheress leaped upon his words
And carried them into her cavern heart.

She seized upon each word in order that it may be
stored in her memory. Satyavan will be soon gone, and all
that will remain for her will be the storehouse of memory.
She must fill it up as fast as she can. And so she did not
allow even a single word of Satyavan to fly away anywhere.
Like a pantheress she leaped upon every word, for, this was
more precious than even gold. But suddenly Satyavan
felt unwell. The poet says:

But as he worked, his doom upon him came.
The violent and hungry hounds of pain
Travelled through his body biting as they passed.

He was suddenly seized with excruciating pain. A
severe attack came but the violent seizure for the time
being left.

Reborn to strength and happy ease he stood,
Rejoicing and resumed his confident toil
But with less seeing strokes.

Somehow Satyavan was feeling a weakness in his body.
He had recovered from the earlier attack of pain, but even
then his strength seemed to be ebbing out. There was
not that force in the use of his axe as was visible earlier.
For, as the poet says:

....Now the great Woodsman
Hewed at him and his labour ceased: lifting

His arm he flung away the poignant axe
Far from him like an instrument of pain.
She came to him in silent anguish and clasped,
And he cried to her, "Savitri, a pang
Cleaves through my head and breast as if the axe
Were piercing it and not the living branch.
Such agony rends me as the tree must feel
When it is sundered and must lose its life.
Awhile let me lay my head upon thy lap
And guard me with thy hands from evil fate:
Perhaps because thou touchest, death may pass"

Then Savitri sat down, away from the tree which Satyavan was felling. She wanted to be far from the hurt tree which Satyavan had cleaved with his axe. With Satyavan lying in her lap,

She guarded him in her bosom and strove to soothe
His anguished brow and body with her hands.

Savitri was completely calm, free from all fear. She knew that the hour had struck and that the doomed moment was fast approaching. But she was ready to meet the challenge of Death. She will meet him, come what may. The poet says:

Griefless and strong she waited like the gods.
But now his sweet familiar hue was changed
Into a tarnished greyness and his eyes
Dimmed over, forsaken of the clear light she loved.
He cried out in a clinging last despair,
"Savitri, Savitri, O Savitri,
Lean down, my soul, and kiss me while I die"

Savitri is all alone, and the heavy footsteps of death are near, very near. Satyavan's life is fast ebbing out. He cries out in a clinging last despair. He still hoped that perhaps if Savitri kissed him, the death could be warded off. The poet says:

And even as her pallid lips pressed his,
His failed, losing last sweetness of response;
His cheek pressed down her golden arm. She sought
His mouth still with her living mouth, as if
She could persuade his soul back with her kiss.

But Savitri soon realized what had happened. The
dreaded footsteps were heard, for he had come to snatch
Satyavan away. Savitri

....grew aware they were no more alone.
Something had come there conscious, vast and dire.
Near her she felt a silent shade immense
Chilling the noon with darkness for its back.
An awful hush had fallen upon the place:
There was no cry of birds, no voice of beasts.
A terror and an anguish filled the world.

Savitri soon felt that she was not just with Satyavan.
Some one had come and intervened in their privacy. This
"some one" had cast an immense shadow making even the
fierce noon dark and chilly. His presence had made entire
Nature silent with awe and fear. Even the birds and the
beasts, the trees and flowers, felt that something ominous
was happening. They felt that some cruel giant had come
and broken up the play of the two lovers. The poet says:

As if from a Silence without form or name
The Shadow of a remote uncaring god
Doomed to his Nought the illusory universe.

Suddenly the Shadow seemed to grow. It was the
shadow of an uncaring god, one that was remote from the
feelings and the joys of humanity. It looked as if this entire
illusory universe was doomed to nothingness under his
powerful spell. Savitri saw the Shadow growing into immense proportions and rendering everything dark under its
influence. The bright noon was changed into a dark night
due to the presence of this Dark God. Savitri realized that
he had come, he who was threatening to come all the time.

The fateful dawn was indeed the herald of the arrival of the Doom. Savitri was calm and composed. The poet says:

> She knew that visible Death was standing there
> And Satyavan had passed from her embrace.

Satyavan had passed on from her hands into the cruel grip of Death. In that silent forest she and Death were face to face with each other with Satyavan lying cold and helpless. Will not Savitri break down, will she not entreat death, will she not pray to him for the return of one whom she loves and without whom her life seems dry and barren? The poet says:

> So was she left alone in the huge wood,
> Surrounded by a dim unthinking world,
> Her husband's corpse on her forsaken breast.
> She measured not her loss with helpless thoughts,
> Nor rent with tears the marble seals of pain:
> She rose not yet to face the dreadful god.
> Over the body she loved her soul leaned out
> In a great stillness without stir or voice,
> As if her mind had died with Satyavan.
> But still the human heart in her beat on.
> Aware still of his being near to hers,
> Closely she clasped to her the mute lifeless form
> As though to guard the oneness they had been
> And keep the spirit still within the frame.

CHAPTER XXI

THE COLLAPSE OF SPACE

Life is not a problem to be solved, it is a mystery to be unravelled. But such is this mystery that it has to be unravelled constantly, from moment to moment. One cannot unravel the mystery of life once for all, for, the moment one unravelling is done, there arises a fresh mystery. The joy and the romance of life consists in this constant unravelling, for, thus alone is one faced with a never-ceasing spectacle of awe and wonder. But the mystery of life becomes all the more mysterious due to the phenomenon of Death. The mystery of life can be comprehended only in the context of Death. But man, in his ignorance, isolates death from the act of living, and with such isolation makes death into something terribly frightening. In fact, by regarding death as opposed to living, he has made both life as well as death into complex problems. The mind of man breaks up everything into two conflicting opposites. It has made life and death as two opposites of existence. In such context of opposites, man regards life as the negation of death, and death as the negation of life. But the fact of the matter is that life and death co-exist, and can never be separated. It is in their co-existence that both life and death become meaningful. It is death that gives meaning to life, and also in true act of living death abides from moment to moment. But when the two are broken up into conflicting opposites, then the shadow of death seems to intervene the very act of living. Life fulfils itself only in death, and without death the act of living must remain a mere stagnant existence. Death is a discontinuity existing in the midst of continuity which obviously is the process of living. And the meaning of life as well as death can

263

be found only when one comprehends discontinuity in the midst of continuity. But having separated death from life, man is afraid of the phenomenon of death. He sees in death the end of all existence. It is this fear that prevents him from looking at death. He who does not know death in the very act of living must for ever remain a stranger to death. For him death is a negation of living and therefore a happening to be feared. And so man has never looked death in the face. He has covered up this fear by subterfuges of a diverse nature. After all, a belief in life after death can never explain the mystery of death; nor can reincarnation tell one the secret of the mysterious phenomenon known as death. Death is its own explanation, and therefore it can never be explained by anything else. For this, one has to listen to death as it unveils its mystery. As Yama tells Nachiketa in the Kathopanishad—he who does not know death while living returns again and again from death, empty handed. Since in the very act of living abide moments of death, one must know the mystery of death in the process of living itself. Only such a man knows how to live completely, needing no future for the fulfilment of the psychologically unfulfilled past. For him there is no unfulfilled experience and therefore finds death as the refreshing moment of living itself.

In Kathopanishad, we find Nachiketa, while alive, going to the palace of Death. In Sri Aurobindo's Savitri, it is Savitri who walks with Death and enters those regions which Death has declared as out-of-bounds for the mortal man. The purpose of Nachiketa's enquiry is limited, for, he wants to know the secret of Death. Savitri's objective is much wider, for, she wants to vanquish death in his own region. Death can be vanquished only in its own region and nowhere else. And without vanquishing Death, how can man know his immortality? Savitri had come down with a mission, and that was to see that the Mortal puts on Immortality. But for this, Death must be vanquished so that it casts no spell of fear in man's act of living. To

break the spell of death was the mission with which
Savitri had come down. If death is to cast no spell on man
then man must look death straight in the face. And this
is what Savitri does when she finds that Death had come
to take Satyavan away. The Lord of Death came slowly,
but as He came nearer and nearer a huge shadow was
cast, transforming the scorching heat of the noon into
freezing chill of the night. Even when Death came close
by Savitri did not get up immediately. Instead, she clasped
the dead body of Satyavan and pressed it against her
bosom. And then gently she lay down the body of her
husband and got up completely calm and unruffled. The
poet says:

> Then suddenly there came on her the change
> Which in tremendous moments of our lives
> Can overtake sometimes the human soul
> And hold it up towards its luminous source.
> The veil is torn, the thinker is no more:
> Only the spirit sees and all is known.

How does one face the fact of life? How did Savitri
face the unalterable fact of Death? The poet tells us that
only when the thinker was no more that she could look at
Death in the face. One can look at the facts of life only
when, in the midst of looking, neither the thinker
nor the thought intervenes. When the thinker and the
thought enter, then the facts of life can never be seen.
The thinker sees only its own projections of thought; the
perceiver sees only the perceived. One can look at things
as they are only when the act of perception is free from
the touch of the thinker and the thought. As long as the
thinker and the thought remain, so long the perception
is veiled. Right perception demands that the veil of projection be torn. The poet says in the above lines: "The
veil is torn, the thinker is no more". If thought had entered then Savitri could not have looked Death in the face.
It is the thinker, through the projections of its thoughts,

that distracts. The poet says that when the thinker is no more then "Only the spirit sees and all is known". As Savitri rose quietly, laying gently the body of Satyavan, there came a change, a tremendous and a sudden change. What was the nature of this change? It was a change where the thinker was no more and therefore Savitri could look at Death without any quiver. Savitri faced Death not merely with her own strength, but when the thinker was no more there entered into her being strength more potent than what she could command. The poet says:

> The passionate instrument of an unmoved Power.
> A Presence was there that filled the listening world,
> A central All assumed her boundless life,
> A sovereignty, a silence and swiftness
> One brooded over abysses who was she.
> A force descended trailing endless lights;
> Linking Time's seconds to Infinity
> A halo of Wisdom's lightnings for its crown
> It entered the mystic lotus in her head,
> A thousand-petalied home of power and light.
> Immortal leader of her mortality,
> Doer of her works and fountain of her words,
> Invulnerable by Time, omnipotent,
> It stood above her calm, immobile, mute.

When the thinker was no more, then there came into existence enormous space in the virgin-pure consciousness of Savitri. Into this space entered Power greater than what Savitri could call from within her own resources. This Power stood above her, calm, immobile, mute. It has been the experience of all saints and mystics that in moments of dire necessity, power enters their being from somewhere, enabling them to do things which they by their own strength would never have been able to achieve. It is this which are described as miracles in the lives of the truly spiritual. It is given to all to see such miracles in their lives—but the condition is that the doer and the thinker must be no more. In the above lines the poet says that it was this Power which was the "doer of her works and fountain of her words". Having being en- dowed with this strength, invulnerable by Time, ' Savitri was now ready to cross swords with the Lord of Death himself. This was the supreme moment in the life of Savitri, the moment about which the poet says:

> All in her mated with that mighty hour,
> As if the last remnant had been slain by Death
> Of the humanity that once was hers.

It is the unveiled perception of Death that has worked this great miracle in which even the last remnant of Savitri's humanity was slain, so that she had come into her true Divine estate. We never allow the fact to operate upon us. We in our pride and arrogance believe that we could alter the unalterable facts. The effort of man is puny. If only he would allow the facts of life to operate, instead of he operating on the facts, then tremendous energies from within himself will be released enabling great changes to take place without he being the doer and the thinker. To allow the facts of life to operate is to experience a supreme moment of Surrender. And surrender is the secret of the great miracle of life. In Savitri such a miracle had taken place when the last remnant of humanity was slain. But though paradoxical it may seem, Savitri showed un- surpassed beauty of humanity even when the last rem- nant of humanity was being slain in her. The poet says:

> A moment yet she lingered motionless
> And looked down on the dead man at her feet;
> Then like a tree recovering from a wind
> She raised her noble head; fronting her gaze.

Even when Savitri rose to confront Death, she had a lingering look at the body of Satyavan who was lying dead at her feet. It is in this lingering look that we see Savitri still intensely human even at that hour when the last remnant of humanity was to drop away from her being. After this lingering look she recovered like a tree that recovers from the storm in which it may have been caught. In the violent breeze the tree bends and it appears as if the raging storm would uproot the tree, but soon the tree recovers and assumes its majestic stature. In the same manner, even though the strong breeze of human emotions raged, Savitri recovered her true stature. She raised her noble head and saw Death straight in the face. And what was the face of Death that Savitri saw? The poet says:

> Something stood there, unearthly, sombre, grand,
> A limitless denial of all being
> That wore the terror and wonder of a shape
> In its appalling eyes the tenebrous Form
> Bore the deep pity of destroying gods.
> A sorrowful irony curved the dreadful lips
> That speak the word of doom.
> His shape was nothingness made real . . . .

The poet describes Death as the "limitless denial of all being". In the Kathopanishad, Nachiketa calls Yama as *Antaka*, one who brings everything to an end. No more apt description of Death could there be than what the poet has stated in the above lines—"nothingness made real". The two—Savitri and Death—met and faced each other. The poet says:

> The two opposed each other with their eyes,
> Woman and universal god: around her,
> Piling their void unbearable loneliness
> Upon her mighty unaccompanied soul,
> Many inhuman solitudes came close
> Vacant eternities forbidding hope
> Laid upon her their huge and lifeless look
> And to her ears silencing earthly sounds,
> A sad and formidable voice arose.

To look into the face of Death is to enter into the depths of utter loneliness. Savitri stood all alone, facing this limitless denial of all being. No human voice could be heard in that inhuman solitude. Who would come near this unearthly sombre form of Death? No human being had dared to look Death in the face. To Death, too, this was a strange experience that a Woman should confront him and challenge his presence. And so he spoke to Savitri in a stern and commanding voice. He said:

Unclasp
Thy passionate influence and relax, O slave
Of Nature, changing tool of changeless Law,
Who vainly writhst rebellious to my yoke,
Thy elemental grasp; weep and forget.
Entomb thy passion in its living grave
Leave now the once-loved spirit's abandoned robe
Pass lonely back to thy vain life on earth.

But Savitri remained unmoved. These stern words of Death made no impression on her. She kept Satyavan under her clasp as if the words of Death meant nothing to her. And so Death spoke again, and said:

Wilt thou for ever keep thy passionate hold,
Thyself, a creature doomed like him to pass
Denying his soul death's calm and silent rest?
Relax thy grasp; this body is earth's and thine
His spirit now belongs to a greater power.
Woman, thy husband suffers.

With these words Savitri, as it were, woke up from her dazed condition and looked around. It appeared that now for the first time she listened to the words of Death, displaying only sternness of power devoid of tender feelings. And so realizing what Death wanted, she:

Drew back her heart's force that clasped his body still
Where from her lap renounced on the smooth grass
Softly it lay, as often before in sleep

When from their couch she rose in the white dawn
Called by her daily tasks: now too as if called
She rose and stood gathered in lonely strength,
Like one who drops his mantle for a race
And waits the signal, motionlessly swift.

Savitri left her hold on Satyavan's body. She had herself
put his body softly on the grass from her lap where Satyavan had been lying during his last moments. Savitri rose
as she used to rise everyday early morning leaving Satyavan lying on his bed. She had to get up so as to attend to
her daily tasks. Here, too, when she heard the voice of
Death, she rose as if ready to take up her work, whatever
it may be. She dropped her mantle in readiness for the
race in which she will soon enter. She was waiting for
the signal so that the race may start. And her preparedness
for the race has been beautifully described when the
poet says she was "motionlessly swift" so that she would
waste no time when the signal for the race comes. In
spiritual life one has indeed to be motionlessly swift. It
shows remarkable awareness born of intense sensitivity
so that no signal of life, not even the faintest, is missed.
Savitri is going on a great spiritual adventure where it is
essential that she should be aware of even the faintest signal
of life, of almost the inaudible whisper of the soul. When
Savitri released her hold on the body of Satyavan, then,
as the poet says:

> . . . . Death, the king, leaned boundless down, as leans
> Night over tired lands when evening pales
> And fading gleams break down the horizon's walls,
> Nor yet the dusk grows mystic with the moon.

The night leaning over the pale evening—it is thus that
Death leaned over the spot where Satyavan was lying.
And surely Death comes only in that interval of discontinuity. In that interval of discontinuity Death leaned over
the body of Satyavan. Until then Death had not actually
touched Satyavan. When Savitri gave up the hold on

Satyavan, realizing that she could do no further, that Death touched Satyavan. It is only now that Savitri comprehends for the first time what Death can mean. The real experience of the presence of death comes to Savitri only in this moment of the interval. As long as she was clasping the body so long there was as it were the continuity of the day with evening becoming paler and paler. But when she left her hold then did metaphorically the night swoop down even before the dusk could grow mystic with the appearance of the moon.

As Death leaned and touched the body of Satyavan, Savitri saw that "another luminous Satyavan arose" forsaking the poor mould of dead clay. She saw that he was standing between her and Death. The poet says:

> Luminous he moved away; behind him Death
> Went slowly with his noiseless tread, as seen
> In dream-built fields a shadowy herdsman glides
> Behind some wanderer from his voiceless herds,
> And Savitri moved behind eternal Death,
> Her mortal pace was equalled with the god's.
> Wordless she travelled in her lover's steps,
> Planting her human feet where his had trod,
> Into the perilous silences beyond.

Satyavan followed by Death, and Savitri following the eternal Death—this was the procession that moved into the silences beyond. The poet says that the tread of Death was noiseless. He always comes noiselessly taking people unawares. In this movement of the Three, great issues were involved. The main question was: Who will finally claim Satyavan—Death or Savitri? It is to settle this issue that Savitri moves on following Death into lands strange to her but over which the Lord of Death ruled with unquestioned authority. It was a strange experience to Savitri, for, she was moving into regions with which she was unfamiliar. While Death was moving into lands

familiar to him, to Savitri it was something utterly strange.
The poet says:

> Across some boundary's intangible bar,
> The silent god grew mighty and remote
> In other spaces and the soul she loved
> Lost its consenting nearness to her life.
> Into a deep and unfamiliar air
> Enormous, windless, without stir or sound,
> They seemed to enlarge away. . . .

Such was the unfamiliar ground on which Savitri was
moving that somehow she felt that she was losing her grasp.
The poet says that "Thought, time and death were absent
from her grasp". She was moving on, on the violent ocean
of will where lived

> Her aim, joy, origin, Satyavan alone.
> Her sovereign prisoned in her being's core
> A treasure saved from the collapse of space.

While the whole space was collapsing, Satyavan was
the only treasure which Savitri had saved. And it was to
guard that treasure, in the midst of the collapse of space,
that she was moving, not knowing where Death was
leading her. The poet says:

> Around him nameless, infinite she surged,
> Her spirit fulfilled in his spirit, rich with all Time,
> As if Love's deathless moment had been found,
> A pearl within eternity's white shell.

The Three moved on into weird lands. Savitri was
wondering whether Death would escape with Satyavan
leaving her alone. And so she kept pace with the other two
lest they escape where no traces of their movement could
be found. On their journey they came to a point beyond
which any movement by a mortal would be regarded as a
trespass by the Lord of Death. At that point Satyavan looked at Savitri feeling that they had come to a place where

he and Savitri must part for ever as Savitri would be forbidden to move further. Seeing Satyavan looking meaningfully at Savitri, Death cried out to Savitri:

> O mortal, turn back to thy transient kind;
> Aspire not to accompany Death to his home,
> As if thy breath could live where Time must die.
> Only in human limits man lives safe.
> Impermanent creatures, sorrowful foam of Time,
> Your transient loves bind not the eternal gods.

What will Savitri do? Must she go back to the lonely existence in the hermitage? Will she enter the forbidden zone? Will she trespass into the territory declared out-of-bounds by Death? The above words of Death were harsh and merciless. But to these words Savitri gave no reply. The poet says:

> The Woman answered not....
> Stood up in its sheer will a primal force.
> Still like a statue on its pedestal,
> Lone in the silence and to vastness bared,
> Against midnight's dumb abysses piled in front,
> A columned shaft of fire and light she rose.

Death did not know of what metal Savitri was made. As against the harsh and cruel words of Death, Savitri stood still like a statue on pedestal, and rose like a column of fire and light. The Three travellers were standing on the dreadful edge of night. The poet says:

> Awhile on the chill dreadful edge of Night
> All stood as if a world were doomed to die
> And waited on the eternal silence' brink.
> As thoughts stand mute on a despairing verge
> Where the last depths plunge into nothingness
> And the last dreams must end, they paused. . . .

The three travellers had come to the brink of silence where thoughts stand mute on a despairing verge. There

D.-18

was utter nothingness in front of them. Death must have
thought that at least at this point Savitri out of fear would
retreat. But all hopes of Death were dashed to the
ground, for, as the poet says:

> The Woman first affronted the Abyss
> Daring to journey through the eternal Night.
> Armoured with light she advanced her foot to plunge
> Into the dread and hueless vacancy;
> Immortal, unappalled her spirit faced
> The danger of the ruthless eyeless waste.

The poet says that the Woman first affronted the
abyss. The use of the word "affront" is most significant.
Death must have regarded the action of Savitri as a great
affront to his authority. How could she dare to enter his
kingdom? If she was the first to put her foot on that soil
of ruthless and eyeless waste, then surely she had hurled
an insult at Death and his supreme authority. The poet
describes this land where Savitri had set her foot in the
following lines:

> In the smothering stress of this stupendous Nought
> Mind could not think, breath could not breathe,
>   the soul
> Could not remember or feel itself; it seemed
> A hollow gulf of sterile emptiness,
> A zero oblivious of the sum it closed,
> An abnegation of the Maker's joy
> Saved by no wide repose, no depth of peace.

The poet here describes as to what it means to enter
the kingdom of Death while still alive. It was a land
utterly barren with sterile emptiness. There were no
intervals of relief. In this land there could be no moments of
repose. There was not only stress, it was smothering stress
where even breathing was impossible. Savitri had entered
this unrelieved darkness where even the next step was not
visible. The darkness was so dense that she could not see

either the giant figure of Death or the luminous Satyavan.
The poet tells us:

> As disappears a golden lamp in gloom
> Borne into distance from the eye's desire,
> Into the shadows vanished Savitri.
> There was no course, no path, no end or goal:
> Visionless she moved amid insensible gulfs,
> Or drove through some great black unknowing Waste,
> There was none with her in the dreadful Vast:
> She saw no more the vague tremendous god,
> Her eyes had lost their luminous Satyavan.

And yet Savitri moved on undaunted by these
experiences of the dreadful Vast. The poet has described
Savitri's journey through the Night in a language most
graphic, as he alone could have used. As one reads this
description one is reminded of the description found in
the Bhagavad Gita where Sri Krishna unveils to the eyes
of Arjuna his Universal Form. The description given by
Sri Aurobindo fills one with great dread, and so one
wonders how Savitri could have travelled alone in this
darkness not knowing where Satyavan was, and not
knowing where the Lord of Death had vanished. The
poet says:

> Her limbs refused the cold embrace of Death,
> Her heart-beats triumphed in the grasp of pain,
> Her soul persisted claiming for its joy,
> The soul of the beloved now seen no more.

Then she heard the treading of Death, felt some
movement afar and also had a faint glimpse of Satyavan
in that darkness. Savitri felt that after all Satyavan had
not vanished from her sight and that Death too was near.
But before she could feel the joy of the recovery of
Satyavan in that darkness, she once again heard the stern
voice of Death. It said:

This is my silent dark immensity,
This is the home of everlasting Night,
This is the secrecy of Nothingness
Entombing the vanity of life's desires.
Hast thou beheld thy source, O transient heart,
And known from what the dream thou art was made?
Hopest thou still always to last and love?

Savitri gave no reply, for, a sense of greater confidence
was growing within her. As the poet says "She saw the
undying fountains of her life, she knew herself eternal
without birth". To know oneself without birth is to
commune with one's eternal self. To know oneself as the
unborn and the Unmanifest is to transcend all limitations
of the manifested existence. And yet the poet tells us:
"Death, the dire god, inflicted on her eyes the immortal
calm of his tremendous gaze". To be able to stand the
gaze of Death demands great courage and inner confidence. Death once again speaks to Savitri:

Although thou hast survived the unborn void
Which never shall forgive, while Time endures
This sorrowful victory only hast thou won.

Death informs Savitri that her victory is only tem-
porary, and soon, very soon, she will realize the tremendous authority of Death against whom she cannot last
long. Death wants to impress Savitri with his unquestioned
power telling her that he alone is supreme. Death mocks
at the puny efforts of man against the vast authority of
his kingdom. He says:

A fragile miracle of thinking clay,
Armed with illusions walks the child of Time,
To fill the void around he feels and dreads,
The void he came from and to which he goes,
He magnifies his self and names it God.
He calls the heavens to help his suffering hopes.

Death says that after all the gods whom man worships—what have they given to him ? What is the highest
gift that they have bestowed on mankind? Death reminds
humanity, through Savitri, that these gods at whose shrines
man worships,

Have given to man the burden of his mind;
In his unwilling heart they have lit their fires
And sown in it incurable unrest.
His mind is a hunter upon tracks unknown;
Amusing Time with vain discovery
They gave him hungers which no food can fill
They cast for fodder grief and hope and joy :
His pasture ground they have fenced with Ignorance.
Into his fragile undefended breast
They have breathed a courage that is met by death,
They have given a wisdom that is mocked by night,
They have traced a journey that foresees no goal.

Having said this, Death thought now he could cajole
Savitri and thus persuade her to go back from the forbidden
land. In the above passage, we find Death showing to man
his utter incapacity to deal with the authority of Death.
Death thought that Savitri must now feel greatly humbled
and not attempt to do something which is outside the
scope of a mere mortal. Death says to Savitri :

Aimless man toils in an uncertain world
Lulled by inconstant pauses of his pain,
Scourged like a beast by the infinite desire,
· Bound to the chariot of the dreadful gods.
But if thou still canst hope and still wouldst love,
Return to thy body's shell they tie to earth,
And with thy heart's little remnants try to live.
Hope not to win back to thee Satyavan.
Yet since thy strength deserves no trivial crown,
Gifts I can give to soothe thy wounded life.

Death wanted to pacify Savitri by offering gifts. He realized that mere sternness would be of no avail, and so Savitri must be pacified. Death was still nursing a hope that by these gifts Savitri would be persuaded to go back and give up the fruitless journey. Having heard Death, Savitri at last spoke and the poet says that "her voice was heard by Night". Savitri said:

> I bow not to thee, O huge mask of Death,
> Black lie of night to the cowed soul of man,
> Conscious of immortality I walk.
> A victor spirit conscious of my force,
> Not as a suppliant to thy gates I came :
> Unslain I have survived the clutch of Night.
> My unwept tears have turned to pearls of strength:
> I have transformed my ill-shaped brittle clay
> Into the hardness of a statued soul.
> I stoop not with the subject mob of minds
> Who run to glean with eager satisfied hands
> And pick from its mire mid many trampling feet
> Its scornful small concessions to the weak.
> Mine is the labour of the battling gods:
> Imposing on the slow reluctant years
> The flaming will that reigns beyond the stars.

Savitri tells Death in no mistakable terms that he was not dealing with a mere weakling who would be satisfied with some small concessions that he may choose to throw. Death has to realize that in Savitri he was confronting a spirit strong and obstinate, the one that can battle like gods, burning with a flaming will that reigns beyond the stars. And so in reply to Death's offer of gifts, Savitri says that her demand was that whatever Satyavan wanted during his lifetime but could not achieve should be given. Satyavan wanted that his parents should once again live in comfort and that his father should gain back his eyesight. This is what Satyavan wanted above everything else. Savitri says to Death: "Give, if thou must, or if thou canst, refuse". Savitri is placing a demand before Death, for, she had not gone to death as a suppliant, seeking some small relief. She tells Death that if he must give then let him give a life of comfort to Satyavan's parents. But she again says: "if thou canst, refuse". It is left to Death to decide, for, Savitri is unconcerned about the small concessions that Death may be pleased to offer. Death, too, must have wondered at the audacity of Savitri. He must have thought that surely that was not the way of receiving gifts. But Death gives this boon by which Satyavan's parents would be restored to their old status and King Dyumatsena be in possession of his eyesight. Having done this Death felt that now he had a right to ask Savitri to go back so that he may be unfettered in his movement carrying Satyavan to his rightful abode after shedding the earthly robe. Death addresses Savitri thus:

Go, mortal, to thy small permitted sphere!
Hasten swift-footed, lest to slay thy life
The great laws thou hast violated, moved
Open at last on thee their marble eyes.

Death asks Savitri to return to her permitted sphere, and if she did not then the laws that she had violated would turn their eyes on her. Death was holding out a threat to Savitri. He felt that having granted the desire of Satyavan, now Savitri would hasten back. But Savitri replied to him saying:

World-spirit, I was thy equal spirit born.
I am immortal in my mortality.
I tremble not before the immobile gaze
Of the unchanging marble hierarchies
That look with the stone eyes of Law and Fate.
My soul can meet them with its living fire.
Out of thy shadow give me back again
Into earth's flowering spaces Satyavan
I will bear with him the ancient Mother's load,
I will follow with him earth's path that leads to God.

Else........
Wherever thou leadst his soul I shall pursue.

Death must have felt stunned at these words of
Savitri. Never in his long career had Death met such a
mortal who was afire with immortality, who accepted no
defeat and who was ready to cross swords with him in his
own kingdom. Death had never met such a challenge. His
threats have proved futile, his gifts too have not tempted
Savitri. Death thought he must impress upon Savitri that
it was futile to challenge his might, and that, by thus challenging, she was exposing herself to dire   consequences.
Having heard what Savitri had said, the poet says, there
arose "the almighty cry of Universal Death".

> Hast thou god-wings or feet that tread my stars,
> Frail creature with the courage that aspires,
> Forgetting thy bounds of thought, thy mortal role?
> Flee clutching thy poor gains to thy trembling breast
> Pierced by my pangs Time shall not soon appease.
> Turn nor attempt forbidden happy fields
> Meant for the souls that can obey my law
> Depart in peace, if peace for man is just.

Death is telling Savitri that if she does not withdraw
from the forbidden territory then she will arouse the furies of
law. And these furies once aroused cannot be easily pacified.
The demand of this fury is such that "hell cannot slake nor
heaven's mercy assuage". He tells her that if she does not
act in accordance with the inscrutable law, then "thou
come bleeding to me at the last, thy nothingness recognised, my greatness known". But the poet says, Savitri
"answered meeting scorn with scorn". The mortal woman
said to the dreadful Lord:

> My God is Will and triumphs in his paths,
> My God is Love and sweetly suffers all.
> Love's golden wings have power to fan thy void:
> The eyes of Love gaze starlike through death's night,

The feet of love tread naked hardest worlds
He labours in the depths, exults on the heights;
He shall remake thy universe, O Death.

She spoke these words, and, there was silence, for no·
immediate reply came from Death. They travelled through
the trackless night, silently, without a word. Savitri told
Death that his universe was most defective, and that it will
have to be remade. She says that it is Love that shall remake the universe of Death. These were challenging words
to which Death replied after a pause. It was a deep and
a perilous pause in "that unreal journey through blind
Nought". Then did Death speak to Savitri saying:

What is thy hope? To what dost thou aspire?
....a vain oneness seeking to embrace
The brilliant idol of a fugitive hour.
And thou, what art thou, soul, thou glorious dream
Of brief emotions made and glittering thoughts,
A thin dance of fireflies speeding through the night,
A sparkling ferment in life's sunlit mire?
Death only lasts and the inconscient Void.
I only am eternal and endure.
I am the shapeless formidable Vast,
I am the emptiness that men call Space,
I am a timeless Nothingness carrying all,
I am the Illimitable, the mute Alone,
I, Death, am He; there is no other God.
Man has no other help but only Death;
He comes to me at his end for rest and peace.
I, Death, am the one refuge of thy soul.
That which thou seest as thy immortal self
Is a shadowy icon of my infinite
I am the immobile in which all things move.

Having given threats and found them of no avail,
having tempted with gifts and found them spurned by
Savitri, Death now follows the path of reason. It believes
that perhaps by reason, Savitri could be pursuaded to

return. Death tells Savitri that "because thou callest me to wrestle with thy soul, I have assumed a face, a form, a voice" For in the true sense of the term, Death is formless. His region is such that:

> ....There love
> Came never with his fretful eyes of tears,
> Nor Time is there nor the vain vasts of Space.
> It wears no living face, it has no name,
> No gaze, no heart that throbs, it asks no second
> To aid its being or to share its joys.

Death asks Savitri to see the real nature of this Nameless Being. It says that if Savitri is immortal then why does she need a second to help her to complete her work? It says:

> If thou desirest immortality,
> Be then alone sufficient to thy soul:
> Live in thyself; forget the man thou lov'st.
> My last grand death shall rescue thee from life,
> Then shalt thou rise into thy unnamed source.

Death tells Savitri that immortality should be sufficient unto itself. If immortality needs something else to fill its insufficiency then surely it is not immortal. Savitri told Death:

> O Death, who reasonest, I reason not,
> Reason that scans and breaks, but cannot build
> Or builds in vain because she doubts her work.
> I am, I love, I see, I act, I will.

Savitri here ridicules the approach of reason. She says that reason knows how to break, it never knows how to build. And, if, perchance, reason builds then its building tumbles down, for, in that building there is no living touch of faith. Savitri says to Death: "I love" and that should be enough. Love cannot be understood by reason, and so Death's reasoning is in vain. It may

reason as profoundly as it likes, but by it Death will never
be able to know what Love is. But Death says to Savitri
that while she talks of love, she must not be oblivious of
Knowledge, for, it says:

> Know also. Knowing, thou shalt cease to love
> And cease to will, delivered from thy heart,
> So shalt thou rest for ever and be still,
> Consenting to the impermanence of things.

But Savitri was more than a match for Death, for,
she says to Death: "When I have loved for ever, I shall
know". Here Savitri utters a profound truth. She indicates to Death that all knowledge is in vain if it has not
arisen in the soil of Love. She says "Love in me knows
the truth all changings mask". Here she tells Death that
behind all changings is the mask that tries to cover the
face of truth. Death represents the factor of change, and
Savitri tells him that she knows that all the activities
towards change in which Death indulges is only an effort
to mask the face of truth. It is Love that pierces through
the mask and looks at the glorious face of truth. All
efforts of Death fail when Love abides, for, love tears off
the mask of death. She tells Death that

> ......man was born among the monstrous stars
> Dowered with a mind and heart to conquer thee.

When Savitri uttered these words, the poet says:
"Death answered not again". Death stood in silence
and "in darkness wrapped". And so once again the
three moved on silently, covering the areas of the Night.
Death could not prevent Savitri from travelling further.
His threats and temptations, his cajoling and reasoning—
all failed. And so this intrepid traveller walked with
Death, and with Satyavan ahead—a journey in eternal
night, but with the voice of Darkness stilled for awhile.
The poet says:

Once more a Wanderer in the unending Night,
Blindly forbidden by dead vacant eyes,
She travelled through the dumb unhoping vasts.
Around her rolled the shuddering waste of gloom,
Resentful of her thought and life and love.

CHAPTER XXII

A MALADY OF THE MIND

THERE is an old adage which says: "Love conquers all". In Sri Aurobindo's Savitri it is the all-conquering power of Love that is described. Man feels powerless under the impact of Death. Does man have any weapon with which to fight the onslaught of death? His reason will be of no avail. His mind is too feeble to battle with Death. If only man will be imbued with Love then will he know that Death has no victory over him. Love, and Love alone, can make blunt even the sharpest weapon of Death. Savitri was not in search of the secret of Death; she was out to defeat Death in its own kingdom. And for this she had no other weapon but the weapon of Love. The mind of man can never know what Immortality is. It may revel in the theory of immortality, but such a theory is of no avail, for, it topples down at the faintest intimation of death. Immortality for the reasoning mind is only everlastingness. But immortality is not an everlasting continuity. In fact, it does not belong to Time at all. The eternal and the everlasting are not identical. While the former is Timeless, the latter is an expression of an endless continuity in the sphere of Time. The Timeless is where the Time is not. It is in the constant cessation of Time, that the Eternal and the Immortal can be comprehended. He who seeks the explanation of Death in terms of Time will never know what Death is. Death reveals its secret in the Timeless Moment. The mind which can function only in the realm of Time can never know what the Timeless Moment is. It is only when mind ceases, that the Timeless Moment arrives. And it is in the cessation of the mind that the experience of Love comes. Man is afraid of Death because he is a stranger to the experience of Love. Love is a communion with the Unborn and the Unmanifest. In this experience, Death is known as the Nameless. It is hardly necessary to state that Name exists in the field of the known and the continuous. As long as one calls death by a name, so long death must evoke fear. Death, the Nameless, is known only by Love, and that is why Love and Fear of Death do not, and cannot, exist together. A communion with the Nameless is indeed the experience of Death. A communion with the Nameless is indeed the experience of Death—and it is also the experience of Love. Love and Death are friends, and so in the presence of Love, Death is completely transformed. Sri Aurobindo in his Savitri has dealt with the problem of Death not in terms so much of vanquishing death as transforming death. Savitri talks not of destroying the universe of Death, but of remaking it. She tells death that Love shall remake his universe. When death is transformed, then it becomes the close companion of life. In such a relationship Life and Death become the two inseparables. In their co-existence, one discovers the secret of Life as well as of Death. Savitri's journey through the eternal night is a journey for transforming death itself so that man no longer regards it as fearsome. It becomes the closest friend of man—the one that shows him the way of full and complete living. But before man knows Death as the closest friend of Life, he has to journey into the land of darkness, and that too in the company of death. Savitri is journeying into this land of darkness. The poet describes this country in the following lines:

> All still was darkness dread and desolate;
> There was no change nor any hope of change.
> In this black dream which was a house of Void,
> A walk to Nowhere in a land of Nought,
> Ever they drifted without aim or goal;
> Gloom led to worse gloom, death to an emptier death,

In some positive Non-Being's purposeless Vast
Through formless wastes dumb and unknowable.

A journey through this dark night must seem meaningless, for, it was a "walk to Nowhere in a land of Nought". Such a journey must needs appear too long and
endless. There seemed to be no aim, no goal, a movement through formless wastes, dumb and unknowable.
To move in such regions would require tremendous courage. Was Death purposely moving through such regions
in order to tire the patience and the courage of Savitri?
Even when some faint glimpses of light were seen, they
seemed unreal, for, the only reality was unrelieved darkness. Light, however feeble, seemed out of place here.
In fact, such light made darkness all the more pronounced. Death is a land of ceaseless negations. It symbolises total negation, so that not even a vestige of existence
can remain there. And does not Love flower in the soil
of total negation? If Love is to triumph, then Savitri
must go through the darkness of total negation. Savitri,
while moving in this land of darkness and negation, says
to herself that

.... she must pay now her debt
Her vain presumption to exist and to think,
To some brilliant Maya that conceived her soul
This most she must absolve with endless pangs,
Her deep original sin, the will to be.

Moving in this land of Nothingness, Savitri must absolve herself of the "original sin". What indeed is this original
sin? As the poet says, it is the will-to-be. As long as the
will-to-be remains, so long there is no Love. And where
Love is not, Death must triumph. To exist and to think is
a vain presumption which must be cast away, for, thus alone
the debt to Maya can be paid. When the debt is paid then
the veil of Maya is rent asunder—but not until this is done.
The soul about which one speaks is itself the product of
the brilliant Maya. When one is caught in this Maya

then one presumes that this so-called soul is permanent
in the midst of everything that is fleeting. But the question arises: Is there nothing else but Maya? How can
one know an answer to this question unless one pierces
the veil of Maya itself? Keeping the veil of Maya un-
pierced, any thought of soul is itself the product of that
very Maya. It is only when the thinnest, the irredicent
veil of Maya, is rent asunder that there comes to view
What Is. But for this veil after veil of Maya has to be
negated, even the subtlest veil of the image, the ideal, the
concept of the soul. The poet says that "Maya is a veil
of the Absolute". The Absolute is for ever the Unmanifest, and so, as the veils of the manifest are negated that
which shines in all its glory is the Absolute. The poet
says:

> The Inconscient is the Superconscient's sleep.
> An unintelligible Intelligence
> Invents creation's paradox profound;
> All here is a mystery of contraries;
> Darkness a magic of self-hidden light ,
> Suffering, some secret rapture's tragic mask,
> And death an instrument of perpetual life.

Existence seems paradoxical because mind can never
understand the co-existence of things. Mind functions only
in the framework of Time and Space. And so in the
language of the mind there is no explanation for co-existence. A co-existence is not two things put in   juxtaposition.
It means two things existing at the same place and at
the same time. The mind can express this only in terms
of paradoxes. The poet in the above passage refers to
these paradoxes. How can death and life exist together?
To the understanding of the mind this would mean one
negating the other, and so the result would be nothingness. The poet tells us:

> Although Death walks beside us on Life's road,
> A dim bystander at the body's start

And a last judgment on man's futile works,
Other is the riddle of its ambiguous face.

Although death is a bystander at the very start of life, its face for ever remains ambiguous. The poet says it is "a grey defeat pregnant with victory". A defeat pregnant with victory is surely a paradox, a riddle which the mind cannot solve. The poet has entitled the Canto One of Book Ten as "The Dream Twilight of the Ideal". When the three travellers moved on in the darkness of the night there came a point where "the intolerant darkness paled and drew apart". The rays of the dawn were beginning to be visible. But still this dawn had a great adversary in the last remnants of the night. As the poet says, this was the

Adversary of the slow struggling Dawn
Defending its ground of tortured mystery,
It trailed its coils through the dead martyred air
And curving fled down a grey slope of Time.

In their journey they came to a dawn. The poet says: "God's long nights are justified by dawn". The dawn was a pleasant experience. The heaviness of the dark night had passed away and the travellers had come to the fresh and light air of the dawn. The poet says:

Passed was the heaviness of the eyeless dark
And all the sorrow of the night was dead.

Perhaps the author here is referring to what the Buddhists have called *Sukhavati*, or what is otherwise known as the Heaven world. These are the conditions described regarding the after-death state in religions that have declared their belief in life after death. Savitri finds herself in this realm of the dawn where the Lord of Death had brought them after the grim experience of the night. But here she found that everything was fleeting. It was pleasant to look at the conditions of this new world, but
D.-19

there was nothing that remained, everything was moving away. The poet says:

> These fugitive beings, these elusive shapes
> Were all that claimed the eye and met the soul,
> The natural inhabitants of that world.
> But nothing there was fixed or stayed for long;
> No mortal feet could rest upon that soil
> No breath of life lingered embodied there,
> In that fine chaos joy fled dancing past
> And beauty evaded settled line and form,
> Yet gladness ever repeated the same notes
> And gave the sense of an enduring world.

This new world seemed enduring, but in reality it was not. It was the repetitive nature of things that created the illusion of permanency. Things were moving so fast that they appeared to be steady. Things repeated themselves in such continued movement that an appearace of an enduring world was created. Perhaps the heaven of the after-death condition seems enduring due to this movement of unceasing recurrence. The poet tells us:

> All in this world was shadowed forth, not limned,
> Like faces leaping on a fan of fire
> Or shapes of wonder in a tinted blur,
> Like fugitive landscapes painting silver mists.
> Here vision fled back from the sight alarmed,
> And sound sought refuge from the ear's surprise,
> And all experience was a hasty joy.

Everything in the world was ephemeral. And the heaven of the after-death condition is indeed such; otherwise why should man return to earth after the joys of the heaven are over. And the poet says that here all experience was a hasty joy. Obviously there is an element of incompleteness in all experiences of joy in this realm. Describing the state of existence in this world, the poet says:

Always the same and always unfulfilled
....all could last, yet nothing ever be.

To last and yet not to be—this is a strange phenomenon. Of what use is that lasting where there is no
experience of being? There may be glory in this realm,
but a glory that is unreal. A world of mere attractive
appearances, a world where shadows danced with no
substance behind. In this world of false appearances,
Savitri saw Satyavan, and what is it that she saw?

Dressed in its rays of wonder Satyavan
Before her seemed the centre of its charm,
Head of her loveliness of longing dreams
And captain of the fancies of her soul.

Savitri moved on in this soil of enchantment. She
felt greatly intrigued by the spectacle of this realm, full
of wonder and charm. While she was in this land of
seeming wonder, there pealed the calm and inexorable
voice. What did this Voice do? The poet says:

Abolishing hope, cancelling life's golden truths,
Fatal its accents smote the trembling air.
That lovely world swam thin and frail, most like
Some pearly evanescent farewell gleam
On the faint verge of dusk in moonless eves.

This calm and inexorable Voice shattered to pieces
that seemingly grand edifice of the enchanting world in
which Savitri was moving. The world itself was ephemeral. Savitri was suddenly brought to the awareness of the
unreality of that world. The Voice said:

Prisoner of Nature, many-visioned spirit,
Thought's creature in the ideal's realm enjoying
Thy unsubstantial immortality
The subtle marvellous mind of man has feigned,
This is the world from which thy yearnings came.
When it would build eternity from the dust,

Man's thought paints images illusion rounds
Prophesying glories it shall never see,
It labours delicately among its dreams.
A rapture of things that never can be born,
Hope chants to hope a bright immortal choir;
Cloud satisfies cloud, phantom to longing phantom
Leans sweetly, sweetly is clasped or sweetly chased.
This is the stuff from which the ideal is formed;
Its builder is thought, its base the heart's desire,
But nothing real answers to their call.
The ideal dwells not in heaven, nor on the earth,
A bright delirium of man's ardour of hope
Drunk with the wine of its own phantasy.

Death has indeed demolished the entire house of
ideals by describing it as a bright delirium of man's
ardour of hope. He says that the ideal exists neither in
heaven nor on earth–it abides only in mind's imagination.
Ideal is built by thought and its base is the desire of the
heart. In fact, ideals are man's attempts to seek fulfilment of the unfulfilled desires. Death tells Savitri not to
attach much importance to these ideals, for, they are only
the constructs of the mind. He tells Savitri:

This angel in thy body thou callst love
Who shapes his wings from thy emotion's hues,
In a ferment of thy body has been born
And with the body that housed it it must die.
It is a passion of thy yearning cells,
It is flesh that calls to flesh to serve its lust;
It is thy mind that seeks an answering mind
And dreams awhile that it has found its mate.

Savitri had been moving in the so-called heaven world
which after the darkness of the night seemed very attractive. In the midst of this attraction, Death utters solemn
and sombre words destroying the world of ideals and laying bare its falseness. He tells Savitri that her love is
also an idealistic delirium produced by the mind. Death

tells Savitri that her so-called love is nothing but her effort
to cover up her loneliness. He says:

In the Alone there is no room for love.
In vain to clothe love's perishable mud
Thou hast woven on the Immortal's borrowed loom
The ideal's gorgeous and unfading robe.
The ideal never yet was real made.

Death uses harsh words, for, he says that her so-called
love has been given gorgeous robes of ideals—and this robe
has been woven on the borrowed loom. Immortality as
a mere concept is indeed a borrowed loom, and on that
loom man weaves many a gorgeous robe. But such robes
cannot hide the ugliness of man's selfish love. Death says:

How can the heavens come down to unhappy earth
Or the eternal lodge in drifting time?
How shall the Ideal tread earth's dolorous soil
While life is only a labour and a hope?
Vain was the sage's thought, the prophet's voice
In vain is seen the shining upward Way.

The fervour of the ideal withers away, and the so-called
love of man cools down in the course of time. These
idealistic feelings are short-lived. They have a momentary
existence. Death tells Savitri:

If Satyavan had lived, love would have died;
But Satyavan is dead and love shall live
A little while in thy sad breast, until
His face and body fade on memory's wall
Where other bodies, other faces come.

He tells Savitri that she will soon get over this infatuation regarding Satyavan, for, love on earth is no more
than a mere infatuation lasting for a while. Savitri is
told by Death that her love was a "sensual want refined"
—it was only a hunger of the body and the heart.

He says to her: "Thy want can tire and cease or turn elsewhere, or love may meet a dire and pitiless end." And so Death informs Savitri that he has indeed been kind to her and Satyavan by taking away Satyavan. If Satyavan had lived, he would have been very unhappy seeing her love cooling off in the passage of time. And now that Satyavan is dead, she too can be free from the embarrassing situation of Satyavan feeling unhappy. He says:

> Death saves thee from this and saves Satyavan:
> He now is safe, delivered from himself;
> He travels to silence and felicity.
> Call him not back to the treacheries of earth
> And the poor petty life of animal Man.

Savitri finds Death speaking a different language from the one that it spoke earlier. No more is there a threat nor a rebuke. He speaks now a honeyed language, solicitous of the welfare of both Savitri and Satyavan. Savitri is quick to see this, and tells Death in a firm voice:

> ....I forbid thy voice to slay my soul.
> My love is not a hunger of the heart
> My love is not a craving of the flesh;
> It came to me from God, to God returns.
> Even in all that life and man have marred
> A whisper of divinity is still heard,
> A breath is felt from the eternal spheres.

Savitri tells Death that love, even when it is most carnal, has in it the touch of the divine and the eternal. Love is never profane. She also tells Death that her love is not a craving of the flesh nor is it a hunger of the heart. About Satyavan, she says that they both have not met for the first time; they have been together from the very beginning of time. She says:

> We are man and woman from the first,
> The twin souls born from one undying fire.
> Did he not dawn on me in other stars?

How has he through the thickets of the world
Pursued me like a lion in the night
And come upon me suddenly in the ways
And seized me with his glorious golden leap!
He rose like a wild wave out of the floods
And dragged me helpless into seas of bliss.

Savitri tells Death that he had better keep mum
where love is concerned, for, what does he know about
love? He is the Lord of Darkness: how can he speak
about the glorious dawn of love? She says to Death:

If there is a yet happier greater god,
Let him wear the face of Satyavan
And let his soul be one with him I love;
For only one heart beats within my breast
And one god sits there throned. Advance, O Death,
Beyond the phantom beauty of this world;
For of its citizens I am not one.

Savitri asks Death to move on from the phantom
beauty of the world to which he has brought the travellers.
Savitri says that she is not a citizen of the phantom
world. There is only one god that sits throned in her
heart—and that is Satyavan. But Death too is persistent,
and says to Savitri that "A bright hallucination are
thy thoughts" He reminds her that "vain is thy longing to build heaven on earth". Death tells Savitri that
after all Mind is the only instrument that she has, and
what can this Mind, a child of Matter, do? He says:

....Mind, a glorious traveller in the sky,
Walks lamely on the earth with footsteps slow;
Hardly he can mould the life's rebellious stuff
Hardly can he hold the galloping hooves of sense
All thy high dreams were made by Matter's mind
To solace its dull work in Matter's jail,
Its only house where it alone seems true.

> Thy soul is a brief flower by the gardener Mind
> Created on thy Matter's terrain plot.

The dreams and ideals of the mind are just the toys with which it plays to break the monotony of its jail life. It lives in a prison and is merely interested in decorating the prison walls. Its dreams and ideals are only in the nature of such decorations. The mind may soar into the skies, but on earth it walks with slow footsteps. It is unable to translate what it dreams and aspires. And so Death tells her:

> Turn not thy gaze within thyself to look
> At visions in the gleaming crystal, Mind,
> ......open thy eyes......and see
> The stuff of which thou and the world are made.

Death asks Savitri not to be carried away by the false visions and dreams of the Mind. He is intent to break the entire structure of Savitri's ideals and dreams. Death is eager that she should return to earth, and not pursue him into realms that do not belong to her. He says:

> ....where is room for soul or place for God
> In the brute immensity of a machine?
> A transient Breath thou takest for thy soul,
> A magnified image of man's mind for God.

When the mind of man thinks of God, it creates an image of magnified man. What else can it do? The mind is like an immense machine which has no need either for soul or for God. Death has been telling Savitri that the world of the mind is utterly false and ideals belong to the realm of the mind. They are the products of thought and hence completely undependable. Death says to Savitri:

> The Ideal is a malady of thy mind,
> A bright delirium of thy speech and thought,
> A strange wine of beauty lifting thee to false sight,
> A noble fiction of thy yearnings made
> Thy human imperfection it must share.

The mind of man builds an ideal and dresses it up with gorgeous robes, and then begins man's struggle to translate that ideal into everyday action. But this translating can never be done. It is mind that creates a distance between Ideal and Action. It has to be remembered that action belongs to the realities of life, and life is eternally in a state of flux. But the Ideal is something static, a fixed point created by the mind. How can a bridge be constructed between two such points—one that is static and the other which is intensely dynamic? Mind creates an ideal in order to escape from the grim realities of life. And so Death tells Savitri to leave this false world of ideals and face the realities of life. He says:

O soul misled by the splendour of thy thoughts,
O earthly creature with thy dream of heaven,
Obey resigned and still, the earthly law,
Accept the light that falls upon thy days;
Take what thou canst of Life's permitted joy,
Submitting to the ordeal of Fate's scourge,
Suffer what thou must of toil and grief and care.

He asks Savitri to retire into the hush of the earth from where she had gone so far. Death has used all the weapons in his armoury to send back Savitri, and to allow him to move on with Satyavan. But all threats and persuasions have proved fruitless. The question still remains: Who will claim Satyavan? Will Death claim him, or will Savitri claim her lover and her husband and walk down to earth hand in hand with him? Shall Death conquer, or shall Love establish its victory over the almighty Lord of Destruction? The issue still remains unsettled, and, in the meanwhile, the travellers must proceed into lands familiar to Death but utterly strange to Savitri.

CHAPTER XXIII

THE ETERNAL BRIDEGROOM

The Bhagavad Gita says that not even for one moment can man remain without performing action, for, to live is to act. Life is relationship, and to be related is to act. But if we examine the nature of our actions, we will find that they are not actions at all, they are only reactions. Such reactions may be in terms of physical movements or of words or of thoughts. There is a fundamental difference between an action and a reaction. A reaction emanates from a fixed centre in one's consciousness. It may be called a centre of habit or of memory. Action, however, arises from no centre at all, and that is why it is always spontaneous and natural. A reaction is habitual, but an action is natural. Thus an action does not arise from a centre of thought. To put it differently, an action always precedes thought. Such an action is not a thoughtless action in the sense that it is impulsive. It remains untouched by thought. In such pure action thought is used only to explain as to how one acted. As we have stated above, an action can be at any level. To look at something is itself an action. But true looking is possible only if thought does not intervene. And so the action of looking must precede thought, if there is to be a true looking. This applies to all categories of actions. When thought intervenes then the experience is broken up. True relationship is possible when the action of relationship precedes thought. With regard to Savitri's encounter with Death, Sri Aurobindo says that a sudden change came over her where "the thinker was no more". That is why her meeting with Death was complete, leaving no residue behind. Our so-called actions are incomplete, and, therefore, in such actions there is always the looking to the future. The whole process of psychological time is created by our incomplete actions. These incomplete actions are verily the reactions. It is reaction which is the begetter of psychological time with all its frustrations and anxieties. It needs to be understood that Love alone is total action. Love is completely free from all trace of reaction. A reaction arises when an outer challenge stimulates the centre of memory or of habit. But Love needs no stimulation of outer challenge. Its action is free from all compulsions, whether outer or inner. We are either compelled by the factors of outer environment or by the inner factors of ideals and images. An action arising from an ideal is a reaction. And so all efforts to translate ideals into actions are an exercise in futility, for, they keep one chained to an endless process of reactions. Such efforts to translate generate only incomplete actions, and therefore create the need for psychological time. In any effort to translate ideals into actions there comes into existence this factor of psychological time. It is not for nothing that Sri Aurobindo deals with the problem of Ideals in a comprehensive manner in the course of Death's dialogue with Savitri, He calls ideals as the malady of the mind or the bright delirium of thought. We have seen how Death ridicules Savitri's idealistic stance. It is in this context that he rules out all sentiments regarding love, calling it only another expression of the same futile idealistic ferver. Death tells Savitri to face the realities of life and not get lost in mere idealistic glamour of love. But Savitri was not a person who could be easily disposed of by Death through such intellectual discussions and moral discourses. Savitri was remarkably quick-witted, and so replied almost immediately to the long oration of Death. She said:

> O dark-browed sophist of the universe
> Who veilst the Real with its own Idea,
> Hiding with brute objects Nature's living face

> Masking eternity with thy dance of death,
> Thou hast woven the ignorant Mind into a screen
> And made of thought error's purveyor and scribe
> And a false witness of mind's servant sense;
> Champion of a harsh and sad philosophy,
> Thou hast used words to shutter out the Light
> And called in Truth to vindicate a lie;
> O Death, thou speakest Truth but Truth that slays,
> I answer to thee with the Truth that saves.

Savitri calls Death a sophist, meaning a mere quibbler. She says that Death tries to veil the Real with its own dark and dismal contrivance. He invokes Truth to vindicate a lie. According to Savitri, Death is an adept at distorting things. Out of this distortion he utters a truth that slays. Savitri tells Death that she speaks the Truth that saves. Death is a past-master at misrepresenting facts. Savitri says:

> The Timeless took its ground in emptiness,
> And drew the figure of a universe,
> That the spirit might adventure into Time
> And wrestle with adamant Necessity
> And the soul pursue a cosmic pilgrimage.

Savitri gives to Death lessons in evolution and reminds him as to how the universe took its birth and how evolutionary stream moved on. She says that the whole purpose of evolution is to see that spirit adventures in Time, and wrestles with Necessity. It was not to submit to Necessity that the spirit took its birth in time. And surely the greatest symbol of Necessity is Death. Savitri says that the spirit is born not to submit to the dictates of Death. She says:

> O Death, thou lookst on an unfinished world,
> Assailed by thee and of its road unsure,
> Peopled by imperfect minds and ignorant lives
> And sayest God is not and all is in vain.
> How shall the child already be the man?

Savitri says that Death is looking at the unfinished world. Here Sri Aurobindo has indicated the dynamic concept of Godhead. God did not create a finished world, and is now resting on His oars. The creation of the universe is a continuing process, and there is none more dissatisfied with his creation than the Creator himself. If Death would only understand the movement of evolution, then he would realize that the child cannot suddenly become a man. The fallacy in Death's reasoning consists in the fact that he is assailing an unfinished universe regarding it as a finished product. Savitri says to Death that the child cannot suddenly become a man, and tells him further:

Because he is infant, shall he never grow?
Because he is ignorant, shall he never learn?
In a small fragile seed a great tree lurks,
In a tiny gene a thinking being is shut,
A little element in a little sperm,
It grows and is a conqueror and a sage.
In God concealed the world began to be,
Tardily it travels towards manifest God:
The infinite holds the finite in its arms,
Time travels towards revealed eternity.

From the Unmanifest to the Manifest, this is the movement of evoluion. The Unmanifest is continually establishing new contacts for its manifestation. The expression of the Unmanifest can never be finished. Even a thousand names of God cannot fully describe him, similarly the Unmanifest goes on, age after age, expressing itself in the Manifest. Never will the Creator say: My world is over and I have created a finished product as my creation. Savitri says to Death:

He has built a world in the unknowing Void.
His forms he has massed from infinitesimal dust,
His marvels are built from insignificant things.
If mind is crippled, life untaught and crude,

If brutal masks are there and evil acts,
They are incidents of his vast and varied plot,
His great and dangerous drama's needed steps.

The poet says that the entire universe is the Creator's
passion-play. Death only looks at isolated incidents, and not
at the whole play. He pities the man as he is today, but
does not see the tremendous potentiality lying concealed
in his nature. Let him not deride the role of man, for, if
till now he was a tool in the hands of Death, tomorrow he
may rise to his full stature and challenge his might.
Savitri indicates that in her challenge, Death must see
the future of humanity. Savitri says that as evolution
proceeds, the Creator wishes man, his highest creation, to
take a greater and greater initiative, and not be a child
eternally spoon-fed by the mother. She says:

His knowledge he disguised as Ignorance,
His Good he sowed in Evil's monstrous bed,
Made error a door by which Truth could enter in,
His plant of bliss watered with Sorrow's tears.

The Creator expressed himself in contraries, so that man
may make his way with full understanding. Savitri says:
"A dual Nature covered the Unique". The One became
the Many so that the Many may return to the One,
bringing a rich harvest of a multi-coloured experience.
She says:

In this meeting of the Eternal's mingling masques,
This tangle-dance of passionate contraries.
Locking like lovers in a forbidden embrace
The quarrel of their lost identity.

In this world the quarrel and the conflict that are
visible are indeed due to lost identity. It is a part of the
growth of man. A point comes when man moves away
from the lost identity to his real nature. When a child
grows to the stature of man, he passes through numerous
ways of error and mistake. But thus alone can he grow

and come to real maturity. Man stumbles again and again, but thus alone can he acquire strength and vigour. Evolution proceeds from Instinct to Intellect. It is true that instinct is pure and innocent, while intellect displays many a time corruption and vile. But intellect is only an interlude, just a pause of the evolutionary stream before it turns to the glory of Intelligence or Intuition. In the interlude perchance many perversions occur, but they are just passing incidents on the onward journey. Intellect gives to man a sweep and a range of expression which the subhuman creatures do not have in spite of the innocence of their instinctual living. But the possibility of perversion does not invalidate the state of purity. Savitri says:

> Our knowledge walks leaning on Error's staff,
> A worshipper of false dogmas and false gods,
> Or fanatic of a fierce intolerant creed,
> Or a seeker doubting every truth he finds,
> A sceptic facing Light with adamant No
> Or chilling the heart with dry ironic smile,
> A cynic stamping out the god in man.

Here the poet describes the many perversions and aberrations of the whole phenomenon of Creation. To look at the whole requires a different approach from one that only examines part by part. Savitri says that Death lacks that approach of the Whole and so is unable to see the real significance of things. It is Love alone that can comprehend the Whole, and the meaning of life is vouchsafed only to one who sees it as a Whole, and not as a synthesis made up of the parts. Savitri says:

> There is the mystic realm whence leaps the power
> Whose fire burns in the eyes of seer and sage;
> A lightning flash of visionary sight,
> It plays upon an inward verge of mind:
> Thought silenced gazes into a brilliant Void.

The experience of mystic communion or Love comes when "thought silenced gazes into the brilliant Void". The evolutionary drama is leading man to that state through the labyrinth of mind and its activities. Savitri says to Death that it is only during the interlude from intellect to intelligence that his reign can last. And during this interlude, Death has taken full advantage to confuse man. She says:

> Thy mask has covered the Eternal's face,
> The Bliss that made the world has fallen asleep.
> Abandoned in the Vast she slumbered on:
> An evil transmutation overtook
> Her members till she knew herself no more.

Sri Aurobindo's philosophy rests on the thesis of Bliss and Joy being the undercurrent of all life on earth. For him, to be a spiritual pilgrim is not to be a candidate for woe. Unfortunately during the interval between intellect and intelligence, death has wrought such havoc that "the bliss that made the world has fallen asleep". It is this inherent joy of life that has to be awakened, but for this the power of Death must be vanquished. Savitri says:

> But now the primal innocence is lost
> And Death and Ignorance govern the mortal world.

Savitri tells Death that even though he has wrought havoc with the life of the mortal, there are still intimations of the Real to be felt even in the midst of the fallen existence. She says:

> Earth still has kept her early charm and grace,
> The grandeur and the beauty still are hers,
> But veiled is the divine Inhabitant.

It is this divine Inhabitant that has to be awakened, for, once he wakes up, no more can Death and Ignorance rule the world. Nature has still kept her charm and grace, it is the mind of man that has come under the sway of the veil cast by Death. Savitri tells Death:

Although God made the world for his delight,
An ignorant Power took charge and seemed his Will
And Death's deep falsity has mastered life.
All grew a play of Chance stimulating Fate.

She says that what has mastered life is Death's deep
falsity. Once this falsity is laid bare the rule of Death will
be no more. And Savitri is addressing herself to this
great task of laying bare the falsity of Death. The first
move in this game is to look Death in the face and challenge
its might. She says:

A hidden Bliss is at the root of things.
A mute Delight regards Time's countless works:
To house God's joy in things Space gave wide room,
To house God's joy in self our souls were born.
Indifferent to the threat of karmic law,
Joy dares to grow upon forbidden soil,
Its sap runs through the plant and flowers of Pain:
It thrills with the drama of fate and tragic doom,
It tears its food from sorrow and ecstasy,
On danger and difficulty whets its strength;
It wallows with the reptile and the worm
And lifts its head, an equal of the stars.

It is Joy that underlies everything, for, it raises its head
even in the midst of doom and destruction. It is this Joy
which is the will to live. This will can never be smothered.
It lifts its head even under dire circumstances and asserts
its equality with the stars. Savitri says that "our earth
starts from mud and ends in sky". When this transfiguration comes, then is seen the end of Death as also
of the Night. She tells Death:

....Love that was once an animal's desire
Becomes a wide spiritual yearning's space.
A lonely soul passions for the Alone,
The heart that loved man thrills to the love of God.

D.–20

The secret of man's transmutation lies in Love. The poet says here that he alone can respond to love of God who has loved man. He who has never known human love must remain a stranger to the love of God. Savitri says to Death:

A Lover leaning from his cloister's door
Gathers the whole world into his single breast.
O Death, I have triumphed over thee within;
I quiver no more with the assault of grief;
A mighty calmness seated deep within
Has occupied my body and my sense.
O Death, not for my heart's sweet poignancy,
Nor for my happy body's bliss alone
I have claimed from thee the living Satyavan,
But for his work and mine, our sacred charge.

Here once again we see the poet depicting Savitri both as human and divine at the same time. Savitri says to Death that "not for my happy body's bliss alone" she asks for living Satyavan. Here the indication is that her human happiness is certainly involved in her demand. But there is the greater demand for the fulfilment of the work which they together have to accomplish. She says that this work is their sacred charge. But what is this work they together can do? Cannot Savitri do it alone? The work obviously is the making of a new world where man can rise to his full spiritual stature. In this great work the masculine and the feminine aspects of consciousness must work together, for, then alone it can lead to the integration of man. Savitri says:

....I the Woman am the force of God,
He the Eternal's delegate soul in man.
My will is greater than thy law, O Death;
My love is stronger than the bonds of Fate:
Our love is the heavenly seal of the Supreme.
I guard that seal against thy rending hands.
Love must not cease to live upon the earth;

For Love is the bright link twixt earth and heaven,
Love is man's lien on the Absolute.

Savitri says she is guarding the seal of the Supreme
which the Supreme has put on their love. Her great mission
on earth is to see that Love does not cease to exist upon
this earth. Love is not a mere sentimentality; nor is it just
emotionalism. The plant of Love flowers only when the
masculine and the feminine co-exist. It is only when
there is a simultaneous existence of the Strength symbolising the masculine consciousness, and Grace symbolising
the feminine consciousness, that Love can be born.
Savitri says that "Love is man's lien on the Absolute".
It is only through Love that man can keep this lien. And
Love is the only link that exists between Man and God.
But Death was a tough customer; he refused to be taken
in by these words of Savitri. And so Death replied to
Savitri saying:

....men cheat the Truth with splendid thoughts,
Thus will thou hire the glorious charlatan Mind,
To weave from his Ideal's gossamer air
A fine raiment for thy body's nude desires,
Daub not the web of life with magic hues;
O human face, put off mind-painted masks;
Accept thy futile birth, thy narrow life,
For truth is bare like stone and hard like death.

There can be no more apt description of the mind
than the epithet given here by the poet wherein he calls it
a "charlatan" meaning a quack or a pretender. Mind is a
quack, administering spurious medicines having no relevance to the ailment. Death tells Savitri that he regards
all her talk as mere effervescence, a sentimental sob-stuff.
He asks her to accept the unpleasant reality, for, "truth
is bare like a stone, and hard like death". But Savitri
immediately retorts and gives a fitting reply to Death's
taunting words. She says:

Yes, I am human. Yet shall man by me,
Since in humanity waits his hour the God,
Trample thee down to reach the immortal heights,
Yes, my humanity is a mask of God:
He dwells in me, the mover of my acts,
In me are the Nameless and the secret Name

Here the poet has introduced two seemingly contradictory expressions, the Nameless and the Secret Name. God's name is indeed a secret which He conveys only to him who goes to him, shedding all false names. When the names given by the mind are dropped away, then the Reality is rendered truly Nameless. It is in the Nameless that the secret Name is conveyed. The Nameless is the *Nirguna* even as the Name is the *Saguna*. The poet says that God is both *Nirguna* as well as *Saguna*, both the Nameless and having a secret Name. But Death continues the dialogue and demolishes argument after argument presented by Savitri. Death tells her:

O priestess in Imagination's house,
Persuade first Nature's fixed immutable laws.
How canst thou force to wed two eternal foes?
Irreconcilable in their embrace
They cancel the glory of their pure extremes:
An unhappy wedlock maims their stunted force.

One may ask: Who are these two eternal foes whom Savitri proposes to join in wedlock? They are Matter and Spirit. Death says that if Matter is all then Spirit is a dream, and if Spirit is all then Matter is a lie. He says: The Real with the unreal cannot mate. Death wants Savitri to make up her mind. If she regards Spirit as supreme, then why does she bother about Matter? Why should the material form of Satyavan mean so much to her? If she believes in Matter then she must obey the laws of matter which are inscrutable. Death indicates to Savitri that she should be consistent in her argument. How can Spirit and Matter be brought together in a wedlock, for, such marriage is bound to prove most unhappy? Savitri replies to God:

My heart is wiser than the Reason's thoughts,
My heart is stronger than thy bonds, O Death
It sees the cosmic Spirit at its work
In the dim Night it lies alone with God.
My heart's strength can carry the grief of the universe
And never lose the white spiritual touch.

The dialogue between Death and Savitri is most illuminating and tremendously scintillating. They seem to be equals and hence cross their swords freely. Death found in Savitri some one who was proving more than a match for him. The arrows of Death, however sharp they may be, fail utterly to hit Savitri.

Death tells Savitri that if she is so strong and powerful then let her show her freedom from the inscrutable laws of fate. She says that surely she will ultimately succeed and that the plans of Death will be foiled. Death the great Nihil contemptuously asked her to prove her strength, and if she does, then,

I will give thee all thy soul desires,
All the brief joys earth keeps for mortal hearts.
Only the one dearest wish that outweighs all,
Hard laws forbid and thy ironic Fate.
My will once wrought remains unchanged through
Time,
And Satyavan can never again be thine.

Here we are reminded of the dialogue between Yama and Nachiketa in the Kathopanishad. Yama tells Nachiketa to choose whatever joys and pleasures of life he liked, but not press him to reveal the secret of Death. In Sri Aurobindo's Savitri, we find Death willing to grant all earthly pleasures to Savitri but Satyavan can never again be hers. But Savitri spurns these flimsy offers of Death, and says:

> If the eyes of Darkness can look straight at Truth,
> Look at my heart and, knowing what I am,
> Give what thou wilt or what thou must, O Death.
> Nothing I claim but Satyavan alone.

The poet says that after these words uttered by Savitri, there was a hush, a poignant silence. Death had never come across such resoluteness on the part of a mortal being. His threats and explanations, his philosophical reasonings and offers of gifts, having failed, Death still attempts to wean Savitri away from the path she has chosen. And so Death tells Savitri:

> I give to thee, saved from death and poignant fate
> Whatever once the living Satyavan
> Desired in his heart for Savitri.
> Bright noons I give thee and unwounded dawns,
> Daughters of thy own shape in heart and mind,
> Fair hero sons and sweetness undisturbed.
> Return, O Child, to thy forsaken earth.

But Savitri is not slow to reply, for, how can these wishes be fulfilled, if Satyavan is not returned to her alive? She says:

> ....Thy gifts resist.
> Earth cannot flower if lonely I return.

But Death too was not to be weaned away from his path. And so he angrily cries out to Savitri:

> What knowest thou of earth's rich and changing life
> Who thinkest that, one man dead, all joy must cease?
> ....grief dies soon in the tired human heart;
> Soon other guests the empty chamber fill.

Death tells Savitri that everything on earth is in a state of flux. Nothing is permanent, and so she too will soon forget Satyavan and his place will be taken by others. He says that grief dies soon in the tired human heart. Savitri tells Death:

Give me back Satyavan, my only Lord.
Thy thoughts are vacant to my soul that feels
The deep eternal truth in transient things.

Savitri knows that life is in a flux and everything is transient. But she reminds Death that she has the insight to comprehend the Eternal in the midst of the transient. She can fathom the permanent even in the ceaseless flux of life. Her love for Satyavan was born when she perceived the Eternal in the bosom of Time itself. But Death says that she is pursuing something that is utterly false. If she returns to earth she will soon find other men as loveable as Satyavan. She will feel happy in the company of the other men, and "Satyavan shall glide into the past, a gentle memory pushed away from thee by new love and thy children's tender hands". Death reminds Savitri that after all life is "a constant stream that never is the same". In the stream of life, fresh waters come every moment, and so events of the past glide into memory. Satyavan too will be one of those events that will get pushed into the recesses of memory. But Savitri tells Death:

Why dost thou vainly strive with me, O Death,
A mind delivered from all twilight thoughts
To whom the secrets of the gods are plain?
All shall be seized, transcended; there shall kiss
Casting their veils before the marriage fire
The eternal bridegroom and eternal bride.

At these words of Savitri, the poet says, the twilight trembled like a bursting veil. There was a deep silence cast over the region where the Three stood. Then they moved without any exchange of words, journeying onward through the drifting ways. The poet describes this further journey in the following words:

The mortal led, the god and spirit obeyed
And she behind was leader of their march
And they in front were followers of her will.

In this further journey, Death brings the travellers to a spot where the twilight of the ideal recedes and the twilight of the earthly real comes into view. Death purposely does this so that Savitri may see clearly what the earthly real is. He feels that perhaps in this environment of the earthly real, Savitri will be able to free herself from the illusions of the idealistic world. Standing on this slope that slowly downward sank, Death once again addresses Savitri and says:

> Behold the figures of this symbol realm!
> Here thou canst trace the outcome Nature gives
> To the sin of being and the error of things
> And the desire that compels to live
> And man's incurable malady of hope.
> Where Nature changes not, man cannot change,
> His mind is pent in circling boundaries:
> For mind is man, beyond thought he cannot soar.
> If he could leave his limits he would be safe:
> He sees but cannot mount to his greater heavens;
> Even winged, he sinks back to his native soil.
> He is a captive in his net of mind
> And beats soul-wings against the walls of life.

The poet says that the limits of man have been set by his mind. He is unable to soar beyond the limits of thought, for, he is a captive in the net of the mind. He fruitlessly beats his soul-wings against the walls of life. But the poet says, somewhat paradoxically, that man would be safe if he could leave his limits. But he appears to feel safe only within his limits. This safety, however, is unreal. His real safety lies in breaking through the supposed safety of the mind. Death tells Savitri that after all she too is the creature of this mind. He asks her that even though she may profess to see the Eternal in the transient, how is she going to bring down that Eternal? He says:

> Hope not to call God down into his life:
> How shalt thou bring the Everlasting here?
> There is no house for him in hurrying Time.

Death tells Savitri that Truth cannot come down to the transient earth, for, how can the Everlasting live in the house of Time? Time is hurrying fast, and so in that flux, where will the Everlasting live? He says to her that she is caught in the illusions of the mind. Death wants to impress upon Savitri that Matter alone exists: Mind has no independent existence. Mind may talk big, but all its talk is empty chatter. And so he says to Savitri:

> If Mind is all, renounce the hope of bliss;
> If Mind is all, renounce the hope of Truth.
> For Mind can never touch the body of Truth
> And Mind can never see the soul of God
> Truth comes not there but only the thought of Truth;
> God is not there but only the name of God.

Death tells Savitri: How can she know God with the mere instrument of mind? The Self can never be known by the mind, and if she is the Self then she must remember that it is Unborn. She must then enter the state of the Unborn. For this she must die and enter the realm of the Spirit only through the gateway of Death. Death tells her:

> ....thou must die to thyself to reach God's height:
> I, Death, am the gate of immortality.

Death brings Savitri to the point that even if she wants to live the life of the Spirit, she and all others must pass through his gate. And so Death is supreme. It is supreme in the field of Matter; and it is also supreme for those who desire to enter the world of the Spirit. Without passing through his gate none can reach the realm of God. Thus must Savitri accept the supreme overlordship of Death. What is the use of Savitri crossing swords with this Almighty Death? Death has now started talking of things that belong to the world of the Spirit. But here Savitri is on a firmer ground, and so tells Death:

> The world is a spiritual paradox
> Invented by a need in the Unseen,

A poor translation to the creature's sense
Of That which for ever exceeds idea and speech,
A symbol of what can never be symbolised,
A language mispronounced, misspelt, yet true.

She says that the world by itself makes no meaning, for,
it can never speak the language of the Spirit. We may describe the world as the symbol of the Real, but the Real
can never be put in a symbol. But even though the world
mispronounces and misspels the language of the Spirit,
there are hidden in it the intimations of the true and the
real. She says that "the world is not cut off from Truth
and God" She tells Death:

In vain thou hast dug the dark unbridgeable gulf,
In vain thou hast built the blind and doorless wall:
Man's soul crosses through thee to Paradise
Heaven's sun forces its way through death and night,
Its light is seen upon our being's verge.
How sayst thou Truth can never light the human mind
And Bliss can never invade the mortal's heart
Or God descend into the world he made?
I have discovered that the world was He;
I have met Spirit with spirit, Self with self,
But I have loved too the body of my God.
I have pursued him in his earthly form.
A lonely freedom cannot satisfy
A heart that has grown one with every heart:
I am a deputy of the aspiring world,
My spirit's liberty I ask for all.

Savitri tells Death that however dark may be his night,
there is always to be seen a ray of light. Such perception
comes to one who can penetrate his veil. To such a one
Transcendence is visible even in the Immanence. God is
not invisible; he is intangible. He is to be found in the
very creation that he has made. Surely one can discover the Creator in the Creation itself; not away from
it. Savitri says that "I have discovered that the world was

He". And so one who discovers the Spirit, does not reject the Body. Savitri says: "I have loved too the body of my God".

Under the incessant assault of Savitri, Death shows signs of thawing and starts adopting a different line. If persuasion and wits fail, then what is he to do? He tries to flatter Savitri by saying that since she is so wise and strong why should she then waste her·precious energies for a cause that is so earthly and mundane? Death tells her:

> Because thou knowest the wisdom that transcends
> Both veil of forms and the contempt of forms,
> Arise delivered by the seeing gods.....
> Use not thy strength like the wild Titan souls!
> Touch not the seated lines, the ancient laws,
> Respect the calm of great established things.

Death tells Savitri that her wisdom transcends both the veil of forms and the contempt of forms. She is neither attached to forms, nor is she repulsed by them. It is a wisdom rare among the mortals, and so Death appeals to her not to dissipate her strength for things that are small and petty. He says that she should not use her powers like wild Titan souls. Death speaks an appealing language, showing great respect for the strength and wisdom of Savitri. He tells her not to disturb the calm of established things. If she uses her strength to disturb the functioning of ancient laws then there would be utter confusion. But Savitri is not taken in by these flattering words of Death, and so she says to him:

> What is the calm thou vauntst, O Law, O Death?

She says what is this calm about which he seems to be boasting so much? If it is the calm of established law then surely such calm is only an expression of something inert and soulless. She tells Death:

> Vain the soul's hope if changeless Law is all:
> Ever to the new and the unknown press on

The speeding aeons justifying God.
What were earth's ages if the grey restraint
Were never broken and glories sprang not forth?
Impose not upon sentient minds and hearts
The dull fixity that binds inanimate things.

Here Savitri speaks of the fundamental urge pressing on the evolutionary stream. If changeless Law is
everything then there is no hope for man. If the grey
restraint of Law is not broken, how can the new glories
spring forth? In Mutations, both biological and psychological, it is these grey restraints of law that are broken.
And it is only thus that new species can be born. The
evolutionary movement can never be fully explained in
terms of the changeless Law. They can explain varia-
tions, but, for, mutations they have no explanation in
the framework of law. Savitri is concerned with spiritual
mutation, not with a mere psychological variation. She
says to Death:

I trample on thy law with living feet;
For to arise in freedom I was born.
If I am mighty let my force be unveiled
Equal companion of the dateless powers,
Or else let my frustrated soul sink down
Unworthy of Godhead in the original sleep.

Death is indeed overawed by these words, but still
tries to hold his own ground, perhaps in vain. He says
to Savitri:

Child, hast thou trodden the gods beneath thy feet
Only to win poor shreds of earthly life
For him thou lov'st cancelling the grand release,
Keeping from early rapture of the heavens
His soul the lenient deities have called?
Are thy arms sweeter than the courts of God?

Savitri says to Death that since he has been praising
her for her might, he should realize that she would like

her force to be fully unveiled and seen as an equal companion of the dateless powers. The "dateless powers" are indeed the powers of Death, for, death comes without any prior appointment. Listening to these words, Death asks Savitri why she should deprive her lover, Satyavan, from the joys of heaven. Is she going to use her powers for that, cancelling the grand release of Satyavan? And then Death taunts Savitri by putting the question: "Are thy arms sweeter than the courts of God?" He has placed a very awkward question before Savitri. Does Savitri regard herself as greater than God himself? How can Savitri say: YES; but how can Savitri also say: No? If she says YES, then surely she makes God inferior to her, and if she says, NO, then she should allow Satyavan to proceed to the courts of God where he will know the rapture of the heaven. Savitri is on the horns of a dilemma.

But Savitri had no hesitation in replying to Death. She said that she was following the path ordained by the Divine, and that she was not deviating in the least from the line indicated by God. She said that perhaps Death did not know that God created man not in order that he may be a mere puppet, a toy, in the hand of the Creator. He created man so that he may become a collaborator with God. But for this man has to be completely free. So long as he is not free, he will be afraid of Death and become a mere plaything in the hands of Fate. It is only as a completely free individual that he can co-operate with God in the fulfilment of his great plan. Savitri was working to claim this freedom for man. She had gone thus far, challenging Death, because her mission dictated to her that man's freedom depended upon his release from the clutches of Death. Death has denied freedom to man. Savitri says:

What liberty has the soul which feels not free,
Unless stripped bare and cannot kiss the bonds

The Lover winds around his playmate's limbs,
Choosing his tyranny, crushed in his embrace?
To seize him better with her boundless heart
She accepts the limiting circle of his arms,
Bows full of bliss beneath his mastering hands
And laughs in his rich constraints, most bound,
                                            most free.
This is my answer to thy lures, O Death.

Death had taunted Savitri by saying that although
she was so wise she was frittering away her energies in pro-
tecting the demands of earthly love. Savitri refused to be
lured by the flattery of Death. She says that she wanted
to be free in the arms of Satyavan. She tells Death that
in order "to seize him better with her boundless heart
she accepts the limiting circle of his arms". She claims
for man his right to love and to be loved. It is this fundamental right which Death attempts to take away. But
Death tells Savitri:

However mighty, whatever thy secret name
Uttered in hidden conclave of the gods,
Thy heart's ephemeral passion cannot break
The iron rampart of accomplished things
Whoever thou art behind thy human mask,
The Cosmic Law is greater than thy will.
Even God himself obeys the Laws he made:
The Law abides and never can it change,
The Person is a bubble on Time's sea.

There is a fundamental conflict in the approaches
of Death and of Savitri. Death regards the Person as
a mere bubble on the sea of Time, while Savitri regards
the Person as a real entity, a traveller from the Timeless
into the realms of Time. Death tells Savitri that if she
claims to know Truth, can she then communicate that
Truth to him. He asks:

....what is Truth and who can find her form
Amid the specious images of sense
Amid the crowding guesses of the mind
And the dark ambiguities of a world
Peopled with the incertitudes of Thought?
Truth has no home in earth's irrational breast:
Yet without reason life is a tangle of dreams,
But reason is poised above a dim abyss
And stands at last upon a plank of doubt.
Eternal truth lives not with mortal men.

Death demolishes Savitri's claim to know Truth and
to represent it here on earth. He says that reason after
all stands only on the plank of doubt, and without reason
man's life is a tangle of mere dreams. Again Death says
that truth has no home in man's irrational breast. Thus
he indicates that neither by reason nor by unreason can
Truth be found. How can Savitri, a mere mortal, know
about Truth. But if Savitri still claims to know Truth,
then Death tells her,

Show me the body of the living Truth,
Or draw for me the outline of her face
That I too may obey and worship her.
Then will I give thee back thy Satyavan.

Death tells Savitri that if she can draw the outline
of the face of Truth and show the body of living Truth,
then he too will follow that Truth and give back to her
Satyavan. Death has laid down an impossible demand,
for, how can the body of living Truth be shown.
Perhaps Death uses the term "living truth" purposely,
for, one can speak of the body of truth with reference
to something that is crystallised and therefore dead. If
Savitri is able to show the body of living Truth, then
Death is ready to follow it, and even give back Satyavan
to her. Death tells Savitri: "No magic truth can bring
the dead to life, no power of earth cancel the thing once
done". Once again he asks Savitri to leave the dead

Satyavan and rearrange her life accepting that fact.   Then Savitri replied, but as she was speaking her mortality disappeared, and her Goddess self grew visible.   She said:

> O Death, thou too art God and yet not He,
> But only his own black shadow on his path
> All contraries are aspects of God's face.
> The Many are the innumerable One,
> The One carries the multitude in his breast;
> Darkness below, a fathomless Light above,
> Stand face to face, opposite, inseparable
> Two poles whose currents wake the immense World-
> Force.

Savitri speaks to Death about the play of the opposites which underlies all movements in the manifested universe.   There has to be collapse of logic before one can understand Truth as God himself.   Truth and God are not two different things.   Death wants to see the face of Truth, but he forgets that Truth defies Reason.   By reason one can never understand the secret of the Universal Drama which the Universe is.   The One and the Many are not opposed to each other, for, as the poet says in the above lines: "The Many are the innumerable One".   Savitri says to Death:

> ....who can show to thee Truth's glorious face?
> Our human words can only shadow her.
> To thought she is an unthinkable rapture of light,
> To speech a marvel inexpressible.
> O Death, if thou couldst touch the Truth supreme,
> Thou wouldst grow suddenly wise and cease to be.

If Death could touch the supreme Truth then he would cease to be—that is what Savitri assures him.   She says here that Truth cannot be expressed in words nor can become a subject of thought.   Truth has to be directly known, and when this direct knowledge comes then the very ground on which Death stands would give way.

But Death says that if Truth cannot be expressed then
how is a bridge to be constructed between the Unmanifest and the Manifest?   Must this gulf remain unbridgeable ? If so, how can earth receive the blessing of heaven?
Who will bring down the light of heaven on earth?
Here now Death poses a direct question to Savitri.   He
says:

> Is thine that strength, O beauty of mortal limbs,
> O soul who flutterest to escape my net?
> Who then art thou hiding in human guise?
> Thy voice carries the sound of infinity,
> Knowledge is with thee, Truth speaks through
> thy words
> The light of things beyond shines in thy eyes.
> But where is thy strength to conquer Time and
> Death?

There is a challenge to Savitri in these words of
Death. He says to her that while she has knowledge
and light, where is her strength to conquer Death and
Time? Without such strength of what use are Knowledge and Light?   Death throws out a more powerful challenge when he addresses her thus:

> Hast thou God's force to build heaven's values here?
> For truth and Knowledge are an idle gleam,
> If Might comes not to give to Truth her right.
> O human claimant to immortality,
> Reveal thy power, lay bare thy spirit's force,
> Then will I give back to thee Satyavan
> Let deathless eyes look into the eyes of Death
> Transform earth's death into immortal life
> Then can thy dead return to thee and live.

As these words of Death were spoken, the poet says,
Savitri looked on Death and answered not. Then a mighty transformation came over Savitri. The poet says :

D.–21

A halo of the indwelling Deity,
The Immortal's lustre that had lit her face
And tented its radiance in her body's house
In a flaming moment of apocalypse
The Incarnation thrust aside its veil

The transformation in Savitri was such that it was a flaming moment of apocalypse, meaning revelation. It was a supreme moment of revelation where the Incarnation threw aside her veil. Savitri came into her own as the incarnation of the Divine. All human beings are incarnations of the Divine—but we are unable to thrust aside the veil that hides this Divinity. Savitri threw aside the veil and a flaming moment of revelation came. The poet says, she was,

A little figure in infinity
Yet stood and seemed the Eternal's very house,
As if the world's centre was her very soul
And all wide space was but its outer robe.

The poet says that such was the transformation that through her eternity looked into the eyes of Death. There was a silence. Even Death must have stood stunned at this transformation of the mere mortal. Then the aweful silence was broken and a Voice was heard that seemed the low calm utterance of infinity. It said:

I hail thee almighty and victorious Death
Thou grandiose Darkness of the Infinite.
Thou art my shadow and my instrument
But now, O timeless Mightiness, stand aside
And leave the path of my incarnate Force.
Relieve the radiant god from thy black mask;
Release the soul of the world called Satyavan
That he may stand master of life and fate
Man's representative in the house of God,
The mate of Wisdom and the spouse of Light
The eternal bridegroom of the eternal bride.

But Death still put up a resistence even though he knew that he had almost lost the game. As the poet says "Death unconvinced resisted still, although he knew refusing still to know, although he saw refusing still to see". Even though Death knew that he was refusing to know, and still resisted. Surely there is none so blind as one who refuses to see. Death was utterly blind in his resistence. Seeing the game was lost, he made frantic efforts to call all his colleagues for help, but one by one these friends and associates relented, leaving Death all alone. The poet says:

> He called to Night but she fell shuddering back,
> He called to Hell but sullenly it retired,
> He turned to the Inconscient for support,
> From which he was born, his vast sustaining self:
> It drew him back towards boundless vacancy
> As if by himself to swallow up himself:
> He called to his strength, but it refused his call.
> At least he knew defeat inevitable
> And left crumbling the shape that he had worn
> Abandoning hope to make man's soul his prey
> And force to be mortal the immortal spirit.

The associates of Death are Night, Hell and Matter —but all these realizing the predicament in which Death was placed deserted him. They refused to stand by him in his hour of great need. Death disappeared and he took refuge in the retreating Night. Death was unable to stand the onslaught of the transformed Savitri. The Voice that had spoken had shaken him up. His frantic efforts to save himself had failed, and none of his associates was willing to stand by him. And so taking shelter under the retreating Night, he vanished. The poet says:

> The dire universal Shadow disappeared
> Vanishing into the Void from which it came.
> As if deprived of its original cause,

The twilight realm passed fading from their souls,
And Satyavan and Savitri were alone.

With the disappearance of Death into the Void from
where it had come, Satyavan and Savitri were left alone.
No more was there the figure of Death to intervene. While the form of Death was not there, there was something
else which still kept Satyavan and Savitri apart. The
poet says that while Satyavan and Savitri were alone,

But neither stirred: between those figures rose
A mute invisible and translucent wall.
In the long blank moment's pause nothing could move:
All waited on the unknown inscrutable Will.

With the disappearance of Death, if Satyavan and
Savitri were left alone, why could they not come together?
What was it that separated them? The poet says: "a
mute invisible and translucent wall" kept them apart
even when Death had vanished. What was this wall and
why did it not crumble when Death moved away? It
has to be remembered that so far what has happened is
the disappearance of Death in the moment of his defeat.
His moving away in the hour of defeat created a long
blank. It was a moment of blankness, not the moment
of emptiness. In the blankness, the form of death had
gone but his invisible presence was there. The blankness
was haunted by this invisible presence of Death. And it
was this haunting presence which created a wall so that
neither Satyavan nor Savitri could stir. The defeat of
death is not sufficient, for, then he will make his presence
felt invisibly. It is not the conquest of Death that will
lead man to the realization of his Immortality. The invisible presence of defeated Death will still strike terror in
the heart of man. By calling the hidden strength, man
may defeat Death and cause his form to disappear. But
this does not free man from the fear of Death. Death must
be transformed so that he becomes the friend of man, not
a disguised foe. Until Death is transformed there is no

freedom for man from the fear of Death. When Death is transformed then man can live with him even in the midst of his daily avocations. It is in such transformation, that life and death can co-exist. And only in their co-existence, can one find the secret of life as well as death. Savitri's strength had defeated Death—but her Love must still create the miracle of Death's transformation. Only then can she go back to earth with Satyavan, and together they create a new world where man shall move as an Immortal Being.

CHAPTER XXIV

THE MOMENT OF CELESTIAL FATE

IN the great epic poem of Savitri, Sri Aurobindo has dealt with the seemingly insoluble problem of Fate. To the common understanding of man, it is utterly insoluble. But Sri Aurobindo has indicated that man need not despair about the problem of Fate, for, it is within the power of man to be free from it. With Fate is associated the problem of Time, and in the sphere of Time, Death is the supreme lord. Thus are Fate, Time and Death inter-related. When one is solved, the others automatically get dissolved. All the three converge on the problem of Karma. Time is indeed the realm in which Karma operates, and Karma becomes intolerable because of the element of Fate involved in it. Man is afraid of Fate because it seems un-alterable. He feels helpless in the face of Fate because it is governed by the processes of Time. Once again the most distressing factor of Fate is its association with Death. Surely there is nothing more unalterable than Death, and so, the most fierce expression of Fate is none other than Death. If one can conquer Death then Fate ceases to be a problem, for, in the conquest over Death there is implied a conquest over Time itself. And if Time comes under the control of man, then Karma loses its sting completely. In fact, in the midst of the passage of Karma, he can become completely Karmaless. Karma then will mean only a processsion of events without any psychological bondage. In taking up the question of Fate, Sri Aurobindo has touched upon one of the most perplexing problems of man. It is in this that the relevance of *Savitri* to the modern man can be seen clearly. Man is for ever troubled by the problem of Fate. The

326

modern man, in the midst of scientific and technological triumphs, faces the problem of Fate with even greater intensity. He has seen that the triumphs of science and technology have not brought him nearer to the solution of the vexed problem of Fate and Karma. In fact, these psychological problems have become all the more pronounced in this age. Man is unhappy in the midst of mounting comforts. It is this paradox of unhappiness in the midst of increasing comfort that has brought him today face to face with the psychological problem of sorrow and suffering. Fate and Karma are only another name for sorrow and suffering. The two poles of life's movement are Time and Death. It begins with the awareness of Time and ends with the shattering experience of Death. It is in this movement from Time to Death that lie the factors of Fate and Karma. Once the movement begins in Time it must end in Death. Man uselessly struggles against Death, for Death is only the culminating point of Time. If he can conquer Time then the problem of Death has no existence whatsoever. It is Time that brings the operation of Karma, and it is once again Time which confronts man with Fate. The crux of the problem is neither Death, nor Fate nor Karma. It is Time which is the begetter of all psychological problems including the problem of Death. And man must establish his mastery over Time, for, beyond Time, Death has no sway, and beyond Time, Fate and Karma have no existence at all. Since Time is the begetter of all psychological problems, it is the experience of the Timeless that frees man from all sorrow and suffering.

So far in the discussion of Savitri with Death, she has been functioning in the realm of Time. In this realm of Time, she has given a crushing defeat to Death. But still there exists a wall, a translucent wall, that separates Satyavan and Savitri. Although they are just by themselves, they cannot meet because of this wall. The wall has its existence in Time, and Savitri's dialogue with Death

has been in the sphere of Time. How can this wall
of separation be demolished, and how can the two Lovers
meet without anything standing between them? With
the disappearance of Death, the whole environment changes. The darkness of the Night gives place to the light
of the Eternal Day. For Savitri the night is over and she
has stepped into the brightness of the Day. The poet says:

> A marvellous sun looked down from ecstasy's skies
> On worlds of deathless bliss, perfection's home,
> Magical unfoldings of the Eternal's smile
> Capturing his secret heart-beats of delight.
> God's everlasting day surrounded her,
> Her soul stood close to the founts of the infinite.
> Infinity's finite fronts she lived in, new
> For ever to an everlasting sight.

Savitri was now surrounded by the joys of the eternal
day. She now lived in infinity's finite fronts. She was
on the threshold of infinity, but still on this side of the
Unmanifest. It is true that she had reached the utmost
height of the Manifest, but even the highest point of the
Manifest is not the Unmanifest. To indicate this the
poet says that she lived in the finite fronts of infinity. Infinity has no fronts, it is only when infinite enters the
field of time-succession that there arise frontiers and boundaries. The Unmanifest and the Timeless have no frontiers. The finite frontiers of the Infinite denote the intimations of the Timeless in the field of Time, of the Unmanifest in the realm of the Manifest. The poet says
that these finite fronts of the Infinite were such that they
were ever new. In the words of the poet, they were "new
for ever to the everlasting sight". In the finite fronts of
the Infinite there come intimations of the Timeless from
moment to moment, and each intimation is new. And
so one can never get used to these intimations. Such was
the realm of delight and ecstasy to which Savitri came
when Death retreated along with the Night. On this plane

of the Eternal Day, the poet says, "rapture was a common
incident" and "limbs were trembling densities of soul".
The poet tells us:

> There Time dwelt with Eternity as one;
> Immense felicity joined rapt repose.

One may ask: How can Time and Eternity be one?
It indicates that it was difficult to say where Time ended
and where the Timeless began. In the first intimation of
the Timeless, Time seems as one with the Eternal. The
stream of Time is crystal clear, for, here the Timeless descends for the first time into the realm of Time. It is like
the great river Ganga descending on the plains of India
for the first time from the pure regions of the Hima-
layas. At this point the Ganga is absolutely crystal clear.
Similarly, when the first intimations of the Timeless descend into the plains of Time then it appears as if Time
dwells with Eternity as one. As she was standing in this
ecstatic realm there appeared before her the transfigured
form of Death. The poet says:

> One whom her soul had faced as Death and Night
> A sum of all sweetness gathered into his limbs
> And blinded her heart to the beauty of the suns.
> Transfigured was the formidable shape.
> A secret splendour rose revealed to sight
> Where once the vast embodied Void had stood.
> Night the dim mask had grown a wonderful face.

Savitri must have felt utterly amazed seeing this tremendous transformation in Death. Death had vanished
when Savitri had appeared before him in her Divine
Form. All the colleagues of Death had deserted him in
the great hour of his need. And with the vanishing of
Death, night had retreated and Savitri had stepped into
the dazzling light of the Eternal Day. There in that
brilliant light of the day appeared before her the transformed figure of Death with all the sweetness gathered

in his limbs. It was a marvellous form that responded to her gaze. Savitri felt that Death's sweetness justified life's blindest pain;

> All Nature's struggle was its easy price
> The universe and its agony seemed worth-while.

Seeing this transformed form of Death, Savitri felt all her struggles were worth-while; in fact, she realized that she had indeed to pay a very easy price to come to this experience of Death's transfiguration. She was surprised to see that "all grace and glory and all divinity were here collected in a single form". The transformation of Death was so complete that it was difficult for Savitri to believe what she saw. The poet describes what Savitri saw thus:

> In him the fourfold Being bore its crown
> That wears the mystery of a nameless Name,
> The universe writing its tremendous sense
> In the inexhaustible meaning of a word.

In this transformation she saw revealed the mystery of the nameless Name. When the Unmanifest expresses itself in the noblest form of Manifestation then is the mystery of the nameless Name revealed. The Nameless is the unmanifest even as Name signifies the Manifest. In the transformation of Death, the manifest had become so transparent that the intangible unmanifest was almost visible in form. So far Savitri had seen only the crude and the gross form of Death. It was almost the physical form of Death. The physical form vanished when Savitri rose to the Divine stature. When the physical form was no more then did Savitri see Death in the nature of its fourfold Being. What is the nature of the fourfold Being which Savitri sees in the transfiguration of Death? The first aspect of this Being was,

> Virat, who lights his camp-fires in the suns
> And the star-entangled ether is his hold
> Expressed himself with Matter for his speech.

The gross physical form of Death was no more. There appeared instead the Etheric form which exists as the substratum of the dense physical. Savitri is looking at the etheric being of Death whose speech is Matter. Describing this etheric nature, the poet says: "His is the dumb will of atom and clod". The secret of Matter's existence lies in its etheric counter-part. The poet calls this nature as Virat. The Mahabharata story says that after completing twelve years in forest-residence, the Pandavas were required to spend one year *incognito*, and the condition was that they must not be found out during this period. The story says that the Pandavas remained *incognito* in the Kingdom of Virat. Sri Aurobindo's mention about Virat in the context of the four-fold Being of Death is most significant. Savitri saw the etheric form of Death. This etheric form is sometimes called the etheric double, meaning the invisible counterpart of the physical. The poet says in the above lines that Virat has his hold over ether. In the etheric form the dense physical matter remains *incognito*. Although the etheric is the "double" of the physical, it is an invisible counterpart of the dense material. In the four-fold Being of Death, there is thus the mention of what is known in Hindu philosophy as the *Pranamaya Kosha*. It is this which is seen by Savitri as Death transfigured. The etheric counterpart of the physical form of Death was obviously as majestic as the outer body. Describing this etheric double, the poet says:

> Objects are his letters, forces are his words,
> Events are the crowded history of his life,
> And sea and land are the pages of his tale,
> Matter is his means and his spiritual sign.

Surely Matter is the means of the etheric body, for, it expresses itself in dense matter. As the poet says: "In the current of the blood, makes flow the soul". The etheric realm is the realm of forces—those that vitalize the physical body. Savitri saw this majestic form of Death, divested of the physical form. Looking more intently at the transfigured form of Death, she saw him as *Hiranyagarbha*, the Golden Egg, symbolising the creative activity of the mind. This was the *Manomaya Kosha* of the Hindu philosophy. About this aspect of Death, the poet says:

> Hiranyagarbha, author of thoughts and dream,
> Who sees the invisible and hears the sounds
> That never visited a mortal ear.
> A magician with the omnipotent wand of thought.

Savitri sees Death in his stupendous Mental form. In this aspect of the Mind, he is like a magician who moves the wand of thought and builds the secret uncreated worlds, the worlds of imagination. The poet says that Death in this aspect is the "Imagist casting the formless into shape". It is the mind that is the giver of shape to that which is Formless, and this it does with the power of imagination. Then Savitri sees Death in his aspect of the *Vigyanmaya Kosha*, that which lies beyond the mental form. About this aspect, the poet says:

> A third spirit stood behind, their hidden cause,
> A mass of superconscience closed in light,
> Creator of things in his all-knowing sleep
> All from his stillness came as grows a tree;
> He is our seed and core, our head and base.
> All light is but a flash from his closed eyes.
> He is the Wisdom that comes not by thought,
> His wordless silence brings the immortal word.

The *Vigyanmaya Kosha* is known as the sheath of Intelligence, even as the *Manomaya Kosha* is the sheath of Intellect. Savitri sees Death not only as the embodiment of Intellect, but also as the embodiment of Intelligence, or Intuition. In the above lines the poet says: "Creator of things in his all-knowing sleep". Intuition functions only when the intellect is in a state of sound sleep, the condition of *sushupti*. That is why the poet says that "He is the Wisdom that comes not by thought". Surely the wisdom that comes by thought is mere knowledge. While Death is the embodiment of Knowledge, he is also the embodiment of Wisdom. In the words of the poet as possessing this Wisdom, "he is the centre of the circle of God". The circle of God is obviously God in manifestation, or the Brahman with attributes, to use the terminology of the Upanishads. And surely Wisdom is the centre of the circle of God, it is the centre of God manifested. But this was not all. Savitri saw Death in the *Anandamaya Kosha*, the Sheath of Bliss. This was the fourth and the highest aspect of Death's Being that she saw. The poet says:

> The bliss that made the world in his body lived.
> Whatever vision has escaped the eye,
> Whatever happiness comes in dream and trance,
> The nectar spilled by love with trembling hands,
> The joy the cup of Nature cannot hold
> Were waiting in the honey of his laugh.
> The secret whisper of the flower and star
> Revealed its meaning in his fathomless look.

In the four-fold being of Death, Savitri saw the beauty of the non-physical aspect of the god. Death had left behind the fearsome physical form. It could stand no longer against the onslaughts of Savitri. Death showed to her his other form, for, he realized that she had conquered the physical expression of Death. Savitri saw the Etheric, the Mental, the Intuitional and the Bliss body of Death. Even she was taken aback by this tremendous transformation that was visible to her. The poet describes this transfiguration of Death in the following lines:

> As from the harp of some ecstatic god
> There springs a harmony of lyric bliss
> Striving to leave no heavenly joy unsung,
> Such was the life in that embodied Light.
> He seemed the wideness of a boundless sky,

He seemed the passion of a sorrowless earth,
He seemed the burning of a world-wide sun.
Two looked upon each other, Soul saw Soul.

It has to be realized that this transfiguration of Death
can be experienced only by one who has the strength to look
into the lonely eyes of Death as he appears in his terrible
form. The terror of Death disappears when the mere
mortal looks Death straight in the face. The transfiguration of Death meant that Savitri had conquered the fear
of Death, so that Death appeared to her as the passion of
a sorrowless earth and as the wideness of the boundless
sky. One may ask: Has Savitri now come to the journey's end? Will she be able to go back with Satyavan
to reshape the world nearer to her heart's desire? What
can this transfigured Death not do? Surely he can give
back to her living Satyavan. Just when "two looked upon
each other, Soul saw Soul" there was heard a voice. The
poet describes this in the following lines:

Then like an anthem from the heart's lucent cave
A voice soared up whose magic sound could turn
The poignant weeping of the earth to sobs
Of rapture and her cry to spirit song.

Death is usually associated with its physical aspect. It
is a physical event greatly feared because it brings physical
existence to an end. But man is not just a physical being; in fact, the physical part is the outermost part of his
existence. If one would look at the physical face of Death
without any fear then one would be able to see the other
aspects of Death which have no element of fearsomeness
in them. When Savitri was able to see the physical death
in the face, then was she able to look upon the other
aspects which were pleasant and intensely sober. These
aspects have been described by the poet in the four-fold
Being of Death. Usually one speaks of the Five-fold Being,
but here the mention is made of the Four-fold because the
physical part of the Being disappeared when Savitri looked

into the lonely eyes of physical Death without any element of fear. When she saw the Bliss aspect of Death, then
was she greatly awe-struck. It is in this state that she
heard a voice which, as the poet says, could turn the weeping of the earth into sobs of rapture. It is the voice of
Ecstasy that speaks. The voice came from the lucent cave
of the heart. It says:

> I am the inviolable Ecstasy;
> They who have looked on me, shall grieve no more.
> The eyes that live in night shall see my form.

The Voice says that he who is not afraid to live in
the darkness of Night shall see my form. How can one
who is plagued all the time by fear, ever know what ecstasy
is? Fear and Joy cannot go together. The Voice says:

> Two powers from one original ecstasy born
> Pace near, but parted in the life of man;
> One leans to earth, the other yearns to the skies:
> Heaven in its rapture dreams of perfect earth,
> Earth in its sorrow dreams of perfect heaven,
> The two longing to join, yet walk apart,
> Idly divided by their vain conceits;
> They are kept apart from their oneness by enchanted
> fears;
> Sundered mysteriously by miles of thought
> They gaze across the silent gulfs of sleep.

The Voice, however, says that when "the phantom
flame-edge fails undone, then never more can space or
time divide". In the case of Savitri the phantom flame-
edge had failed, for, no more could fear assail her, and
there can be no division by Space and Time of the
"lover from the loved". The Voice says:

> ....Space shall draw back
> Her great translucent curtain,
> ....Time shall be

The quivering of the spirit's endless bliss.
Attend that moment of celestial fate.

The Voice says to Savitri that a great moment of celestial fate had arrived where Space shall draw back her curtain
and Time shall be the quivering of spirit's endless bliss. It
asks Savitri to attend that moment, to be aware of it. In
this state Earth and Heaven are not far away. Here there
is no question of the two longing to join, yet walk apart.
Savitri by the dint of her dauntless courage had made
possible for that moment to arrive. But the Voice says:

Meanwhile you two shall serve the dual law
Which only now the scouts of vision glimpse,
Who pressing through the forest of their thoughts
Have found the narrow bridges of the gods.
Wait patient of the brittle bars of form
Making division your delightful means
Of happy oneness rapturously enhanced
By attraction in the throbbing air between.

But at this moment of celestial fate, Savitri was faced
with a choice. She is told that she and Satyavan will remain
united together in an ecstatic communion, but then they
must follow the dual law of ecstasy. This means they two
must function in different regions as that is how the two
poles of ecstasy operate. She is told to make this division
of work "their delightful means of happy oneness". The
Voice says that this happy oneness will be all the more
enhanced by attraction in the throbbing air between. The
air between them will throb with their love, and so this
separation, willingly accepted, will enhance their feeling
of love and attraction for each other. They will remain
one, and yet be willingly separated for work, for, ecstasy
follows the rule of the opposites. This polarity will be surcharged by their mutual love and attraction, but without
polarity the law of ecstasy cannot function. We must remember that it is still the transfigured Death that speaks,

and Death knows only the plane of duality. All that Death suggests to Savitri is a state of polarity without separation—a polarity that enhances the attraction between the two poles. A polarity without opposition that is the choice that this Voice places before Savitri. But a question may arise: What is the other choice? Supposing Savitri does not accept this polarity where the law of duality operates, what else has the Voice to offer to her? What is the alternative if she rejects this state of polarity enhancing love and attraction between the two poles? The Voice says:

> Yet if thou wouldst abandon the vexed world,
> Careless of the dark moan of things below,
> Tread down the isthmus, overleap the flood,
> Renounce the tie that joins thee to earth-kind,
> Cast off thy sympathy with mortal hearts.
> Ascend, O Soul, into thy blissful home
> Roam with thy comrade splendour under skies
> Spiritual lit by an unsetting sun
> As godheads live who care not for the world
> And share not in the toil of Nature's powers:
> Absorbed in their self-ecstasy they dwell.
> Cast off the ambiguous myth of earth's desire,
> O immortal, to felicity arise.

The Voice tells Savitri to renounce all care and anxiety for the world, and ascend into the realm of bliss and there live eternally with her comrade. The Voice says that it is a land lit by an unsetting sun. The sun will never set there; there will be no darkness of the night. And so Savitri can live with Satyavan without any interruption. But for this she must give up the myth of earth's desire. She must live unmindful of what the creatures of the earth ask or demand. The Voice has placed two alternatives before Savitri. In both these alternatives she will remain united to Satyavan. She can either dwell with her lover in the world of bliss and renounce all responsibility for earth's desires, or, accept the law of polarity so that the two,

D.-22

ever united, still willingly function in two different realms. It will be a polarity, where though separated, they will grow in greater attraction for each other. Let Savitri make her choice. The poet says that on listening these words "a smile came rippling out in her wide eyes", and she said:

> I climb not to thy everlasting Day,
> Even as I have shunned thy eternal Night.
> To me who turn not from thy terrestrial Way,
> Give back the other self my nature asks,
> Thy spaces need him not to help their joy;
> Earth needs his beautiful spirit made by thee
> To fling delight down like a net of gold.
> Earth is the chosen place of mightiest souls
> Earth is the heroic spirit's battlefield,
> Thy servitudes on earth are greater, king,
> Than all the glorious liberties of heaven.

Savitri tells the Voice that she too was an inhabitant of heaven and has wandered in its glamorous regions. She says, "thy wonder-rounds of music I have trod". She has known and experienced the dance of the gods. She says that she has known all that the heaven-world offers, but she has not moved thus far, daring the dangers of the dark night, to be told to renounce the earth and settle down in the sylvan beauties of heaven. She says:

> In me the spirit of immortal love
> Stretches its arms out to embrace mankind.
> Too far thy heavens for me from suffering men.
> Imperfect is the joy not shared by all.
> O thou who soundest the trumpet in the lists,
> Take not the warrior with his blow unstruck.
> Are there not still a million fights to wage?
> Break not the lyre before the song is found,
> Are there not still unnumbered chants to weave?

Savitri tells Death not to separate them under the pretext of the dual law of ecstasy. To do so would be like breaking the lyre before the song is found, it will be like taking away the warrior before the blow is struck. She says to Death:

Weld us to one in thy strong smithy of life.
Thy fine-curved jewelled hilt call Savitri,
The blade's exultant smile name Satyavan.

She says to him, "Part not the handle from the untried steel". For his valiant sword, Savitri will be the curved jewelled hilt and Satyavan will be the blade's exultant smile. Savitri once again wants to remind Death:

I know that I can lift man's soul to God
I know that he can bring the Immortal down.

Savitri will lift the soul of man to God, and Satyavan will bring the immortal down on earth—thus will the gulf between heaven and earth be bridged. Here she speaks about the secret of Ascent and Descent which flows like an undercurrent in Sri Aurobindo's whole philosophy. Savitri tells Death that he can use both Satyavan and herself for his great work. Let him not regard them as enemies challenging his empire, but as collaborators in the great work of bringing heaven and earth together. But Death had still many doubts to be cleared. He said to Savitri:

How shall earth-nature and man's nature rise
To the celestial levels, yet earth abide?
Heaven and earth towards each other gaze
Across a gulf that few can cross; none touch,
The shore that all can see but never reach.
Heaven's light visits sometimes the mind of earth.

Death asks Savitri, how can earth remain earth and still rise to the celestial levels.? Heaven and earth can only gaze at each other. The earth may see the other shore but it can never reach it. He says that from time to time the Light of heaven visits the mind of man, but these are just casual contacts which never last. About earth, he says:

....hers are fragments of a star-lost gleam,
Hers are but careless visits of the gods.
They are a Light that fails, a Word soon hushed
And nothing they mean can stay for long on earth.
There are high glimpses, not the lasting sight.

Death wants Savitri to remember that these touches
of heaven are only the careless and casual visits of the
gods. Now and then some great genius may bring down
the light of heaven but then it soon fades away, for,
nothing that comes from heaven can stay long on earth.
He says:

Men answer to the touch of greater things:
Or, raised by some strong hand to breathe heaven-air,
They slide back to the mud from which they climbed.

Here Death is telling Savitri the story of what the
mystics and the prophets have achieved. They may have
pushed humanity to the heights of heaven for the time being,
but very soon man returns to the mud from where he had
risen. Death says that she should not strive to invest the
common man with uncommon things. It is good that man
remains common so that he functions within the campus
of his own nature. If too much violence is done to this
nature of man then "the settled balance of created things"
would be disturbed. Death says:

To be the common man they think the best,
To live as others live is their delight.
For most are built on Nature's earthly plan
And owe small debt to a superior plane;
The human average is their level pitch,
A thinking animal's material range.

And so it is better if Savitri does not disturb this normal
run of man by introducing factors which he cannot as-
similate. Each creature must perform his appointed task.
She must understand what the normal task of man is.
Any effort to ask man to step out of his normal range

would be disastrous. Man may have the powers of the mind but they are limited. And more than mind he does not possess. Death says:

> His mind is closed between two firmaments.
> He seeks through words and images the Truth,
> Even his Knowledge is an Ignorance.
> He is barred out from his own inner depths;
> He cannot look on the face of the Unknown.

How can man overstep his own limits? It is futile to seek to do something that is impossible. Savitri should leave things to shape themselves, and not try to hasten too much. He advises Savitri not to expect too much from a mere mortal. By hastening too much the balance of things would get disturbed resulting in greater sorrow for man. One is reminded here of the first Discourse of the Bhagavad Gita where Arjuna speaks of *Kula-kshaya* which is nothing but a disturbance in the balance of things. Death tells Savitri:

> O too compassionate and eager Dawn,
> Leave to the circling aeon's tardy pace
> And to the working of the inconscient Will,
> Leave to its imperfect light the earthly race:
> All shall be done by the long act of Time.

Death wants Savitri to leave the problems of the earth to be solved by the processes of Time. She need not bother about them. She can rise to the realms of heaven to which she essentially belongs and live there in a state of eternal bliss with Satyavan. Formerly the plea of Death was that Savitri should return to earth and spend her days as best as she could. But now the appeal is different. Death is willing to see that Savitri and Satyavan are never separated, but for this Savitri must release herself from her obligations to the earth. He says to her:

> Break into eternity thy mortal mould,
> Then shalt thou know the Lover and the Loved,

Leaving the limits dividing him and thee.
Receive him into boundless Savitri,
Lose thyself into infinite Satyavan,
O miracle where thou beganst, there cease.

Death asks Savitri to step over the line that divides him
and her. He says that she should end her play where she
began. She came down from heaven, let her play also cease
in heaven. After all she did not want to be separated from
her Lover. What greater joy can there be than that the
Two could be united in the everlasting bliss of heaven?
Let not Savitri limited by Time receive Satyavan; rather
let the boundless Savitri receive her lover. Once again
let not the lover be bound by the limitations of earth, but
let him be infinite Satyavan. Death wants boundless
Savitri to remain united with infinite Satyavan. But for this
earth must be left behind. Surely the boundless and the
infinite cannot abide in the limitations of the earth. But
Savitri replied to the transfigured godhead, that was Death,
thus:

In vain thou temptst with solitary bliss
Two spirits saved out of a suffering world;
My soul and his indissolubly linked
In the one task for which our lives were born,
To raise the world to God in deathless Light,
To bring God down to the world on earth we came.
I keep my will to save the world and man;
Even the charm of thy alluring voice,
O blissful godhead, cannot seize and snare.
I sacrifice not earth to happier worlds.

In the common understanding of man, Liberation, or
Moksha or *Nirvana* is regarded in terms of personal salvation. There really can be no personal salvation at all. It is
only when the person vanishes like the dew-drop slipping into the shining sea, that Liberation can come.
There is no liberation for the person; it is only when the
person disappears that Liberation can be realized. And

so all talk of personal salvation is meaningless. Savitri
tells Death that she cannot be allured and tempted by
talks of solitary bliss. She cannot be weaned away from her
promise given to mankind. To raise the world to God and
to bring God down on earth—this dual task of Ascent and
Descent is the assignment given to her, and she will fulfil
it. Nothing can tempt her away from this Divine Mission
to which she is committed. Savitri says to Death that if
man cannot rise to the rarefied air of heaven, then man
must transcend himself and break down the limitations
that bind him. She says:

> Since God has made earth, earth must make in her God:
> What hides within her breast she must reveal.
> If man lives bound by his humanity,
> If he is tied for ever to his pain,
> Let a greater being then arise from man,
> The superhuman with the Eternal mate
> And the Immortal shine through earthly forms.

The whole emphasis in Sri Aurobindo's philosophy is
for the creation of a New Man. If man is bound by the
limitations of the mind, then let man break into the lands
of the Supermind. Man is not destined to live within the
limitations imposed by the mind. The New Man must
arise, but he will come only when the circle of mind is broken and the never-ceasing contact with the Supermind is
established. The birth of the Supermind is the New Dawn
to which the poet refers as he speaks of the New Man, free
from the tortures of his own limitations. Savitri recognizes
the imperative need for the arising of the New Man. She
realizes that consciousness, cribbed, cabined and confined
within the limitations of the mind, must be released so
that the Supermind may descend on earth. But Death
tells Savitri:

> In the impetuous drive of thy heart of flame,
> In thy passion to deliver man and earth
> Indignant at the impediments of Time

And the slow evolution's sluggard steps,
Lead not the spirit in an ignorant world
To dare too soon the adventure of the Light
Across the last confines of the limiting Mind
Into the danger of the Infinite.

Death again and again cautions Savitri regarding blind
adventures into the realms beyond the Mind. He tells her
that however slow the process of evolution may be, it is
safe to move along its pace. Daring too soon is dangerous.
But Savitri was a revolutionary and so could not be
dissuaded by words of caution. The border-line between
Mind and Super-Mind may be perilous, but she must
cross it. She must plunge into this adventure, for, the
problems of mankind are urgent and their solution cannot
brook any delay. Realizing the state of urgency in which
Savitri was, Death tells her:

But if thou wilt not wait for Time and God,
Do then thy work and force thy will on Fate.
..........but not here
Can the great choice be made that fixes fate.
Arise upon a ladder of greater worlds
To the infinity where no world can be.

In the above lines, Death declares his own limitations. He says that if Savitri cannot wait for Time to do
its work, then she should take whatever measures she
likes to force her will on Fate, and change that Fate.
Death says Savitri is free to do this. But then the changing
of Fate is not within his jurisdiction. He works on the
plane of Time, and in Time there is no solution to the
problem of Fate. Death says that his work is to carry out
the requirements of Fate. Within those requirements he
can make adjustments, and this he has tried to do by
placing various alternatives before Savitri. He is not em-
powered to change Fate; his power is only to execute Fate.
And so if Savitri wants the Fate to be changed, then she
must rise to a higher dimension of existence. And this

higher dimension is indicated by Death in the above lines
where he says: "Arise......to the infinite where no
world can be". The solution of the problem of Fate lies
not in the manifested realms, but in the Unmanifest where
no world can be. The answer to the problem of Fate is
not with Time, it is with the Timeless. Man has unneces--
sarily made Death into a problem. Death is not the
problem, it is Time which is the problem, for out of Time
arise conditions of Fate. Death is only an expression of
Time. It is in the Timeless that fate ceases to exist. If
Savitri wants to alter Fate, then Death tells her:

Ascend, O soul, into thy timeless self;
Choose destiny's curve and stamp thy will on Time.·

Death had done all he could for Savitri within the realm
of Time. He was unable to give back to Savitri, Satyavan
alive. To do so was outside his powers. He could soften the
blow of fate; he could accommodate Savitri in the realm
where Satyavan must live after discarding his mortal coil.
Death was prepared to make all those adjustments. But
Savitri was not interested in these mere adjustments; her
fight was with Fate itself. She must free man from the
dictates of Fate. She is not concerned with modifications
in the functioning of Fate; she demands man's total freedom from the prison-house of Fate. Death says that Fate
can be changed, but not in the realm of Time. He who
conquers Time is free from the demands of Fate. And so
Death asks Savitri to rise to those realms which are beyond
the frontiers of Time.

One may ask: How did Savitri ascend to the realms
of the Timeless? Of course, to describe this ascent as a
movement into the realms of the Timeless is a contradic-
tion in terms. The Timeless has no realm; it is somewhat
like a mathematical point which has position but no
magnitude. To talk of the realm of the Timeless is to put
it into the framework of Space. Time and Space are not

two different things. They are only two different approaches pointing to the same phenomenon. Where there is Space, Time too is involved; and where there is Time, Space is inevitably indicated. And so the Timeless is a state which can be experienced, but cannot be defined. The question is: How did ·Savitri ascend to that state? What was the secret of her ascent? When one looks at Time with .complete objectivity, allowing no subjective factor to project itself in this perception, then in that very looking at Time, the experience of the Timeless comes. Ordinarily we look at the chronology of Time with the super-imposition of the psychology of Time. To look at chronology of Time without psychological super-imposition is to see its flow. And in thus seeing the flow of Time, one perceives not only the continuity of Time, but one becomes aware of the moments of discontinuity. This awareness of the moments of discontinuity in the flow of Time is the experience of the Timeless. Savitri looked in the face of Death, and Death is indeed the symbol of Time. It is in looking into the lonely eyes of Death, without any subjective projection, that Savitri came to the experience of the Timeless. When Savitri ascended the Timeless state then the poet says:

> He ended and upon the falling sound
> A power went forth that shook the founded spheres
> And loosed the stakes that hold the tents of form
> In the stupendous theatre of Space
> The heaven-worlds vanished in spiritual light.

When Savitri rose to the Timeless state, Death ended. Earlier it was the form of Death that had vanished, and Death returned in a transfigured condition. But now Death ended, for, when Time ends, the very ground of the existence of Death ceases to exist. And when Death ended some mysterious power was released which shook the very foundations of manifested existence, for, it "loosed the stakes that hold the tents of form". The poet says that the heaven-worlds vanished in spiritual light. There is a reference here that a spiritual experience is of a higher dimensional validity than the heavenly or what may be called the occult experience. In the above lines the poet says that the heaven-worlds vanished when Savitri rose to the Timeless experience. The poet says: "The moments fell into eternity". Savitri heard a voice which asked her to choose. She replied:

> Thy peace, O Lord, a boon within to keep
> Amid the roar and ruin of wild Time
> For the magnificent soul of man on earth.
> Thy calm, O Lord, that bears thy hands of joy.

Savitri asks for the Peace of the Divine and the Timeless in the midst of the roar and ruin of Time. This is the first boon that she asks. What does this mean—the peace of the Timeless in the din and noise of Time? This is what is known in Hindu mysticism as the *Salokya Mukti* meaning living in the environment of the Timeless even when engaged in the activities demanded by Time. The Voice replied: "Wide open are the ineffable gates in front". She could pass through these gates and retire into the deep silence of the Timeless. But soon Savitri heard "a million creatures cry to her". The world below shuddered at the thought of Savitri retreating into the realms of Eternal Silence. And so she asked for a second boon and said:

> Thy oneness, Lord, in many approaching hearts
> My sweet infinity of thy numberless souls

In this request for "Thy oneness" there is contained the *Samipya Mukti*, meaning drawing nearer to the reality of things. This is the seeking of His oneness in many approaching hearts. The boon was granted. But at this point there was heard the sobbing of nature. Will Savitri return to humanity only with this feeling of oneness? Will it give her the strength to tackle the vast problems of fate and

time? She may move about with the oneness of the
Lord, but she may be utterly feeble to do anything for the
uplift of man. Then does Savitri ask again, and says:

> Thy energy, Lord, to seize on woman and man,
> To take all things and creatures in their grief
> And gather them into a mother's arm.

The gate was further opened and her boon was granted.
In this asking for the energy of the Lord, there is obviously a reference to the *Sarupya Mukti*, meaning growing into
the likeness of the Lord, so that she can carry the power
and the strength of the Lord himself. But Savitri felt, will
the peace, the oneness and the energy of the Lord enable
her to tackle the vast problems of man? And so she
finally asks:

> Thy embrace which rends the living knot of pain,
> Thy joy, O Lord, in which all creatures breathe,
> Thy magic flowing waters of deep love,
> Thy sweetness give to me for earth and men.

In this last prayer she asks for the embrace of the
Lord. Without Love what will she do? She may have Peace
and Oneness and Energy but these are of no avail without
Love. Here is contained the *Sayujya Mukti*, meaning, Not
I but Thee. In Love there is no existence of the "I"—
in this state only "Thee" exists. And this indeed is the
secret of *Sayujya Mukti*. Savitri must go down to earth
with the Power of Love, "thy magic flowing waters of
deep love". When Savitri spoke these words, there was
a silence, and then arose the blissful Voice which said:

> O beautiful body of the incarnate Word,
> Thy thoughts are mine, I have spoken with thy voice.
> My wi" is thine, what thou hast chosen I choose
> All thou hast asked I give to earth and men.
> Because thou hast obeyed my timeless will
> I lay my hands upon thy soul of flame,
> I lay my hands upon thy heart of love,

I yoke thee to my power of work in Time.
I bind by thy heart's passion thy heart to mine
Now will I do in thee my marvellous works
....thou shalt raise the earth-soul to Light
And bring down God into the lives of men
Men shall be lit with the Eternal's ray
Living for me, by me, in me they shall live.
In the heart of my creation's mystery
I will enact the drama of thy soul,
Inscribe the long romance of Thee and Me.
I will possess in thee my universe
The universe find all I am in thee.
I will use thee as my sword and as my lyre.

Savitri has come to the journey's end; or perhaps it
may be more true to say that her real journey now begins.
So far she had journeyed to God; now she will journey
in God. The Divine Voice says : "I shall possess in
thee my universe, and the universe find all I am in thee".
Savitri will now become the bridge between the Divine
and the Human, between Heaven and Earth. Savitri
began her journey with Death, it was a journey in Time
and with Time. But now with the elixir of the Timeless she will impart to Time a new meaning and a new
significance. A mere movement in Time is meaningless
unless there is the touch of the Timeless. Savitri goes
into the realm of Time now with the secret of the Timeless. Fate can be changed but not by a mere movement
in Time. It can be changed when one moves in Time
impregnated with the secret of the Timeless. The Voice
tells Savitri:

Descend to life with him thy heart desires.
O Satyavan, O luminous Savitri,
I sent you forth of old beneath the stars
A dual power of God in an ignorant world,
Bringing down God to the insentient globe,
Lifting earth-beings to immortality.

In the world of my knowledge and my ignorance
Where God is unseen and only is heard a Name
And knowledge is trapped in the boundaries of mind
And life is hauled in the drag-net of desire,
And Matter hides the soul from its own sight,
You are my Force at work to uplift earth's fate
O Savitri, thou art my spirit's Power,
The revealing voice of my immortal Word,
The face of Truth upon the roads of Time
Pointing to the souls of men the routes to God.

Here the Divine indicates to Savitri why she was
sent to earth, and what is the task that is now assigned
to her. She has to be "the face of Truth upon the roads
of Time pointing to the souls of men the routes of God".
Here in this world, knowledge is trapped in the boundaries
of the mind, and it will be Savitri's task to free knowledge
from the limitations of the mind. This trapping of
knowledge in the boundaries of the mind indicates that
the "Mind in a half-light moves amid half-truths." The
light of the mind is half or insufficient and so what it
makes visible is only half-truth. To be guided by mind is
thus to remain in a realm of half-truths—which is what
is happening to man today. The Divine Voice says:

There are greater destinies mind cannot surmise,
Fixed on the summit of the evolving Path
The traveller now treads in the Ignorance,
Unaware of his next step, not knowing his goal.
Mind is not all his tireless climb can reach.

The Divine Voice tells Savitri that Mind is not the
final point of man's evolution. In fact, the mind of man
is unable to comprehend the greater destinies. To walk
in the light of the mind is to walk in ignorance. Here
Savitri is being given the new marching orders which are
to lead humanity from the prison house of the mind to
the free air of the Super-Mind. That is the main work

of Savitri which she has to achieve on earth in company
with Satyavan. The Voice says:

> There is a consciousness mind cannot touch,
> Its speech cannot utter nor its thought reveal,
> It has no home on earth, no centre in man,
> Yet is the source of all things thought and done,
> The fount of the creation and its works.

It will be the mission of Savitri to work for the descent of this consciousness which mind can never touch.
This is that state of consciousness which has no home
on earth and no centre in man. Savitri must work for
the establishment of this centre in man. But this cannot
be done unless man breaks through the limitations of the
mind. This means that a new race of man must emerge;
there must take place the birth of a New Man. From
the Humanity of the Mind, the evolutionary stream must
move towards the Humanity of the Super-Mind. The
Voice says:

> Some shall be made the glory's receptacles
> And vehicles of the Eternal's luminous power.
> These are the high forerunners, the heads of Time,
> The great deliverers of earth-bound mind,
> The high transfigurers of human clay,
> The first-born of a new supernal race.

The Voice is placing before Savitri the entire picture
of the future of the human race. Savitri's mission is not
just to introduce few modifications in the existing pattern
of things—she has to be the bringer of a new age—the
age of the Super-mind. The New Man will usher in a
New Age where he shall annul "the decree of death
and pain", and,

> Bring back to Nature her early joy to live,
> The metred heart-beats of a lost delight,
> The cry of a forgotten ecstasy,
> The dance of the first world-creating Bliss.

If Savitri goes back to earth with Satyavan then she must know what stupendous work they together must achieve. It is not merely for Satyavan's claim to Immortality that she had entered into a dialogue with Death and transformed him. What she asked for Satyavan was for all humanity, for, man must be released from the bondage to Death. A new dimension of living must open for all who comprise humanity. She is told that the New Man will be,

A point or line drawn in the infinite,
A manifest of the Imperishable.
The super-mind shall be his nature's fount,
The Eternal's truth shall mould his thoughts and acts,
The Eternal's truth shall be his light and guide.
All then shall change, a magic order come
Overtopping this mechanical universe.
A mightier race shall inhabit the mortal's world.

In Sri Aurobindo's philosophy the fundamental emphasis has always been on obliterating the distance between Spirit and Matter, between Heaven and Earth. To spiritualize Matter itself is the high goal he has placed before man. His technique of Integral Yoga is oriented to the fulfilment of this objective. It will be Savitri's task to work for the birth of this new humanity and the emergence of a new order of things. What she has to strive for is indicated in the following lines:

The supermind shall claim the world for Light
And thrill with love of God the enamoured heart,
In earthly hearts kindle the Immortal's fire.
A soul shall wake in the Inconscient's house;
The mind shall be God-vision's tabernacle,
The body intuition's instrument,
And life a channel for God's visible power.

In the new dispensation of the Supermind, the mind and the body too shall be transformed. Man will need both body and mind, but these must become the instruments of the Supermind. The mind at present is the vehicle of its own past, but this must change so that it becomes the tabernacle of God-vision. The body must become the instrument of intuition, and not either of intellect or of instinct. In the subhuman creatures, body acts according to the dictates of instinct; in man today body acts at the behest of intellect. The Voice tells Savitri:

> This world shall be God's visible garden-house,
> The earth shall be a field and camp of God,
> Man shall forget consent to mortality
> And his embodied frail impermanence.
> The Spirit shall be the master of his world.

In this new order of things man will no longer give his consent to mortality and to his frail impermanence. Immortality shall be the birth-right of man. Not Matter, but Spirit shall be the master of the world, for, man will know the secret of spiritualizing matter itself. This will be the age of superman. Savitri is told:

> When superman is born as Nature's king,
> His presence shall transfigure Matter's world;
> He shall light up Truth's fire in Nature's night.

It is true that first the forerunners of this New Humanity will emerge. There must first come the pioneers of the new race, for, it is they that shall lead the common man. In modern sociology we fail to realize that it is the individual that can shape the new race. It is true that society moulds the individual but this moulding is like introducing a modified continuity. All social changes, whether reforms or so-called revolutions, are of this nature. They are mere modification in the patterns that exist. Fundamental changes always come from the individual. Society, in the ultimate analysis is static; it is the individual alone that is dynamic. And for fundamental changes it is the dynamism of the individual that alone is the most effective instrument. The Voice says:

D-23

The higher kind shall lean to lift up man.
Man shall desire to climb to his own heights
The truth above shall wake a nether truth;
Even the dumb earth become a sentient force.
The Spirit shall look out through Matter's gaze
And Matter shall reveal the Spirit's face.
The Spirit shall take up the human play,
This earthly life become the life divine.

To transform earthly-life into Life Divine—that is the great mission to which Savitri and Satyavan together must address themselves. Sri Aurobindo's philosophy rejects neither earth nor heaven. This philosophy stands for an indissoluble marriage between Heaven and Earth. As the poet says: "The Spirit shall look through Matter's gaze, and the Matter shall reveal the Spirit's face". Let Savitri go with Satyavan, hand in hand, but not forget the great work that the two lovers must accomplish. After having drawn this full picture of earth's future, the Voice stopped. The poet says "The measure of that subtle music ceased", and,

Sank like a star the soul of Savitri.
Amidst a laughter of unearthly lyres
She heard around her nameless voices cry
Triumphing, an innumerable sound.
A choir of laughing winds to meet her came.

As she was coming down to earth., humanity was anxiously waiting to meet her. But Savitri that was descending after a successful encounter with Death was totally changed. The poet says:

A face was over her which seemed a youth's,
Symbol of all the beauty eyes see not.

Yes, Savitri was changed, and yet she was the same. She combined in herself Humanity and Divinity with even greater majesty. The poet says: "changed in its shape, yet rapturously the same". Savitri brought the soul of

Satyavan down, for no longer was it in the custody of Death' But the soul of Satyavan was most precious to Savitri. Only when the soul touches the body that the two lovers will be able to move on earth, hand in hand, to rebuild it nearer to their heart's desire. The prone body of Satyavan must rise, but this can happen only when it has the vital touch of the soul which so far Death had kept in his custody. But now the soul of Satyavan was released, and Savitri was enabling it to come down. The poet says:

> Like a flower hidden in the heart of spring
> The soul of Satyavan drawn down by her
> Inextricably in that mighty lapse.

The poet says that the soul of Satyavan was inextricably drawn down by her. The word "inextricable" is most apt, for, indeed the drawing down of the soul of Satyavan by Savitri was most mysterious. It was drawn even as a flower is hidden in the heart of spring. Savitri's descent to earth after her great victory over Death is beautifully described by the poet in the following lines :

> ....Then all the blind
> And near attraction of the earth compelled
> Fearful rapidities of downward bliss.
> Lost in the giddy proneness of that speed,
> Whirled, sinking, overcome she disappeared
> Like a leaf spinning from the tree of heaven,
> In broad unconsciousness as in a pool;
> A hospitable softness drew her in
> Into a wonder of miraculous depths,
> Above her closed a darkness of great wings
> And she was buried in a mother's breast.

Long before man plunged into the adventures of space travel, Sri Aurobindo's imagination seems to have visualized as to how space-ship would return from outer space into earth's atmosphere and its gravitational pull. In

Savitri's descent one is reminded of the return of the
space-ship from adventures into outer space and coming
under the compelling attraction of the gravitational pull of
the earth.   Here the ship of life comes not from outer space
but from the inner space, the space of consciousness.   Savitri returns to the earth consciousness from the stupendous adventure of a super-conscious experience.   And as
she descended to earth she was buried in the mother's
breast.   The mother earth welcomes her and pressed her
to her bosom.   The poet says that Savitri came to earth
like a "leaf spinning from the tree of heaven".   The earth
saw in Savitri's return its own redemption.   With Savitri's
descent the entire earth atmosphere was changed.   The
poet describes this change in his own inimitable manner
in the following exquisite lines:

> Then from a timeless plane that watches Time,
> A Spirit gazed out upon destiny.
> In its endless moment saw the ages pass.
> The prophet moment covered limitless Space
> And cast into the heart of hurrying Time
> A diamond light of the Eternal's peace,
> A crimson seed of God's felicity
> A glance from the gaze fell of undying Love.
> A wonderful face looked out with deathless eyes;
> A hand was seen drawing the golden bars
> That guard the imperishable secrecies.
> A key turned in a mystic lock of Time.
> A power leaned down, a happiness found its home.
> Over wide earth brooded the infinite bliss.

The descent of Savitri after her dialogue with Death
was like the diamond light cast into the heart of hurrying Time; it was as if the glance of undying life fell
from the divine gaze.   In her return to earth there was
born the miracle of Timeless looking on time.   And when
this happens then the moment itself becomes endless, revealing the passage and movement of ages.   The poet says

that with the return of Savitri "a power leaned down,
a happiness found its home". In our present-day world
it is sorrow that has found its home here on earth. But
when Savitri returns with the great secret of man's immortality, then everything is changed. Earth becomes the
home of happiness. The poet says that over the wide
world brooded infinite bliss because Savitri had returned
—not alone, but with Satyavan. The mortal had put
on immortality; the Spirit had triumphed over Matter.

The entire dialogue with Death had taken the whole
day. Satyavan died in the morning, and so from morning till dusk Savitri went on with her dialogue with Death.
Within these few hours was carried on Man's battle for
establishing his claim to Immortality. As the day was
advancing towards evening, the final issue was settled.
The issue was: Will Death claim Satyavan? Or will
Savitri claim him? At last Savitri claimed Satyavan and
won the great battle with Death. The poet says:

> Into the magic secrecy of the woods
> Peering through an emerald lattice-window of leaves,
> In indolent skies reclined, the thinning day
> Turned to its slow fall into evening's peace.

The day had thinned and was reclined in indolent
skies, and it was turning to its slow fall into evening's
peace. It was at that time, where the day was moving
towards its meeting with night, that Savitri came down
and "pressed the living body of Satyavan". What was
the nature of Savitri that had returned after her victory
over Death? The poet says:

> Human she was once more, earth's Savitri,
> Yet felt in her illimitable change.
> A power dwelt in her soul too great for earth,
> A bliss lived in her heart too large for heaven.

CHAPTER XXV

THE MAGIC OF GOLDEN CHANGE

ONE of the great master-pieces of English Literature is *Paradise Lost* by John Milton. This was followed by his *Paradise Regained*. Sri Aurobindo in his monumental epic of *Savitri* has dealt with the self-same problem of paradise lost and paradise regained. But the sweep and range of the subject are different from those of Milton. In the death of Satyavan, Savitri's paradise was lost; but reclaiming Satyavan from Death Savitri regained her lost paradise. In Death mortal man finds the loss of his paradise. Savitri was concerned with regaining the paradise not for herself but for the entire humanity. The poet indicates to us, in canto after canto, that man confined within the limitations of Mind must experience the tragedy of the loss of his paradise. It is only when he is able to bring down the light of the Supermind in his consciousness that he can find his paradise regained. In Savitri we find Sri Aurobindo as a great mystic of mystics. The fundamental note of all mysticism is transcending the realm of Duality. To reject the demands of Duality one by one is the only way that leads the spiritual aspirant to the rich experience of Non-duality. The Way of mysticism is the Way of Love, and surely Love can come into being only when Duality is completely negated. Fear exists only in the realm of duality; in the state of non-duality there is no fear. There is fear so long as the other exists, but when the "other" is not there of what shall man be afraid? In the realm of duality, Death reigns supreme. And so no solution of the problem of Death can ever be found in the field of duality. Savitri conquered Death by Love, and Love is a state of

358

non-duality. Where Love is, there is no fear of Death. In the negation of Love, there is the paradise lost; in the state of Love paradise is regained. Sri Aurobindo's *Savitri* is the saga of Love. It is not just a story of a wife's loyalty and fidelity to her husband as is indicated in the legendary story. Savitri's return to earth, establishing her unchallenged claim over Satyavan, is a great moment of rejoicing for all, for, it is a moment indicating an end of the Empire of Death and the emergence of the Empire of Love. The poet says:

> The whole wide world clung to her for delight,
> Created for her rapt embrace of love.
> Her life was a dawn's victorious opening,
> The past and unborn days had joined their dreams,
> Old vanished eves and far arriving noons
> Hinted to her a vision of prescient hours.

As Savitri descended on earth she naturally tried to pick up the old threads. She had been away for the whole day, and each moment of that day was filled with experiences which were soul-absorbing in range as well as content. She had come back from an entirely different realm. During her absence she had lost trace of what was happening down here on earth. The poet says:

> Half-risen then she sent her gaze around,
> As if to recover old sweet trivial threads,
> Old happy thoughts, small treasured memories,
> And weave them into one immortal day.

She wanted to weave all that happened in the past into the immortal day which she had experienced. What had happened was small and trivial—but then nothing is so small and trivial as cannot be woven in the fabric of love. Savitri wanted to get back into the mood of the earth, for, it is earth she is to serve. As she gazed around, she saw the body of Satyavan lying there as if in fathomless sleep. How could Satyavan rise by his own effort?

Immortality is not an achievement by human effort, for, how far can the mortal go by his own attempts? For the mind of man immortality means only an endless continuity. But that is not what it is. Immortality is experienced by human consciousness in the Timeless Moment. The mind of man, however, functions only within the framework of Time and Space, and, is therefore, a stranger to the Timeless Moment. Satyavan is the victim of Time, while Savitri is the pilgrim from the Timeless regions. It is only when the Timeless touches Time that the sense of Immortality comes. Satyavan by himself cannot rise; he needs the touch of Savitri in order to wake up from the fathomless sleep in which he was. The poet says:

> But soon she leaned down over her loved to call
> His mind back to her with her travelling touch
> On his closed eyelids; settled was her still look
> Of strong delight, not yearning now, but large
> With limitless joy or sovereign last content,
> Pure, passionate with the passion of the gods.

Savitri leaned over Satyavan who was fast asleep. She wanted to wake him with her travelling touch on his closed eyelids. The phrase "travelling touch" is most significant. It obviously means the touch that she had brought from her travels into the Timeless region. In this touch there was no yearning; in it there was no ordinary desire. And yet the touch was not that of aloofness nor of cold indifference. The poet says that it was pure, and, yet, it was passionate with the passion of the gods. When Savitri softly touched the closed eyelids of Satyavan there was absolutely no carnal desire agitating her, and yet there was in that touch the passion of the gods. In the phrase "the passion of the gods", the poet has once again indicated that in Savitri the human and the divine lived together. Even though she had returned from a communion with the Divine, she had not lost touch with the emotions that surge the human heart. The poet says:

> Then sighing to her touch the soft-winged sleep
> Rose hovering from his flower-like lids and flew
> Murmurous away. Awake, he found her eyes
> Waiting for his, and felt her hands, and saw
> The earth his home given back to him once more
> And her made his again, his passion's all.

The poet says that with the soft touch of Savitri, sleep rose sighing and flew away murmuring. It naturally disliked to be asked to leave the flower-like lids of Satyavan on which it was resting. And when the sleep flew away, Satyavan woke up and found that Savitri's eyes were waiting to look at him. He felt her hands, and was happy to know that she was there, "made his again", for, she was this passion's all. She had filled this entire region of passion so that there was none else in that region. The poet tells us:

> With his arms' encircling hold around her locked,
> A living knot to make possession close,
> He murmured with hestitating lips her name,
> And vaguely recollecting wonder cried:
> "Whence hast thou brought me captive back, love-
> chained,
> To thee and sunlight's walls, O golden beam
> And casket of all sweetness, Savitri,
> Godhead and woman, moonlight of my soul?

Satyavan woke up at the soft touch of Savitri, but he was utterly dazed. He could not understand what had happened, for, he had a feeling that he had travelled very far and had visited strange lands and that too in the company of Savitri. He said:

> Together we have disdained the gates of night;
> I have turned away from the celestial's joy
> And heaven's insufficient without thee.

Satyavan was unable to make out as to where they both had been, and what had happened to Death. He had a vague remembrance that it was with the appearance of Death that he had lost all consciousness, but where was that Death now? He asks Savitri:

> Where now has passed that formidable Shape
> Which rose against us, the Spirit of the Void,
> Claiming the world for Death and Nothingness,
> Denying God and Soul? Or was all a dream
> Or a vision seen in a spiritual sleep?

Satyavan wants to know whether the appearance of Death was only a dream, and what he seems to recollect was just a vision that had arisen in his sleep. He wants Savitri to explain to him as to what had happened while he was asleep. Then Savitri replied:

> ....our parting was the dream;
> We are together, we live, O Satyavan
> Look round thee and behold, glad and unchanged
> Our home, this forest with its thousand cries
> And the whisper of the winds among the leaves
> Only our souls have left Death's night behind
> Changed by a mighty dream's reality
> And stood at Godhead's gates limitless, free.

Savitri assured dazed Satyavan that everything was as it had been. While outwardly there was no change, there was a tremendous inward change, for, they had returned leaving the night of Death behind. And surely this was no mean achievement. Having stood at the gate of Godhead they are now free and limitless. No fate can bind them, no stream of Time can carry them away. Satyavan certainly felt immensely re-assured by these words of Savitri. The poet says:

> Then filled with the glory of their happiness
> They rose and with safe clinging fingers locked
> Hung on each other in a silent look.

But he with a new wonder in his heart
And a new flame of worship in his eyes.

The poet says that it was a different Satyavan that
rose from the fathomless sleep. There was a new flame
of worship in his eyes. Needless to say this flame of worship was for Savitri. With a new wonder in his heart,
Satyavan said:

What high change is in thee, O Savitri? Bright
Ever thou wast, a goddess still and pure,
Yet dearer to me by thy sweet human parts.
But now thou seemst almost too high and great
For mortal worship; Time lies below thy feet
And thou lookst on me in the gaze of the stars,
My human earth will still demand thy bliss:
Make still my life through thee a song of joy
And all my silence wide and deep with thee.

Satyavan found Savitri risen much higher in stature.
He said to her that she was always a goddess still and pure,
but she was dearer to him by her sweet human parts. He is
wondering whether in the new stature of Savitri, she has
lost the human touch and become supremely divine. He
says to her that whatever may have been the change
brought about in her, he will need her to make his life a
song of joy. But Savitri puts all doubts of Satyavan at rest.
The poet says:

She clasped his feet, by her enshrining hair
Enveloped in a velvet cloak of love,
And answered softly like a murmuring lute:
"All now is changed, yet all is still the same.
Lo, we have looked upon the face of God,
Our life has opened with divinity.
Our love has grown greater by that mighty touch
And learnt its heavenly significance,
Yet nothing is lost of mortal love's delight.
Heaven's touch fulfils, but cancels not our earth:

Still am I she who came to thee mid the murmur
Of sunlit leaves upon this forest verge;
All that I was before, I am to thee still,
Close comrade of thy thoughts and hopes and toils,
I am thy kingdom even as thou art mine,
The sovereign and the slave of thy desire,
Our wedded walk through life begins anew,
No gladness lost, no depth of mortal joy
Let us go through this new world that is the same
We have each other found, O Satyavan,
In the great light of the discovered soul.

Here we find the poet giving us a picture of the fusion
of contraries. Savitri having risen to greater heights of divinity is still the same, intensely human. All is changed and
yet all is still the same. Savitri asks Satyavan to rise so that
the two can walk through the new world which is still
the same. Savitri tells Satyavan that she is both the sovereign and the slave of his desire. What greater assurance
can Satyavan need? Savitri tells him that it is true that
they have touched the gates of Divinity, however, "heaven's touch fulfils, but cancels not our earth". To seek
the fulfilment of heaven without cancelling the earth—
this is truly the very core of Sri Aurobindo's philosophy.
Savitri tells Satyavan that their earth will not be cancelled,
and yet they will keep the pristine purity of heaven. Then
Savitri says to Satyavan: "Let us go back, for eve is in the
skies". They must go back to the hermitage, for, evening
was growing and soon it will be dark. The parents must
be worrying, for, they both had started out early in the
morning, and now the night was nearing. The poet says:

She closed her arms about his breast and head
As if to keep him on her bosom worn
For ever through the journeying of the years.
So for a while they stood entwined, their kiss
And passion-tranced embrace a meeting point
In their commingling spirits, one for ever,

Two-souled, two-bodied for the joy of Time.
Then hand in hand they left that solemn place
Full now of mute unusual memories,
To the green distance of their sylvan home
Returning slowly through the forest's heart:
Round them the afternoon to evening changed;
Light slipped down to the brightly sleeping verge
And the birds came back winging to their nests
And day and night leaned to each other's arms.

Savitri and Satyavan slowly wended their way to the hermitage. It was a time when day and night leaned on each other's arms. And the two lovers too moved hand in hand, for, it is thus with their spirits commingled that they will reshape the mortal life of man. As they proceeded towards their home they were met by a resplendent company of people bringing a stream of unknown faces. Large number of people came clad in colourful costumes. There were also strong warriors in their glorious armour in this company as also proud-hooved steeds trampling through the wood. Both Satyavan and Savitri must have wondered how such a throng could come to receive them, and that too with warriors and steeds. But their wonder must have disappeared soon, for, as the poet says:

In front King Dyumatsena walked, no more
Blind, faltering-limbed, but his far-questing eyes
Restored to all their confidence in light
Took seeingly this imaged outer world;
Firmly he trod with monarch steps the soil.
By him that queen and mother's anxious face
Came changed from its habitual burdened look
Which in its drooping strength of tired toil
Had borne the fallen life of those she loved.
Her eyes were first to find her children's forms.

King Dyumatsena and the Queen were leading this vast throng of men and women who had started on their quest for Satyavan and Savitri, for, the two had been

away the whole day, and now the night was drawing close.
When the mother saw the children, she and the King
hurried to meet them, and the parents were beside themselves with joy. Then the King spoke to Satyavan, chiding
him, and said:

> The fortunate gods have looked on me today,
> A kingdom seeking came and heaven's rays.
> But where wast thou? Thou hast tormented gladness
> With fear's dull shadow, O my child, my life.
> What danger kept thee for the darkening woods?
> Or how could pleasure in her ways forget
> That useless orbs without thee are my eyes
> Which only for thy sake rejoice at light?

And the King also mildly rebuked Savitri, for he said
to her:

> Not like thyself was this done, Savitri,
> Who ledst not back thy husband to our arms,
> Knowing with him beside me only is taste
> In food and for his touch evening and morn
> I live content with my remaining days.

Although the rebuke to Savitri was couched in mild
words, it was sufficiently strong. The King felt that
Satyavan's behaviour on that day was unlike hers. But how
could Savitri reply, and so it was Satyavan who said with
smiling lips:

> Lay all on her; she is the cause of all.
> With her enchantments she has twined me round.
> Behold, at noon leaving this house of clay
> I wandered in far-off eternities, ·
> Yet, still, a captive in her golden hands,
> I tread your little hillock called green earth,
> And in the moments of your transient sun
> Live glad among the busy works of men".

All who heard these words of Satyavan were wondering as to what had happened; where had he gone, and

what regions he had traversed as a captive in the golden
hands of Savitri.   They could not make out anything.
They all turned in the direction of Savitri. She was standing behind Satyavan with

> A deepening redder gold upon her cheeks,
> With lowered lids the noble lovely child.

She stood there with lowered lids, for, Satyavan had
thrown all the blame upon her. But as the people gathered
there turned to her, they all felt like saying:

> What gleaming marvel of the earth or skies
> Stands silently by human Satyavan
> To mark a brilliance in the dusk of eve?
> If this is she of whom the world has heard
> Wonder no more at any happy change.

While this was the general feeling in the hearts of the
large throng that had assembled, there was one who
looked like a priest and a sage addressed Savitri directly,
thus giving expression to what others were secretly feeling
in their hearts.

> O woman soul, what light, what power revealed,
> Working the rapid marvels of this day,
> Opens for us by thee a happier age?

Everyone was eager to know what noble purpose had
induced Savitri to come down to earth from the dizzy
heights of Heaven. What will· be the new age of happiness
that she will usher in along with Satyavan? Everyone
realized that the presence of Savitri was like a brilliance
in the dusk of eve. Savitri replied to the sage:

> Awakened to the meaning of my heart,
> That to feel love and oneness is to live
> And this the magic of our golden change
> Is all the truth I know or seek, O sage.

In these four lines the poet has summed up the entire mission of Savitri. To feel love and oneness is to live, this is the magic of the golden change. She has come down on earth so that in company with Satyavan she may show to humanity the Miracle of Love. Savitri says that this is all that she knows or seeks. To bring in a new age inspired and nourished by Love—this is her mission. And what greater mission can there be than this? Is not the world in need of this healing balm of Love, and without Love all that man does is utterly futile and meaningless? But Love demands the fusion of the masculine and feminine aspects of consciousness. In the commingling of Satyavan and Savitri there is the fusion of the two aspects of consciousness. Satyavan represents the noblest character of masculine consciousness. He is the symbol of humanity reaching its apex in the culture of the mind. But mind cannot solve the problems of the present day civilization. And yet mind is a necessary instrument for bringing about changes. But mind can become a fitting instrument of the Super-mind only when it dies. Out of the death of the old mind is born the New Mind which alone can work in collaboration with the Super-mind. And mankind's salvation lies today in mind's collaboration with the Super-mind. Savitri is the representative of the Super-mind. But before Savitri and Satyavan can work in close collaboration, the old Satyavan must die. The death and the renewal of Satyavan is a pre-condition for the emergence of the new age of the Super-mind. When the old mind dies then is born in human consciousness the living flame of Love. Savitri and Satyavan together are destined to enkindle the Flame of Love in all humanity. Where the Flame of Love burns bright there all problems of sorrow and suffering vanish into thin air. Savitri says that they will establish this Kingdom of Love here on earth.

When Savitri stopped speaking, conveying the great mission of their life, the poet says: "Westward they turned in the fast gathering night". The entire assembly turned westward as the night was gathering fast. It is significant that the poet speaks here of the westward movement. The Light always comes from the East, and moves towards the West. The entire assembly had heard the inspiring words of Savitri which were truly the words of light, then they all turned towards the west to share with others the light that they had received. Savitri was the bringer of New Light. She and Satyavan must now move westwards to shed the light of Wisdom in the darkened world of man. In the following lines the poet describes the movement of Satyavan and Savitri towards the west. The description refers not merely to physical surroundings—in fact, it refers to the psychological environment of man through which the Two Redeemers are moving so as to dispel the darkness that has enveloped humanity. The poet says:

> From the entangling verges freed they came
> Into a dimness of the sleeping earth
> And travelled through her faint and slumbering plains.
> Murmur and movement and the tread of men
> Broke the night's solitude. The neigh of steeds
> Rose from the indistinct and voiceful sea
> Of life and all along its marchings swelled
> The rhyme of hooves, the chariot's homeward voice.
> With linked hands Satyavan and Savitri,
> Hearing a marriage march and nuptial hymn,
> Where waited them the many-voiced human world.
> Numberless the stars swam on their shadowy field
> Describing in the gloom the ways of light.
> Then while they skirted yet the southward verge,
> Lost in the halo of her musing brows
> Night, splendid with the moon dreaming in heaven
> In silver peace, possessed her luminous reign.
> She brooded through her stillness on a thought
> Deep-guarded by her mystic folds of light,
> And in her bosom nursed a greater dawn.

The journey together of Savitri and Satyavan was towards a greater dawn which the night nursed in her bosom.

Their movement was like "describing in the gloom the ways of light". They we e the beacon light of Divinity calling man to rise to the realms of Immortality. They had to make their way through the dimness of the sleeping earth—but then that has been the lot of all redeemers of humanity. The prophets and sages have always had to travel through faint and slumbering plains. The birth of Savitri indicated the arrival of a Dawn for humanity, but the work of Savitri and Satyavan together indicates a journey towards a Greater Dawn. In the birth of Savitri the Supermind touched the earth consciousness, but in the journey of Savitri and Satyavan there is the prospect of the Supermind reshaping the earth itself so that the seemingly unbridgeable gulf between Heaven and Earth may be bridged for ever. It is to this great work of bridging the gulf between Heaven and Earth that Savitri and Satyavan have been called, and they together shall achieve what otherwise seems impossible. Their common endeavour shall lead humanity to heights never scaled before. As the poet says:

> Then man and superman shall be at one
> And all the earth become a single life.
> Even the multitude shall hear the Voice
> And turn to commune with the Spirit within
> And strive to obey the high spiritual law:
> This earth shall stir with impulses sublime,
> Humanity awake to deepest self,
> Nature the hidden godhead recognise.
> Even the many shall some answer make
> And bear the splendour of the Divine's rush
> And his impetuous knock at unseen doors.
> Thus shall the earth open to divinity
> And common natures feel the wide uplift,
> Illumine common acts with the Spirit's ray
> And meet the deity in common things.

THE SCIENCE OF MEDITATION

THIS WORK treats the philosophy and psychology of Meditation from a purely practical standpoint. The theme of Meditation is discussed in terms of the three main constituents, namely, the Brain, the Habit mechanism and the Mind. The revitalisation, the modification and the transformation of the triad respectively would usher in the wholeness of spiritual life. It is sincerely hoped that a practical treatment of the subject of meditation will help man to lead a healthy and creative life amidst his baffling psychological life.

ISBN: 81-208-0297-7 (Cloth); ISBN: 81-208-0298-5 (Paper)

J. KRISHNAMURTI AND THE NAMELESS EXPERIENCE

J. KRISHNAMURTI is one of the most revolutionary thinkers of our age. To listen to him or to read his books is an experience by itself. He challenges every norm and value of individual as well as social life. He is not interested in mere outer changes; he stands for a fundamental transformation, what he calls the Mutation of the Mind. He states that there must arise first the New Man before a New Society can be brought into existence.

The present book deals comprehensively with all aspects of Krishnamurti's teachings, his philosophy, his psychology and a practice of no-practice. Krishnamurti says: Society is always static; only in the individual can there be a radical revolution.

ISBN: 81-208-0589-5 (Cloth); ISBN: 81-208-0590-9 (Paper)

J. KRISHNAMURTI AND SANT KABIR

FROM KABIR to Krishnamurti is a far cry. For, they are separated one from the other by over five centuries. But quantitative measurement of this distance has a qualitative aspect which cannot be measured in any time-scale. Two great seers lived in two completely different worlds—with no comparison between the two. And yet they expressed their thoughts and experience not only in a similar language but almost in identical terms.

In these two streams of thought represented by Kabir and Krishnaji, the author notes a fascinating parallelism. These streams run parallel to each other—and yet they meet from time to time— at the intersections between the two approaches to life. *J. Krishnamurti and Sant Kabir* focuses on these meeting points between the two approaches to life. The book also presents the intersections between the writings and sayings of Kabir and Krishnaji.

ISBN: 81-208-0667-0 (Cloth); ISBN: 81-208-0668-9 (Paper)

THE SECRET OF SELF-TRANSFORMATION

THE CENTRAL theme of discussion in this monograph revolves round the problem of man's self-transformation in the midst of an artificial and soulless civilization. According to the the author, the solution to the problem lies in a synthesis between 'the two principal traditions of India'—Yoga and Tantra which he defines as philosophy and practice. In his view, only on a successful synthesis between the two depends the full flowering of the individual, and only 'a transformed individual... can become a nucleus for fundamental social change'.

The Secret of Self-Transformation is at once an indictment of all sorts of monstrosities that go under the banner of modern science and a call for revolutionary change within man himself. The call also goes not for restructuring the world in such a way that man does not become a creature of technology but rises up as a master of his true self. The discussion takes place within a compass of twenty chapters. The richness of ideas, presented in a lucid and convincing style, attracts readers of all shades.

ISBN: 81-208-0381-7 (Cloth); ISBN: 81-208-0402-3 (Paper)

FROM MIND TO SUPER-MIND

THE MESSAGE of the *Gita* has an important and a practical bearing on the problems of the modern age. It shows a way out of the complexities of the mind to complete and unfettered freedom of the Super Mind. This path is not meant only for the few, it can be trodden by all who seek freedom from life's entanglements.

Modern man is indeed besieged with great inner conflict and it is this conflict which has caused the utter disintegration of his psychological life. The disintegration within has caused unhappiness without. He is verily in search of inner integration and perhaps, for this, there can be no better guide than the teaching of the *Bhagavad Gita*. The creation of an Integrated Individual is indeed the purpose of the intensely dynamic message of the *Gita*.

In an age where the individual is becoming more and more insignificant due to the impacts of political, economic and social forces, the *Gita* brings to man a message of hope and cheer, for it shows a way of life which leads to the regaining of his lost significance, and the spiritual regeneration of man is indeed the way to the creation of a happy society.

ISBN: 81-208-0964-5 (Cloth); ISBN: 81-208-0965-3 (Paper)